JBoss™ at Work
A Practical Guide

Other Java™ resources from O'Reilly

Related titles

Head First Design Patterns
Head First EJB™
Hibernate: A Developer's
    Notebook™
Java™ in a Nutshell
Java™ Enterprise in a Nutshell

JBoss™: A Developer's
    Notebook™
Real World Web Services
Spring: A Developer's
    Notebook™
Tomcat: The Definitive Guide
WebLogic: The Definitive
    Guide

Java Books Resource Center

java.oreilly.com is a complete catalog of O'Reilly's books on Java and related technologies, including sample chapters and code examples.

OnJava.com is a one-stop resource for enterprise Java developers, featuring news, code recipes, interviews, weblogs, and more.

Conferences

O'Reilly brings diverse innovators together to nurture the ideas that spark revolutionary industries. We specialize in documenting the latest tools and systems, translating the innovator's knowledge into useful skills for those in the trenches. Visit *conferences.oreilly.com* for our upcoming events.

Safari Bookshelf (*safari.oreilly.com*) is the premier online reference library for programmers and IT professionals. Conduct searches across more than 1,000 books. Subscribers can zero in on answers to time-critical questions in a matter of seconds. Read the books on your Bookshelf from cover to cover or simply flip to the page you need. Try it today with a free trial.

JBoss™ at Work
A Practical Guide

Tom Marrs and Scott Davis

O'REILLY®

Beijing · Cambridge · Farnham · Köln · Sebastopol · Taipei · Tokyo

JBoss™ at Work: A Practical Guide
by Tom Marrs and Scott Davis

Published by O'Reilly Media, Inc., 1005 Gravenstein Highway North, Sebastopol, CA 95472.

O'Reilly books may be purchased for educational, business, or sales promotional use. Online editions are also available for most titles (*safari.oreilly.com*). For more information, contact our corporate/institutional sales department: (800) 998-9938 or *corporate@oreilly.com*.

Editor:	Mike Loukides
Production Editor:	Colleen Gorman
Cover Designer:	Karen Montgomery
Interior Designer:	David Futato

Printing History:

October 2005:	First Edition.

 This book uses RepKover™, a durable and flexible lay-flat binding.

ISBN: 978-0-596-00734-8
[M]

Table of Contents

Preface

Are you curious about the cool, new features of JBoss 4 and J2EE 1.4? Are you frustrated with all the simplistic "Hello World" examples? Do you want to see a realistic application deployed on JBoss?

As practitioners, we've seen that most people struggle with the following issues when deploying J2EE applications on JBoss:

- Real application deployment involves many J2EE and JBoss deployment descriptors, and it's difficult to make them all work together.
- Developers new to JBoss need a way to get started.
- Most projects don't have a packaging and deployment strategy that grows with their application.
- Class Loaders are confusing and can cause problems when developers don't know how to use them.

This book shows you how to use JBoss with the latest Open Source Java tools. By building a project throughout the book with extensive code examples, we cover all major facets of J2EE application deployment on JBoss, including JSPs, Servlets, EJBs, JMS, JNDI, Web Services, JavaMail, JDBC, and Hibernate.

With the help of this book, you'll:

- Implement a full J2EE application and deploy it on JBoss.
- Discover how to use the latest features of JBoss 4 and J2EE 1.4, including J2EE-compliant Web Services.
- Master J2EE application deployment on JBoss with EARs, WARs, and EJB JARs.
- Understand the core J2EE deployment descriptors and how they integrate with JBoss-specific descriptors.
- Deploy JSPs, Servlets, EJBs, JMS, Web Services, JavaMail, JDBC, and Hibernate on JBoss.
- Base your security strategy on JAAS.

Although this book covers the gamut of deploying J2EE technologies on JBoss, it isn't an exhaustive discussion of each aspect of the J2EE API. This book is meant to be a brief survey of each subject aimed at the working professional with limited time.

Audience

This book is for Java developers who want to use JBoss on their projects. If you're new to J2EE, this book will serve as a gentle introduction. But don't mistake this book for a true J2EE reference manual. There is a reason those books are 1,000+ pages long—they cover each technology in exhaustive detail. This book gives you enough to get a simple example up and running quickly.

If you've worked on J2EE projects but are new to JBoss, this book covers familiar concepts, introduces you to key J2EE 1.4 issues including Web Services, and shows you how to make them work with JBoss. If you've worked with JBoss before, this book will get you up to speed on JBoss 4, JBoss WS (Web Services), and Hibernate 3.

About This Book

This book starts with a simple web page and iteratively shows you how to add the various J2EE technologies to develop an application that runs on JBoss. Rather than getting stuck in the details of every possible J2EE API or J2EE/JBoss deployment descriptor, we focus on learning by doing. We introduce you to each topic, show what we're going to do, do it, and recap what we did. By taking an iterative approach, we keep things short, sweet, and to the point so that you can put JBoss to work on your projects.

Assumptions This Book Makes

We assume that you've worked with Java and are familiar with Open Source tools such as Ant and XDoclet. We show you how to download and install them. We provide you with Ant scripts for compiling and deploying the application.

Conventions Used in This Book

The following typographical conventions are used in this book:

Plain text
> Indicates menu titles, menu options, menu buttons, and keyboard accelerators (such as Alt and Ctrl).

Italic
> Indicates new terms, URLs, email addresses, filenames, file extensions, pathnames, directories, and Unix utilities.

Constant width

Indicates commands, options, switches, variables, attributes, keys, functions, types, classes, namespaces, methods, modules, properties, parameters, values, objects, events, event handlers, XML tags, HTML tags, macros, the contents of files, or the output from commands.

Constant width bold

Shows commands or other text that should be typed literally by the user.

Constant width italic

Shows text that should be replaced with user-supplied values.

 This icon signifies a tip, suggestion, or general note.

 This icon indicates a warning or caution.

Using Code Examples

This book is here to help you get your job done. In general, you may use the code in this book in your programs and documentation. You do not need to contact us for permission unless you're reproducing a significant portion of the code. For example, writing a program that uses several chunks of code from this book does not require permission. Selling or distributing a CD-ROM of examples from O'Reilly books *does* require permission. Answering a question by citing this book and quoting example code does not require permission. Incorporating a significant amount of example code from this book into your product's documentation *does* require permission.

We appreciate, but do not require, attribution. An attribution usually includes the title, author, publisher, and ISBN. For example: "*JBoss at Work: A Practical Guide,* by Tom Marrs and Scott Davis. Copyright 2005 O'Reilly Media, Inc., 0-596-00734-5.'

If you feel your use of code examples falls outside fair use or the permission given above, feel free to contact us at *permissions@oreilly.com.*

Safari Enabled

 When you see a Safari® enabled icon on the cover of your favorite technology book, that means the book is available online through the O'Reilly Network Safari Bookshelf.

Safari offers a solution that's better than e-books. It's a virtual library that lets you easily search thousands of top tech books, cut and paste code samples, download chapters, and find quick answers when you need the most accurate, current information. Try it for free at *http://safari.oreilly.com*.

Comments and Questions

Please address comments and questions concerning this book to the publisher:

O'Reilly Media, Inc.
1005 Gravenstein Highway North
Sebastopol, CA 95472
(800) 998-9938 (in the United States or Canada)
(707) 829-0515 (international or local)
(707) 829-0104 (fax)

We have a web page for this book, where we list errata, examples, and any additional information. You can access this page at:

http://www.oreilly.com/catalog/jbossatwork

We also have a companion web site for this book, where we have an FAQ, links to resources, and bonus materials. Please visit:

http://www.jbossatwork.com

To comment or ask technical questions about this book, send email to:

bookquestions@oreilly.com
tom@jbossatwork.com
scott@jbossatwork.com

For more information about our books, conferences, Resource Centers, and the O'Reilly Network, see our web site at:

http://www.oreilly.com

Acknowledgments

Many people contributed to this book's development. We're grateful to Mike Loukides, our editor, for his experience, guidance, and direction. We'd like to thank him for believing in us and being patient with two first-time authors as we learned our craft.

We had a great team of expert technical reviewers who helped ensure sure that the material was technically accurate, approachable, and reflected the spirit of the JBoss, J2EE, and Open Source communities. Our reviewers were Norman Richards, Greg Ostravich, Andy Ochsner, and Dan Moore. Their suggestions and corrections greatly improved the quality of the book. We're especially thankful to Norman Richards of

JBoss, Inc. for his quick turnaround on show-stopper issues and for all his great advice.

We owe a great debt to the Open Source community who made the tools for this book:

- To JBoss, Inc. for creating and maintaining JBoss, an outstanding and reliable J2EE application server that we use on our jobs every day. JBoss is great and we love it. We hope that the concept of Professional Open Source will continue to blossom and grow.
- To the Ant, XDoclet, Log4J, Apache Jakarta, Hibernate, and (numerous) Apache and SourceForge projects—you guys rock! Your tools keep the Java community going.

Tom's Acknowledgments

I am especially thankful to Scott Davis, my co-author, for exhorting me to finish the book, holding me accountable, and for pushing me to improve my writing style. This book would've been impossible without him.

Thanks to Richard Monson-Haefel, Sue Spielman, Bruce Tate, Brett McLaughlin, Frank Traditi (my business coach), the Denver Java Users Group (DJUG—*http:// www.denverjug.org*), and everyone else who encouraged me along the way.

Thanks to Jay Zimmerman, coordinator of the "No Fluff Just Stuff" (*http://www. nofluffjuststuff.com*) conferences, for enabling me to take my message on the road.

Thanks to The One Way Café in Aurora, CO—keep the lattes and good advice flowing.

Most importantly, I am deeply grateful to my wife, Linda, and daughter, Abby, for supporting me during the writing process. I love you and look forward to spending more time together.

Scott's Acknowledgments

Tom came to me with an opportunity to co-author a book for O'Reilly. How could I possibly turn down a gig like that? Tom and I have known each other for years, and we knew from the start that we brought complementary skills to the table. This book was a collaborative effort in every sense of the word, but it never would have happened if Tom hadn't planted the first seed.

What started out as a wildly optimistic (and in retrospect, totally unrealistic) attempt to map out the entire known world of Open Source J2EE development eventually got distilled down to the book you are now holding. Even though this book is far more modest in scope than our original idea, I think that it still captures the spirit of what we set out to accomplish. Without getting bogged down in the whole commercial versus free versus open source quagmire, we wanted to show you that it is possible to create a production-quality application using nothing but freely available tools.

Thanks go out to the Denver and Boulder JUG communities—hanging out with all of you (too numerous to mention individually) has made me a better programmer and a better person. When I was a lone wolf contractor, your emails and IMs, phone calls and lunches, but *especially* the post-meeting pints and horror story-swaps are what kept me sane through all of it. When I was new to a city and a programming language, you made me feel like I belonged.

A very warm thanks goes out to Jay and the whole NFJS crew (Ted, Bruce, Erik, Jason, James, Mike, Stu, Justin, Glenn, David, Eitan, Dion, Ben, Dave, and the rest of y'all). After attending my first conference, I knew that I wanted to be a part of it professionally. The collective talent and charisma of the speakers is breathtaking. During a Fourth of July celebration, my three year-old son Christopher said in awe, "Daddy, the fireworks are too big for my eyes." No exaggeration—I feel the same way when I'm on the NFJS tour.

But my deepest thanks and love goes to my family: Kim, Christopher, and little soon-to-be-born Baby X. I did my best to keep my writing hours limited to after bedtime and during naptime (Mom's and son's both), but I know that it crept into the waking hours as well. Thanks for pretending for my benefit that it didn't matter. You are my everything.

CHAPTER 1

Getting Started with JBoss

Have you noticed that simply saying "I am a Java programmer" isn't enough these days? It conveys a little bit of information, but not enough to make any serious decisions. It's kind of like saying, "I play sports" or "I like food." A recruiter can assume that a Java programmer has a passing familiarity with curly braces and semicolons, but little else.

The Java programming language runs on an incredibly diverse set of hardware—from cell phones and PDAs down to embedded chips on a credit card; every major desktop and laptop, regardless of operating system or hardware manufacturer; entry-level workgroup servers up to clusters of high-end servers; and even mainframes.

The mantra in the heady early days of Java was, "Write once, run anywhere." The original ideal of having the same application run anywhere from a cell phone to a large-scale cluster of servers turned out to be more marketing hype than business reality, although the "run anywhere" part of the slogan has proven remarkably prescient.

Modern Java developers often define themselves by the hardware they specialize in. J2ME developers eke amazing functionality out of resource-starved micro-devices with limited networking capabilities. J2SE programmers have mastered daunting but robust GUI frameworks such as Swing and SWT for rich desktop application development. And J2EE software engineers are masters of the server-side domain.

Saying that you are a J2EE programmer begins to narrow the field a bit, but our hypothetical recruiter still doesn't have enough information to place you in the proper job. J2EE is a loose collection of server-side technologies that are related, but are by no means homogenous.

Some J2EE experts specialize in web-related technologies—JSPs, Servlets, and the diverse landscape of web frameworks such as Jakarta Struts or Sun's Java Server Faces. Others are back-end specialists that focus more on the transactional integrity and reliability of business processing that uses technologies such as EJBs, JMS, and relational databases. (We'll define these acronyms later in the book.) There is even a new breed of Web Services specialists that use the J2EE product suite and a host of related XML technologies, such as SOAP and WSDL, to offer a Service Oriented Architecture to Java and non-Java clients alike.

Asking any one specialist to describe the J2EE toolkit brings to mind the story of the blind men and the elephant. Each blind man describes the elephant based on the part he touches—the one holding the trunk describes a very different animal than the one holding the tusk or the ear.

This book attempts to describe the whole elephant in the context of JBoss, an open source J2EE container. Like the technology it implements, JBoss is not a single monolithic application. Rather, it is a family of interrelated services that correspond to each item in the J2EE collection.

Each chapter in this book explores one of the J2EE services, but unlike the blind men, we show how one technology works in conjunction with the others. A J2EE application is often greater than the sum of its parts, and understanding the J2EE collection means understanding how each piece is interrelated.

Why "JBoss at Work"?

Before we get too far into things, we should explain why we chose the title *JBoss at Work* for this book. Understanding the authors' backgrounds should help.

Both of us are practicing software engineers who have worked together off and on for years. More importantly, both of us are former presidents of the Denver Java Users Group (*http://www.denverjug.org*). When we polled the group for potential interest in a given subject, the same phrase came up over and over again: "I don't want to be an expert in it, I just want to make it work."

"I just want to make it work" really resonates with us because we feel the same way. An ever-growing number of technologies fall under the J2EE umbrella, and there are at least two or three competing implementations of each. Just trying to keep up is a never-ending battle.

There is a 1,000-page book out there for each topic we cover in only 20 to 30 pages. *JBoss At Work* isn't intended to be an exhaustive discussion of every facet of the J2EE collection. This book is meant to be a brief survey of each subject aimed at the working professional with limited time—"Give me an overview, show me some working code, and make it snappy...." (Think of it as 12 months of JUG presentations collected in a single volume, minus the PowerPoint slides and cold pizza.)

Why JBoss?

JBoss fits the "I just want to make it work" gestalt to a T. Depending on the speed of your Internet connection, you can have it downloaded, unzipped, and running in less than five minutes. Turning services on and off is as simple as adding or removing files from a directory. The fact that it's free means that you don't get bogged down with per-seat or per-CPU licensing costs. JBoss is both a great learning tool and a production-quality deployment environment.

But any tool as powerful as JBoss also has pitfalls and complexities. The biggest disservice we could do is show you how to write applications that are tied to a specific application server, JBoss or otherwise. The "Write Once, Run Anywhere" promise of J2EE development may not happen automatically, but you can take steps to minimize the impact of moving from one application server to the next. In addition to your code being more portable, being a non-partisan J2EE developer means that *you and your skills* are more portable as you move from one job to the next.

The Example: JAW Motors

We have tried to come up with an application that uses each layer of the J2EE collection in some sort of meaningful way. By design, this book is short on academic discussions and long on working code examples. Showing a coherent business application in action will hopefully give you a clearer idea of how the various layers interact, as opposed to a series of disjointed "Hello World" examples exercising each layer in isolation.

The JAW Motors application supports a fictitious automobile dealership. Each chapter progressively adds a new J2EE technology that solves a specific business problem. Viewing cars on a website involves JSP pages and some form of persistence (JDBC or Hibernate). Performing a credit check sends a JMS message and an email response using JavaMail. Purchasing a car requires the transactional support of Stateless Session Beans. Sharing data from the JAW Motors inventory with other dealerships involves setting up Web Services.

In addition to showing how JBoss works, we hope that these examples answer the how and why of each technology: how is it used, and why it should (or shouldn't) be used. Just because a hammer can sink a screw in drywall doesn't necessarily mean that it is the best tool for the job. The measure of a successful J2EE application isn't how many of the technologies it uses; it is how effectively each technology is used.

Source code for the JAW Motors application is available for download from *http://www.jbossatwork.com*. We encourage you to download the files and build them as you follow along in the book. We want you to literally *see JBoss at work*, not just read about it.

Before we get too far, let's make sure that you have all necessary tools to build and deploy the application to JBoss.

The Tools

Making JBoss work involves more than just downloading and running JBoss. A cook certainly needs to know how to run the oven, but a lot of preliminary work must happen before the dish is ready for baking.

Professional chefs call this set up process "mis en place." They sharpen knives and place cutting boards within arms' reach. They prepare ahead of time ingredients they can safely cut up and measure before the dinner rush. Everything that can be done in terms of efficiency is handled up front so the culinary artist isn't distracted by mundane details.

Similarly, making JBoss work effectively requires you to do a bunch of work up front. Code must be compiled and packaged up in a specific way. You must wade through endless deployment descriptors. If one tiny piece of information doesn't match up with its companion in another file, the application will not deploy properly, and all of your hard work will be for nothing.

The mis en place of JBoss development involves other tools that make it easy to handle the mundane details of building and deploying your application. As in JBoss, you can download and use all of these tools for free:

- Java
- Ant
- XDoclet

Let's talk briefly about how to install and configure them.

Installing Java

It probably goes without saying that the first thing you'll need is a working installation of Java. JBoss 4.0.2 is compatible with J2SE 1.4 or higher. We use J2SE 1.4.2 in this book, although nothing should prevent you from running the examples in Java 5.

Download the full JDK (Java 2 Development Kit) from Sun's web site (*http://java. sun.com*). Follow Sun's instructions for installing the JDK on your operating system. Next, create an environment variable called *JAVA_HOME* that points to the Java installation directory. Finally, add *$JAVA_HOME/bin* to the system path so you can run Java from the command line.

To verify your Java installation, type java -version at a command prompt. You should see Example 1-1.

Example 1-1. Output of java -version

```
rosencrantz:~ sdavis$ java -version
java version "1.4.2_07"
Java(TM) 2 Runtime Environment, Standard Edition (build 1.4.2_07-215)
Java HotSpot(TM) Client VM (build 1.4.2-50, mixed mode)
rosencrantz:~ sdavis$
```

Installing Ant

We use Ant 1.6.5 to compile, package, and deploy the examples in this book. You can download it from *http://ant.apache.org*.

To install Ant, simply unzip the downloaded file to the directory of your choice. Next, create an environment variable called *ANT_HOME* that points to the Ant installation directory. Finally, add *$ANT_HOME/bin* to the system path so you can run Ant from the command line.

To verify your Ant installation, type ant -version at a command prompt. You should see Example 1-2.

Example 1-2. Output of ant -version

```
rosencrantz:~ sdavis$ ant -version
Apache Ant version 1.6.5 compiled on June 2 2005
rosencrantz:~ sdavis$
```

Installing XDoclet

We use XDoclet 1.2.3 to generate J2EE deployment descriptors, web.xml, and various other J2EE configuration files for the JAW Motors application. XDoclet is a combination of custom Ant tasks and special attributes that you include in your source code. You can download it from *http://xdoclet.sourceforge.net*.

To install XDoclet, unzip the downloaded file into the directory of your choice. Next, create an environment variable called *XDOCLET_HOME* that points to the XDoclet installation directory.

To verify your XDoclet installation, change to the *$XDOCLET_HOME/samples* directory and type ant at a command prompt. You should see Example 1-3.

Example 1-3. Output of ant

```
rosencrantz:/Library/xdoclet-1.2.3/samples sdavis$ ant

[many lines deleted for clarity]

compile:
     [echo] +--------------------------------------------------+
     [echo] |                                                  |
     [echo] | C O M P I L I N G   S O U R C E S                |
     [echo] |                                                  |
     [echo] +--------------------------------------------------+
    [javac] Compiling 109 source files to
            /Library/xdoclet-1.2.3/samples/target/classes

jar:
     [echo] You can find the generated sources in the /samples/target/gen-src
     [echo] directory and the compiled classes in the /samples/target/classes
     [echo] directory. Enjoy!
```

Example 1-3. Output of ant (continued)

```
BUILD SUCCESSFUL
Total time: 1 minute 23 seconds
rosencrantz:/Library/xdoclet-1.2.3/samples sdavis$
```

Installing JBoss

Now that we have all prerequisites in place, we can get to the reason why you are here: installing and running JBoss.

Download the JBoss Application Server Version 4.0.2 from *http://www.jboss.org*. Since it is written in Java, the same installation files will work on Windows, Linux, Unix, or Mac OS X. Any platform that has a JVM can run JBoss.

To install JBoss, simply unzip the downloaded file to the directory of your choice. Next, create an environment variable called *JBOSS_HOME* that points to the JBoss installation directory. Finally, add *$JBOSS_HOME/bin* to the system path so you can run JBoss from the command line.

To verify your JBoss installation, type run at a command prompt (run.bat for Windows users, run.sh for Linux/Unix/Mac users). You should see something like this in your terminal window:

```
rosencrantz:/Library/jboss/bin sdavis$ ./run.sh
======================================================================
=========

  JBoss Bootstrap Environment

  JBOSS_HOME: /Library/jboss

  JAVA: /System/Library/Frameworks/JavaVM.framework/home/bin/java

  JAVA_OPTS: -server -Xms128m -Xmx128m -Dprogram.name=run.sh

  CLASSPATH: /Library/jboss/bin/run.jar:/System/Library/Frameworks/
  JavaVM.framework/home/lib/tools.jar


======================================================================
=========

22:14:03,159 INFO  [Server] Starting JBoss (MX MicroKernel)...
22:14:03,177 INFO  [Server] Release ID: JBoss [Zion] 4.0.2
(build: CVSTag=JBoss_4_0_2 date=200505022023)
22:14:03,181 INFO  [Server] Home Dir: /Library/jboss-4.0.2

[many lines deleted for clarity...]

22:14:55,890 INFO  [Http11Protocol] Starting Coyote
HTTP/1.1 on http-0.0.0.0-8080
22:14:56,396 INFO  [ChannelSocket] JK: ajp13 listening on /0.0.0.0:8009
22:14:56,519 INFO  [JkMain] Jk running ID=0 time=0/240  config=null
```

```
22:14:56,530 INFO  [Server] JBoss (MX MicroKernel)
 [4.0.2 (build: CVSTag=JBoss_4_0_2 date=200505022023)]
 Started in 53s:238ms
```

If you don't see any exceptions scroll by, JBoss is up and running when you see the final line: `Started in xx ms`. To stop JBoss, press `ctrl+C`.

Now that we're sure that everything runs, let's explore JBoss a bit more closely.

Touring the JBoss Directory Structure

JBoss has directory structure that resembles most open source projects (as shown in Figure 1-1). We're going to briefly point out what each directory holds, and then quickly move along. You'll rarely need to make changes to them. JBoss is configured and ready to run out of the box. You'll spend most of your time messing around with the *server/* directory. This is where you deploy your application.

Figure 1-1 shows a brief overview of each directory:

`bin/`
> Start up and shut down scripts.

`client/`
> JAR files used by external client applications that remotely access JNDI resources.

`docs/`
> Strangely, the JBoss documentation is not found here. (It can be downloaded from *http://www.jboss.com/products/jbossas/docs*.) Instead, you'll find various subdirectories:

> `dtd/`
>> XML DTDs describing the structure of J2EE standard and JBoss-specific deployment descriptors. In J2EE 1.4, DTDs have been deprecated in favor of Schemas. The DTDs are preserved here to support previous versions of the J2EE. JBoss still uses DTDs for JBoss-specific descriptors.

> `examples/`
>> Subdirectories with sample JBoss descriptors. The most notable among them is the `jca` subdirectory that holds sample DataSource configuration files (`*-ds.xml`) for most of the major relational databases. We'll discuss this directory in more detail in the JDBC chapter.

> `licenses/`
>> Licenses for all the different services.

> `schema/`
>> XML Schemas (XSDs) describing the structure of J2EE 1.4 standard deployment descriptors.

> `tests/`
>> Unit and functional tests for JBoss.

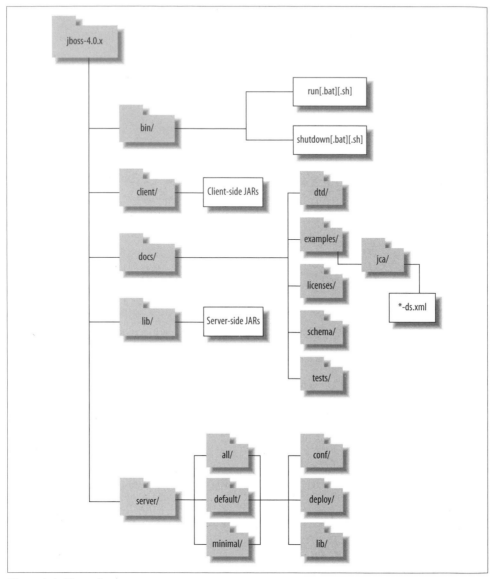

Figure 1-1. JBoss directory structure

lib/
    JAR files that make up JBoss.

server/
    Sub-directories for the various server configurations. This is where you deploy
    your applications.

Server Configurations

The *server/* directory is the most interesting one of the bunch to us as J2EE developers. It is where we configure JBoss services and deploy our applications.

Earlier in the chapter we said that JBoss was a family of interrelated services. This family of services is called a Server Configuration. Three named server configurations are in the *server/* directory: minimal, default, and all. The only difference among the three are the specific services that run at startup.

minimal/

> Includes only JNDI and logging services. As the name implies, it does not include any of the other standard J2EE services (EJBs, JMS, or a web container).

default/

> This is the base J2EE 1.4 configuration. It is what runs if you do not specify a server configuration.

all/

> This is the "kitchen sink" server configuration. It includes everything in the default configuration plus services like clustering.

You can easily create your own Server Configuration by simply copying one of these directories, giving it a unique name, and adding or removing services as you wish. We'll stick with the default ones for this book, but feel free to experiment on your own.

When we started JBoss previously, it ran using the default configuration. Try starting JBoss with the minimal configuration. At a command prompt, type run -c minimal. JBoss should start up in a fraction of the time it took last time. You also should see far fewer lines in the console output than you did last time.

Type ctrl+C at a command prompt to stop JBoss, and then run -c default to run the default server configuration again. Notice all of the additional services that start up in the default configuration.

JBoss is really just a thin JMX (Java Management Extenstions) microkernel. JMX is a framework that allows you to interact with live, running code. You can start and stop services, gather metrics, and even change parameters on the fly. Services that implement the JMX interface are called "managed beans," or MBeans.

Each of the J2EE services that run inside JBoss is an MBean. Log4j, Tomcat, and Hibernate are all MBeans. We'll talk about how to selectively turn them on and off in the next section.

You don't need to know anything about JMX to deploy an application to JBoss. You really don't need to know it to configure JBoss, either—you'll just see the terminology come up from time to time. JBoss is a great example of the power of JMX. (For more information on JMX, see *Java Management Extensions* by J. Steven Perry.)

Touring the Server Configuration Directory Structure

A server configuration has three core subdirectories: *conf/*, *deploy/*, and *lib/*. Like the main JBoss directories, you'll make changes to them only on rare occasions. Generally, you'll simply drop your EAR or WAR file in the *deploy/* directory and let JBoss handle the rest.

conf/
> Includes configuration files for core services such as Log4J and JAAS

deploy/
> Deployment directory for both dynamic JBoss services (MBeans) and your custom applications (EARs and WARs)

lib/
> JAR files to support the dynamic JBoss services (MBeans).

Look around the *default/conf/* directory. The main Server Configuration file is *jboss-service.xml*. The only reason why you might edit this file is to change a port that a specific service runs on. Edit these values with care—the ports assigned to these services are well known. Changing them could cause downstream services to fail.

Change to the *default/lib/* directory. These JAR files make up the J2EE services. You might drop an occasional database driver in here, but all the JARs that your application uses should be included in the WAR or EAR *lib/* directory.

Now change to the *default/deploy/* directory. This is where we'll deploy the JAW application in just a bit. For now, let's play around with the JBoss MBeans.

Make sure that you have JBoss open in one console window and the *default/deploy/* directory open in another. While JBoss runs, it constantly polls this directory looking for changes to the configuration. Let's dynamically undeploy an MBean to see this process in action.

The easiest way to see the process is to create a *$JBOSS_HOME/server/default/undeploy/* directory. (It can be named anything you like, but "undeploy" is a common choice.) Move the *hsqldb-ds.xml* file to the *undeploy/* directory and watch the JBoss console. You should see the Hypersonic database service shut down and all of the related services reconfigure themselves. Now move the file back from the *undeploy/* directory to the *deploy/* directory. Once again, JBoss recognizes the change in configuration and adjusts itself accordingly.

Adding and removing services while JBoss is running is called "hot deployment." As you'll see in the next section, you can hot deploy EARs and WARs as well.

Now that we've played around with JBoss a bit, let's deploy our first application.

Deploying Applications to JBoss

J2EE applications are generally bundled up as Enterprise Archives (EARs) or Web Archives (WARs). JBoss services can be bundled up as Service Archives (SARs). While each application technically is nothing more than a simple Java Archive (JAR), they have special internal directory structures and configuration files that must be present for the sake of the application server. (We will discuss EARs and WARs in greater detail later in the book.)

Knowing when to use these different file types and where to place them can be confusing. Here are some basic principles:

- *$JBOSS_HOME/lib* is for the application server's dependent libraries. These file types should always be packaged as JARs. You should never put your own JARs in this directory.

- *$JBOSS_HOME/server/[server configuration]/lib* is for the Server Configuration's dependent libraries. These, too, should always be JARs. You may add an occasional database driver JAR to this directory.

- *$JBOSS_HOME/server/[server configuration]/deploy* is for SARs, WARs, and EARs. Plain old JARs will be ignored if placed here directly, although all three types of files may themselves contain JARs.

If you haven't done so already, go to *http://www.jbossatwork.com* and download the code examples. Once you've unzipped the downloaded file, copy *jaw.war* from the *ch01/ 01a-test* directory to *$JBOSS_HOME/server/default/deploy*. In the JBoss console window, you should see the deployed test application.

To verify that the application was deployed correctly, open a web browser and go to *http://localhost:8080/jaw* (see Figure 1-2).

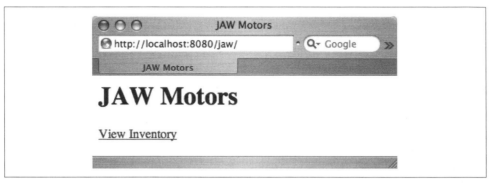

Figure 1-2. JAW Motors web page

Note that our WAR is treated no differently than an MBean. If you move *jaw.war* to the *undeploy/* directory, JBoss will dynamically unload it, as it did with Hypersonic earlier.

Looking Ahead...

Now that you've had a chance to see JBoss at work, let's begin writing our web application. The next chapter walks you through the basics of building and deploying a WAR.

CHAPTER 2

Web Applications

In this chapter, we'll begin writing the JAW Motors application. First, we'll explain some basic architectural principles like the MVC pattern of web development. Then we'll explore the building blocks of the web tier (JSP, JSTL, CSS, and servlets). Finally, we'll use ANT to create WAR files and deploy them to JBoss.

Our goal is not to teach you these technologies and techniques from scratch—they should be familiar to most web developers already. This chapter is meant to be a quick overview and demonstration of the technology working in JBoss. For deeper look into web tier software and development best practices, look at *Head First Servlets & JSP*, by Bryan Basham, Kathy Sierra, and Bert Bates (O'Reilly).

The Servlet Container

The servlet container is the core J2EE technology that powers the web tier. It is considered a container because JSPs and servlets cannot run as standalone applications—they must implement special interfaces and run "inside" the container. The container listens for HTTP requests on a given port, hands the incoming data to your custom components, and uses the resulting output to create a well-formed HTML document to return to the web browser as the response.

The JBoss developers wisely chose not to create their own servlet container to meet this need. A number of excellent ones already are out there. Rather than recreating the wheel, JBoss allows you to integrate the servlet container of your choice.

Tomcat 5.5.9 is the default servlet container included with JBoss 4.0.2. It is deployed as a SAR in *$JBOSS_HOME/server/default/deploy/jbossweb-tomcat55.sar*.

If you are comfortable working with Tomcat, you should have no trouble working in JBoss. All the usual configuration files and JARs are in the Tomcat directory. For example, edit *server.xml* to change the port Tomcat listens on. (8080 is the default.) To change the default session timeout from 30 minutes, edit *conf/web.xml*. (For more information about installing and configuring Tomcat, see *Tomcat: The Definitive Guide* by Jason Brittain and Ian F. Darwin (O'Reilly).)

Thanks to the modular design of JBoss, swapping out Tomcat for another servlet container is easy. Jetty is another option that is fast, mature, and open source. (As a matter of fact, it was the default container included with JBoss 3.x.) Go to *http://jetty.mortbay.org/jetty/download.html* to download a pre-built SAR, ready to drop in and run.

Three-Tier Applications

Before we dive into writing our code, let's take a moment to talk about some architectural principles. This discussion will set the stage for this chapter and the rest of the book.

The parts of a J2EE application fall into three basic tiers:

- The presentation tier is the collection of J2EE components that comprise the UI. For web applications, this tier includes components like Servlets and JSPs.
- The business tier is so named because it is where your business logic lives. The technologies that live here include EJBs and MDBs.
- The persistence tier is where your data is stored for the long term. It generally involves a relational database, but isn't limited to that. You could store your data as XML, serialized JavaBeans, or even plain old ASCII text files.

In a well-engineered application, components in each tier are "highly cohesive" and "loosely coupled". By highly cohesive, we mean that each component should do only one thing. By loosely coupled, we mean that components across the tiers shouldn't depend on one another unnecessarily.

For example, a getCars( ) method call should return only data. The data shouldn't be preformatted into HTML. If it is, your data tier knows too much about the presentation tier. The two tiers are highly coupled.

An unfortunate side effect of this coupling is that deciding to add a new presentation technology later (like a Swing client) will force you to rewrite a portion of your persistence tier as well. If instead your persistence tier returns data and lets the presentation tier concern itself with the formatting, then you can reuse your persistence tier across multiple UIs. Loosely coupled tiers encourage reuse.

You also could argue that the persistence tier fails the highly cohesive test. It is concerned with too many things—data and presentation. A clean separation of concerns is what we are hoping to accomplish.

This notion of tiers guided both the JAW Motors application architecture and the layout of this book. The book starts with the presentation tier in the first few chapters, moves through the persistence tier in the middle chapters and tackles business tier issues in the latter chapters.

Exploring the Presentation Tier

So, here we are at the presentation tier. The same principles of high cohesiveness and loose coupling are as applicable within this tier as they are across tiers. In the presentation tier, it is known as the Model / View / Controller (MVC) pattern.

- The view is the actual screen. It is implemented using JSPs, CSS, and taglibs like the JSTL. It is concerned only about formatting the data in a pleasing way.
- The model is the data. In a "View Cars" screen, the model is a Plain Old Java Object (POJO). In our case, it is a simple JavaBean named CarBean.
- The controller mediates communication between the View and the Model. If a "viewCarList" request comes in, it retrieves the CarBeans from the persistence layer and hands them to the view. In a web application, the controller generally is a servlet.

Why Didn't You Use Framework X?

Perhaps the only thing more contentious among programmers than the argument over which text editor to use is which web framework to use. There are over 30 different Java-based web frameworks out there to choose from.

The dirty little secret of choosing a framework is that they are more similar than they are different. They all follow the same basic MVC pattern. So whether you choose to use Struts, JSF, Webwork, Tapestry, or any of the others, you are doing essentially the same thing—using a MVC framework.

While the frameworks all have similar philosophies, they differ in terms of implementation. Rather than choosing one and risk having you get lost in the details of the specific framework, we took the coward's way out and rolled our own MVC. We felt that this would allow us to clearly demonstrate how each J2EE technology interacts, and hopefully avoid the wrath of the jilted framework aficionado.

On most projects, we generally go with the framework the team has the most experience with, but you shouldn't feel obligated to choose any of them. We'll use a framework if the added functionality merits the additional overhead, but in the spirit of agile development we'll often use the "home grown" framework presented here for quick and dirty prototypes. By adhering to the basic principles of the MVC pattern, moving from our homegrown framework to a "real" one later in the development cycle is reasonably painless.

Building the View Cars Page

Let's begin by implementing the View Cars page. As you can imagine, the first thing most people do when they visit a car dealership is walk around the lot to see which cars the dealer has in stock. In a similar vein, we'll create a view that allows visitors to "walk the lot" via the web.

This view also gives us an excuse to explore the structure of a WAR file. We'll deploy the WAR to JBoss and see it run in container. Once we have that much under our belt, we'll swing back around and do a quick refactoring to implement the model and controller.

Iteration 1: HTML

JSPs are plain HTML files with some templating capabilities that enable us to plug in data dynamically at runtime. Here is an example of our page using static HTML. (We'll add the dynamic content in just a moment.) Example 2-1 should give you a basic feel for what the webpage will look like, and Figure 2-1 shows the result in a web browser.

Example 2-1. carList.html

```
<html>
<body>
  <table border="1">
    <tr>
      <th bgcolor="cccccc" align="left">Make</th>
      <th bgcolor="cccccc" align="left">Model</th>
      <th bgcolor="cccccc" align="right">Model Year</th>
    </tr>

    <tr>
      <td align="left">Toyota</td>
      <td align="left">Camry</td>
      <td align="right">2005</td>
    </tr>


    <tr>
      <td align="left">Toyota</td>
      <td align="left">Corolla</td>
      <td align="right">1999</td>
    </tr>


    <tr>
      <td align="left">Ford</td>
      <td align="left">Explorer</td>
      <td align="right">2005</td>
```

Example 2-1. carList.html (continued)

```
    </tr>
  </table>
</body>
</html>
```

Make	Model	Model Year
Toyota	Camry	2005
Toyota	Corolla	1999
Ford	Explorer	2005

Figure 2-1. carList.html rendered in a web browser

Iteration 2: JSP and JSTL

Now that we see what we are working toward, let's make this page dynamic. To start, we'll fill the data table using pluggable values rather than using static HTML.

While you can include straight Java code in JSPs, this practice is generally frowned upon. First, this "scriptlet" code is not compiled until runtime. This means that your users bear the brunt of missed semicolons and fat-fingered method calls. It also encourages "copy and paste" reuse. Without compiled code, you cannot test it thoroughly, JAR it up, and reuse it across applications. Most importantly, scriptlets aren't tag-based. By relying on them, you mix programming and tag-based technologies.

The solution to all these problems is Tag Libraries (taglibs). Taglibs are compiled Java classes that emit well-formed fragments of HTML. Once you've identified a taglib at the top of your JSP, you can mix the new tags in right along with the native JSP tags. Since taglibs are stored in a JAR file, they can be distributed easily and reused across applications.

The JSP Standard Tag Library (JSTL) allows you to use custom tags to do the dynamic things you'd normally do using code or scriptlets—insert data into the page dynamically, perform do/while loops, and use if/then branches, for example. Two JARs make up the JSTL—*standard.jar* and *jstl.jar*. As you'll see in a moment, you should include these JARs in your WAR's WEB-INF/lib directory.

Here is the same page using the JSTL to populate the table. Don't worry about the scriptlet at the top—we have a bit of a "chicken and egg" situation on our hands. We use the scriptlet only because we don't have a model or controller in place yet. It will be the first thing to go once we implement the remaining parts of the MVC framework. Focus instead on the JSTL code used to populate the HTML table, as in Example 2-2.

Example 2-2. carList-jstl.jsp

```jsp
<%@ taglib prefix="c" uri="http://java.sun.com/jsp/jstl/core" %>
<%
    // DON'T FREAK OUT!!! This scriptlet code will go away once
    // we have a model and controller in place...

    String[ ][ ] carList = {
            {"Toyota", "Camry", "2005"},
            {"Toyota", "Corolla", "1999"},
            {"Ford", "Explorer", "2005"}
    };

    pageContext.setAttribute("carList", carList);
%>

<html>
<body>
  <table border="1">
    <tr>
      <th bgcolor="cccccc" align="left">Make</th>
      <th bgcolor="cccccc" align="left">Model</th>
      <th bgcolor="cccccc" align="right">Model Year</th>
    </tr>

    <c:forEach items='${carList}' var='car'>
      <tr>
      <td align="left">${car[0]}</td>
      <td align="left">${car[1]}</td>
      <td align="right">${car[2]}</td>
      </tr>
    </c:forEach>
  </table>
</body>
</html>
```

Notice that our source code became considerably shorter. We're using a JSTL forEach loop to walk through each value in the string array instead of building out the entire table by hand. By doing so, we have to describe the row only once instead of *for each* car, as in the previous HTML example.

The syntax used to fill in the <td> elements—${car[0]}—is the JSP Expression Language (EL). It's not truly tag-based, but is used often in conjunctions with the JSTL. You can use a <c:out> JSTL tag if you'd prefer to use only tag-based solutions.

Iteration 3: CSS

Our source code has gotten considerably more concise, but we're not done optimizing yet. There still is a lot of repetitive formatting syntax in place. The Don't Repeat Yourself (DRY) principle is in serious violation at this point.

You can solve this problem by incorporating a bit of Cascading Style Sheet (CSS) magic. CSS is not a J2EE technology—it is part of the HTML standard. Even though Java discussions don't mention it much, it should be an indispensable part of any J2EE developer's toolkit. It allows you to separate presentation details from your data by centralizing styling instructions in a single file.

This brings several benefits along for the ride. It keeps your HTML code clean and concise by eliminating all formatting markup. It allows you to create semantic, descriptive styles instead of relying on physical styling. Most importantly, it allows you to change your look and feel globally by modifying a single file. (This is called "skinning" your web site.)

Example 2-3 is a simple example of a CSS-styled JSP page.

Example 2-3. carList.jsp

```
<%@ taglib prefix="c" uri="http://java.sun.com/jsp/jstl/core" %>
<%
    // DON'T FREAK OUT!!! This scriptlet code will go away once
    // we have a model and controller in place...

    String[ ][ ] carList = {
            {"Toyota", "Camry", "2005"},
            {"Toyota", "Corolla", "1999"},
            {"Ford", "Explorer", "2005"}
    };

    pageContext.setAttribute("carList", carList);
%>

<html>
<head>
  <link rel="stylesheet" type="text/css" href="default.css">
</head>


<body>
  <table>
    <tr>
      <th>Make</th>
      <th>Model</th>
      <th class="model-year">Model Year</th>
    </tr>

    <c:forEach items='${carList}' var='car'>
      <tr>
      <td>${car[0]}</td>
      <td>${car[1]}</td>
      <td class="model-year">${car[2]}</td>
      </tr>
    </c:forEach>
```

Example 2-3. carList.jsp (continued)

```
  </table>
</body>
</html>
```

Example 2-4 is a default CSS-styled JSP page.

Example 2-4. default.css

```
table
{
    border-style: solid;
    border-color: #aaa;
    border-width: 1px;
}

th
{
    color: #000;
    background-color: #ccc;
    border-style: solid;
    border-color: #aaa;
    border-width: 1px;
    font-weight: bold;
    text-align: left;
}

td
{
    color: #000;
    background-color: #fff;
    border-style: solid;
    border-color: #aaa;
    border-width: 1px;
    text-align: left;
}

.model-year
{
    text-align: right;
}
```

Notice the link to the stylesheet in the JSP's <head> section. This tells the web browser to download the stylesheet and use it to render the page. If the stylesheet cannot be found at the address provided, the web page still will be rendered without an error message or any indication that there was a problem. This means that you can supply a bogus address up front and drop in a valid CSS file reference later on. (Of course if your page isn't formatted the way you'd expect, the link to the CSS file is a good place to start troubleshooting.)

In the CSS file, you can set up rendering styles for both built-in tags (table, th) and custom names (model-year). If you plan to apply the style to multiple tags, begin the named style with a period. This creates a CSS class. If you want to limit it to a single use per page (like "footer", "copyright", etc.), begin the named style with a hash ("#"), which creates a CSS ID.

We've only scratched the surface of CSS capabilities. In addition to using it for styling, you can use it to precisely position your HTML elements on the screen. This sets the stage for advanced web UI tricks like tabbed interfaces and drag-and-drop. For a more comprehensive discussion of CSS, see *Cascading Style Sheets: The Definitive Guide* by Eric A. Meyer (O'Reilly).

Deploying the Application as a WAR File

Now that our webpage is looking good, let's bundle everything up into a WAR file and deploy it. The WAR file, as you might guess from its name (Web ARchive), is a collection of presentation tier files. Bundling them up into a single file makes it easy to deploy a complete web application. Recall from the last chapter that all you need to do to deploy a web application in JBoss is copy the WAR file into the *$JBOSS_HOME/server/default/deploy* directory.

In the spirit of high cohesiveness, the WAR file should not contain files that pertain to the other tiers (like EJBs or persistence code). The next chapter discusses the anatomy of an Enterprise Archive (EAR) file. The EAR file is a meta-wrapper, bundling your presentation tier WAR with additional JARs that support the persistence and business tiers.

If you haven't done so already, visit *http://www.jbossatwork.com* and download the sample code bundle. Unzip it to the directory of your choice and change to the *ch02* directory. You should see a number of subdirectories—one for each example in this chapter. Change to */02-view/webapp*. Type ant to compile the application and create the WAR file, as in Example 2-5.

Example 2-5. Building the WAR using Ant

```
Buildfile: build.xml

clean:
   [delete] Deleting directory
   /Users/sdavis/Desktop/jbossatwork/ch02/02-view/webapp/build

compile:
   [mkdir] Created dir:
   /Users/sdavis/Desktop/jbossatwork/ch02/02-view/webapp/build
   [mkdir] Created dir:
   /Users/sdavis/Desktop/jbossatwork/ch02/02-view/webapp/build/classes

war:
   [mkdir] Created dir:
   /Users/sdavis/Desktop/jbossatwork/ch02/02-view/webapp/build/distribution
     [war] Building war:
```

Example 2-5. Building the WAR using Ant (continued)

```
/Users/sdavis/Desktop/jbossatwork/ch02/02-view/webapp/build/
distribution/jaw.war
```

```
all:

BUILD SUCCESSFUL
Total time: 2 seconds
```

Copy the resulting WAR file to *$JBOSS_HOME/server/default/deploy* to deploy it. Visit *http://localhost:8080/jaw* to see it in action. Follow the View Inventory link to see the list of cars.

A Deeper Examination of the WAR

Notice that the URL of your web application is the same as the WAR filename. This URL is called the Context Root. The next chapter shows you how to set your Context Root to be anything, independent of your WAR name. To do this, you'll need to package things up in an EAR. Before getting into the complexity of EARs, though, you need a solid understanding of the WAR file structure.

Most graphical zip utilities can display WAR file contents, as in Example 2-6. For fans of the command line, type jar tvf jaw.war.

Example 2-6. Contents of jaw.war

```
     0 Mon Mar 28 21:41:50 MST 2005 META-INF/
   103 Mon Mar 28 21:41:48 MST 2005 META-INF/MANIFEST.MF
   837 Mon Mar 28 21:33:16 MST 2005 carList-jstl.jsp
   637 Mon Mar 28 21:31:56 MST 2005 carList.html
   823 Mon Mar 28 21:28:20 MST 2005 carList.jsp
   448 Mon Mar 28 21:41:40 MST 2005 default.css
   226 Mon Mar 28 21:14:52 MST 2005 index.jsp
     0 Mon Mar 28 21:26:42 MST 2005 WEB-INF/
   399 Mon Mar 28 21:01:44 MST 2005 WEB-INF/web.xml
     0 Mon Mar 28 21:41:50 MST 2005 WEB-INF/classes/
     0 Mon Mar 28 21:41:50 MST 2005 WEB-INF/lib/
 20682 Fri Feb 11 20:05:08 MST 2005 WEB-INF/lib/jstl.jar
393259 Fri Feb 11 20:05:08 MST 2005 WEB-INF/lib/standard.jar
```

The root of your WAR file is your web application root. Notice *index.jsp*—this file is the starting page of your application. You'll see momentarily that this is specified in *web.xml*. Along for the ride are your other JSP and CSS files.

Your compiled java classes and library JARs are stored in the WEB INF directory. Files in *WEB-INF* are hidden from public view—web users cannot see the directory contents or any of its subdirectories from their browser. They can, however, call a resource stored in *WEB-INF* (like a servlet), as long as it was configured in *web.xml*.

As you might have guessed by now, *WEB-INF/web.xml* (Example 2-7) is an important file to be familiar with. It is the main web deployment descriptor file.

Example 2-7. web.xml

```
<?xml version="1.0" encoding="ISO-8859-1"?>

<web-app version="2.4"
    xmlns="http://java.sun.com/xml/ns/j2ee"
    xmlns:xsi="http://www.w3.org/2001/XMLSchema-instance"
    xsi:schemaLocation="http://java.sun.com/xml/ns/j2ee web-app_2_4.xsd">

    <!-- The Welcome File List -->
    <welcome-file-list>
        <welcome-file>index.jsp</welcome-file>
    </welcome-file-list>
</web-app>
```

For now, *web.xml* only identifies the welcome file list. It is common practice to name your main file index.jsp, but you can use any arbitrary name you'd like as long as it is listed here. This file will continue to grow throughout the book. *Web.xml* is where you identify servlets, JNDI lookups, and security options, among many other things.

What About jboss-web.xml?

As you scan the JBoss discussion forums and mailing lists, you'll see an occasional reference to another deployment descriptor—jboss-web.xml.

Web.xml is the standard deployment descriptor for web applications. By design, it is meant to be standard across all Servlet containers. The flip side is that it doesn't allow container-specific settings. Jboss-web.xml fills this gap. As the name suggests, the settings in this file are specific to JBoss deployments.

There is no need for jboss-web.xml right now, so we didn't include it. You'll see it pop up in the coming chapters.

Ant

You could painstakingly assemble the WAR by hand, or simply use the WAR task included in Ant. While you're deciding which path to take, look at the Ant task in Example 2-8.

Example 2-8. WAR Ant Task

```
<target name="war" depends="compile"
        description="Packages the Web files into a WAR file">
        <mkdir dir="${distribution.dir}" />
```

Example 2-8. WAR Ant Task (continued)

```
    <war destFile="${distribution.dir}/${war.name}"
        webxml="${web.inf.dir}/web.xml">
        <!-- files to be included in / -->
        <fileset dir="${web.dir}"  exclude="WEB-INF/web.xml" />

        <!-- files to be included in /WEB-INF/classes -->
        <classes dir="${classes.dir}" />

        <!-- files to be included in /WEB-INF/lib -->
        <lib dir="${lib.dir}" />

        <!-- files to be included in /WEB-INF -->
        <webinf dir="${web.inf.dir}" excludes="web.xml" />
    </war>
</target>
```

In case you're not fluent in XML-ese, this task gathers up all files from their various locations and puts them in the appropriate WAR file spot:

- All JSPs and web files from ${web.dir} are placed in the root of the directory structure
- The classes (servlets and the like) from ${classes.dir} are placed in WEB-INF/ classes
- The supporting JAR files (like the JSTL) from ${jar.dir} are placed in WEB-INF/lib
- The miscellaneous config files from ${web.inf.dir} are placed in WEB-INF

Once the WAR file is pieced together, the Ant task places it in ${distribution.dir} (which in our case is *build/distribution*). Notice the EL-like syntax? It allows us to define variables at the top of the file and reuse them throughout.

Adding a Model and Controller

Now we have a working skeleton. Let's add the model and controller to complete the MVC framework.

The Model

The model is a Plain Old Java Object (POJO). You've built classes like this a thousand times before. CarBean is nothing more than a class with three member variables and the associated accessors and mutators.

As you saw in the previous JSP example, using string arrays for data storage doesn't yield very expressive source code. We use an object-oriented programming language to build objects that have a deeper semantic meaning than a pile of primitive data types. In Example 2-9, you can see that CarBean is nothing more than a class with three member variables and the associated accessors and mutators. Car.make, Car.model, and

Car.modelYear mean something to us, as opposed to the use of string [0], string [1], and string [2].

Example 2-9. CarBean.java

```java
package com.jbossatwork;

public class CarBean
{
    private String make;
    private String model;
    private String modelYear;

    public CarBean(String make, String model, String modelYear)
    {
        this.make = make;
        this.model = model;
        this.modelYear = modelYear;
    }

    public String getMake()
    {
        return make;
    }

    public void setMake(String make)
    {
        this.make = make;
    }

    public String getModel()
    {
        return model;
    }

    public void setModel(String model)
    {
        this.model = model;
    }

    public String getModelYear()
    {
        return modelYear;
    }

    public void setModelYear(String modelYear)
    {
        this.modelYear = modelYear;
    }
}
```

Now that we have a model, let's change our JSP to iterate through an ArrayList of CarBeans instead of a simple string array (Example 2-10). The number of lines of code hasn't really changed, but hopefully the source code is far more readable using the JavaBean. (And yes, that pesky scriptlet code is still around. Once we get our Controller in place, we'll be able to replace it with something a bit more production-worthy.)

Example 2-10. carList.jsp

```jsp
<%@ taglib prefix="c" uri="http://java.sun.com/jsp/jstl/core" %>
<%@ page import="java.util.ArrayList,
               com.jbossatwork.CarBean"%>
<%
    // DON'T FREAK OUT!!! This scriptlet code will go away once
    // we have a controller in place...

    ArrayList carList = new ArrayList( );
    carList.add(new CarBean("Toyota", "Camry", "2005"));
    carList.add(new CarBean("Toyota", "Corolla", "1999"));
    carList.add(new CarBean("Ford", "Explorer", "2005"));

    pageContext.setAttribute("carList", carList);
%>

<html>
<head>
  <link rel="stylesheet" type="text/css" href="default.css">
</head>

<body>
  <table>
    <tr>
      <th>Make</th>
      <th>Model</th>
      <th class="model-year">Model Year</th>
    </tr>

    <c:forEach items='${carList}' var='car'>
      <tr>
      <td>${car.make}</td>
      <td>${car.model}</td>
      <td class="model-year">${car.modelYear}</td>
      </tr>
    </c:forEach>
  </table>
</body>
</html>
```

Notice that our EL has changed to reference the individual attributes of the Java-Bean instead of using array notation. EL automatically calls the getters and setters behind the scenes. We are left with code that is almost plain English—"put the car make here, the car model there."

The Controller

Now the question is how will the JSP get its hands on the populated ArrayList? If you call the JSP directly (as we do in *index.jsp*: `<a href="carList.jsp">`), there's really no way to do the required setup for the view. Oh sure—JSTL tags allow you to make SQL calls directly from your JSPs, but that doesn't sound "highly cohesive," now, does it?

Enter the controller. If our link sends us to the controller instead of directly to the JSP, the controller can get the cars from the database, put them in memory, and redirect us to the JSP. Our new link looks like this: `<a href="controller?action=viewCarList">`. This link calls the controller in Example 2-11, asking it to perform the `viewCarList` action.

Example 2-11. ControllerServlet.java

```java
package com.jbossatwork;

import java.io.IOException;
import java.util.List;
import java.util.ArrayList;
import javax.servlet.*;
import javax.servlet.http.*;

public class ControllerServlet extends HttpServlet
{
    private static final String ACTION_KEY = "action";
    private static final String VIEW_CAR_LIST_ACTION = "viewCarList";
    private static final String ERROR_KEY = "errorMessage";
    private static final String ERROR_PAGE="/error.jsp";

    public void doGet(HttpServletRequest request, HttpServletResponse response)
            throws IOException, ServletException {
        processRequest(request, response);
    }

    public void doPost(HttpServletRequest request, HttpServletResponse response)
            throws IOException, ServletException {
        processRequest(request, response);
    }

    protected void processRequest(
                HttpServletRequest request, HttpServletResponse response)
            throws ServletException, IOException {
        String actionName = request.getParameter(ACTION_KEY);
        String destinationPage = ERROR_PAGE;

        // perform action
        if(VIEW_CAR_LIST_ACTION.equals(actionName))
        {
            List carList = new ArrayList();
            carList.add(new CarBean("Toyota", "Camry", "2005"));
```

Example 2-11. ControllerServlet.java (continued)

```
            carList.add(new CarBean("Toyota", "Corolla", "1999"));
            carList.add(new CarBean("Ford", "Explorer", "2005"));
            request.setAttribute("carList", carList);

            destinationPage = "/carList.jsp";
        }
        else
        {
            String errorMessage = "[" + actionName + "] is not a valid action.";
            request.setAttribute(ERROR_KEY, errorMessage);
        }


        // Redirect to destination page.
        RequestDispatcher dispatcher =
                getServletContext( ).getRequestDispatcher(destinationPage);

        dispatcher.forward(request, response);
    }
}
```

The controller gets the `action` parameter off of the request stack and branches to the appropriate code block. (For now, we have only one action in place: `VIEW_CAR_LIST_ACTION`.) The controller creates the `CarBeans`, sticks them in an `ArrayList` named `carList`, and puts the list into `Request` scope. At the end of the `processRequest( )` method it redirects us to the appropriate JSP.

Now that the controller handles the data setup, we can *finally* remove the scriptlet code from our JSP to get Example 2-12. It's looking pretty lean and mean at this point. (Go back and look at the original HTML-only example we started with to gauge just how far we've come.)

Example 2-12. carList.jsp (Final Version)

```
<%@ taglib prefix="c" uri="http://java.sun.com/jsp/jstl/core" %>

<html>
<head>
  <link rel="stylesheet" type="text/css" href="default.css">
</head>

<body>
  <table>
    <tr>
      <th>Make</th>
      <th>Model</th>
      <th class="model-year">Model Year</th>
    </tr>

    <c:forEach items='${carList}' var='car'>
      <tr>
```

Example 2-12. carList.jsp (Final Version) (continued)

```
      <td>${car.make}</td>
      <td>${car.model}</td>
      <td class="model-year">${car.modelYear}</td>
      </tr>
   </c:forEach>
  </table>
</body>
</html>
```

Notice that the JSTL for loop finds the carList object automatically in the Request scope. We don't have to tell it where to go looking for it.

The last thing we need to do is add the servlet to web.xml. In the coming chapters we'll use XDoclet to dynamically generate this file on the fly. For now, we'll just hand-edit the file in Example 2-13.

Example 2-13. web.xml

```
<?xml version="1.0" encoding="ISO-8859-1"?>

<web-app version="2.4"
    xmlns="http://java.sun.com/xml/ns/j2ee"
    xmlns:xsi="http://www.w3.org/2001/XMLSchema-instance"
    xsi:schemaLocation="http://java.sun.com/xml/ns/j2ee web-app_2_4.xsd">

    <!-- servlet definition -->
    <servlet>
        <servlet-name>Controller</servlet-name>
        <servlet-class>com.jbossatwork.ControllerServlet</servlet-class>
    </servlet>

    <!-- servlet mapping -->
    <servlet-mapping>
        <servlet-name>Controller</servlet-name>
        <url-pattern>/controller/*</url-pattern>
    </servlet-mapping>

    <!-- The Welcome File List -->
    <welcome-file-list>
        <welcome-file>index.jsp</welcome-file>
    </welcome-file-list>

</web-app>
```

The <servlet> section allows us to create an alias for the class. This alias makes it easier to refactor later on. It shields us from class and package name changes, but also means that we can swap entirely different servlet classes in and out for testing purposes, with nothing but a single line change in web.xml.

The `<servlet-mapping>` section exposes hidden *WEB-INF* resources to the public. The `<url-pattern>` allows you to set up any name you'd like. We remapped `com. jbossatwork.ControllerServlet` to simply `controller`.

With all of this in place, we're ready to build and deploy again. Change to the *ch02-mvc* directory and type ant. Copy the new *jaw.war* to the *deploy* directory. Visit *http://localhost:8080/jaw* to see it in action.

Looking Ahead...

As this application matures, the various pieces get pushed into different tiers. Instead of the servlet creating the `CarBeans` out of thin air, it will pass the request to an EJB. The EJB will eventually get the information out of a database. But for now we completed the first step toward a fully realized J2EE application.

If you are familiar with agile development methodologies, you know that having one working application in the hand is worth two that are still stuck in development. Even though the UI is just the tip of the iceberg in terms of the entire application, having this much in place is a huge milestone.

Nothing makes an application seem more real than a working set of screens, even if (as is the case here) it has nothing of substance behind the façade. It allows the user to see the program far more clearly and persuasively than index cards, white board drawings, or cocktail napkins. From the developer's perspective, it gives a clear idea of what blanks still need to be filled in (persistence, business logic, etc.).

Perhaps most importantly, it allows the UI to have the longest usage cycle. By the time the application is fully implemented, you and the users will have spent enough time working with the UI that all the usability and look-and-feel issues will have been long since been hammered out. As one of our customers said, "Because I was working with the screens from the very beginning, by the time the final application was delivered, I felt like I was already an expert."

CHAPTER 3

Building and Deploying an EAR

In the last chapter we introduced you to web applications, but the web tier is just one part of the J2EE spectrum. In this chapter, we'll expand the JAW application from a simple WAR file into a full-fledged EAR.

We'll explore the different parts of an EAR file. We'll build a Common JAR containing classes that can be shared across all tiers of the application. Finally, we'll play with various Ant and XDoclet tasks to create our EAR and dynamically generate the deployment descriptors JBoss needs.

WARs Versus EARs

The WAR file is a convenient way to bundle up all pieces of a web application. All servlet containers know how to deploy a WAR file—they expand the bundle, look for the *WEB-INF* directory, and read the *web.xml* found there for further deployment instructions.

The EAR file provides the same type of functionality for a full-fledged J2EE application. JBoss expands the EAR, finds the required deployment descriptors, and proceeds from there.

An EAR is like a carton of eggs—it keeps everything organized. While the carton doesn't add any direct value to your omelet, it makes getting the eggs home from the store so easy that you wouldn't think about transporting eggs any other way.

Each egg in your EAR carton is a specific piece of the J2EE puzzle. These eggs (or JARs) come in three basic varieties called "modules":

Web module
    A WAR file containing presentation tier components

EJB module
    An EJB JAR file containing the middle-tier components (EJBs, MDBs, etc.)

Java module

A regular JAR file containing classes and libraries that are shared across the entire application. An application client JAR and a common JAR are two examples of Java modules.

An EAR can contain at least one of any of these modules. By the same token, any of them can be safely omitted if they aren't needed. Figure 3-1 shows the structure of an EAR file.

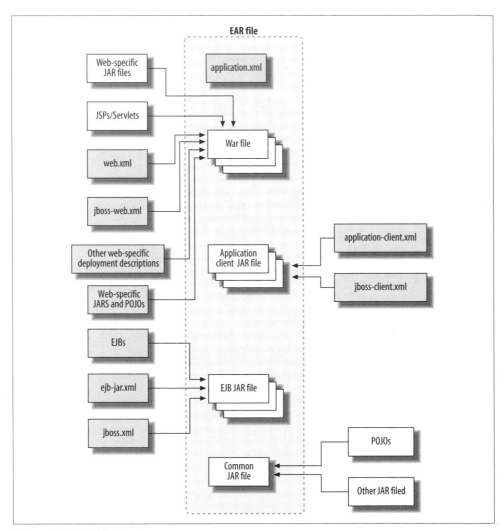

Figure 3-1. EAR file structure

Application.xml

Just as a WAR file contains a *web.xml* deployment descriptor, an EAR file contains a file named *application.xml*. It is essentially a packing list, telling the J2EE server exactly what files the EAR contains and where you can find the files relative to the root of the EAR. The EAR file's *META-INF* directory stores *application.xml*.

Example 3-1 shows the JAW Motors *application.xml* file.

Example 3-1. application.xml

```
<?xml version="1.0" encoding="UTF-8"?>
<application xmlns="http://java.sun.com/xml/ns/j2ee"
        xmlns:xsi="http://www.w3.org/2001/XMLSchema-instance"
        xsi:schemaLocation="http://java.sun.com/xml/ns/j2ee
            http://java.sun.com/xml/ns/j2ee/application_1_4.xsd"
        version="1.4">
  <display-name>JBossAtWorkEAR</display-name>

  <module>
      <web>
          <web-uri>webapp.war</web-uri>
          <context-root>jaw</context-root>
      </web>
  </module>

  <module>
      <java>common.jar</java>
  </module>

</application>
```

The elements in *application.xml* should be pretty self-explanatory. We are telling the application server the name of each JAR and what function it serves.

Notice that Web modules allow you to specify one other value—the <context-root>. Recall from the previous chapter that the context root is your web site's URL. If you deploy a simple WAR file, the name of the WAR will be used as the URL. When your WAR file is deployed inside an EAR, this element allows you to override the physical name of the WAR and use whatever URL you'd like.

Although not shown in this example, <security-role> is another important element in *application.xml*. The <security-role> element describes (what else?) the security roles used throughout a J2EE application for both web and EJB components. Defining security roles in *application.xml* provides a single place to set up J2EE declarative security without duplicating it in *web.xml* and *ejb-jar.xml*. The Security chapter describes <security-role> in greater detail.

Common JAR

In the previous chapter, we created a `CarBean` POJO to hold the various attributes of a car. We stored it in the WAR file because, well, you didn't have any other choice at that time. We should now reconsider the storage location for the `CarBean` to maximize its reuse.

By the end of this book, we will pull cars out of a database in the persistence tier, and hand them to objects in the business tier, which ultimately will pass them up to the presentation tier. An object that is shared across tiers is a perfect candidate for the Common JAR.

In addition to custom domain objects, the Common JAR is a great location to store common libraries such as Log4J or JDOM. While both WARs and EJB JARs have *lib* directories, they are best used for tier-specific libraries. For example, the JSTL JARs belong in the WAR—they have no other purpose than to support the creation of web pages. On the other hand, logging is something that happens throughout the codebase—it really belongs in a common JAR.

Let's factor our `CarBean` out of the WAR and into the Common JAR. In addition to moving directories, we're going to rename it to better describe its purpose in the application.

The suffix "Bean" is a bit overloaded: it includes JavaBeans, Enterprise Java Beans, Session Beans, Message-Driven Beans, JMX MBeans, and the list goes on. The design pattern that best describes the `CarBean`'s function is a Data Transfer Object (DTO), so when we move the bean, we'll also rename it `CarDTO`. The source code will remain the same, but the name will give us a better idea about the true purpose of the class.

Exploring the New Directory Structure

The previous chapter included only the *webapp* directory. If you change to the *ch03/03a-ear* directory, you'll see that we've expanded to a *webapp* directory and a *common* directory.

We also expanded from one to three *build.xml* files. Each subdirectory has its own *build.xml*, and the master build file lives in the top-level directory. The goal is to keep each portion of the application as autonomous as possible. Granted, most of the application will depend on the common sub-project, but by providing individual Ant scripts you have the opportunity to build each portion of the project separately.

The common sub-project

Take a moment to explore the `common` sub-project. It contains a single class—`CarDTO`. We have created a new package structure to store all DTOs—`com.jbossatwork.dto`.

You can build this sub-project by typing ant in the common directory. It compiles the CarDTO class and bundles it up into a JAR file. After you've built the sub-project, change to the *build/distribution* directory and type jar tvf common.jar to verify that the CarDTO class is indeed stored in *common.jar*.

The webapp sub-project

The only change to the webapp sub-project from the previous chapter is the removal of the CarDTO class. To accommodate this change, we now must import the com.jbossatwork.dto package at the top of ControllerServlet.

We also have to change our *build.xml* script to include the *common.jar* in our class-path. Notice that the definition of common.jar.dir uses a relative path to step up one level from the basedir of the webapp sub-project and down into the common sub-project's output directory in Example 3-2.

Example 3-2. webapp build.xml

```
<property name="lib.dir" value="lib"/>
<property name="compile.lib.dir" value="compile-lib"/>
<property name="common.jar.dir" value="../common/build/distribution"/>

<path id="compile.classpath">
    <fileset dir="${compile.lib.dir}">
        <include name="**/*.jar"/>
    </fileset>

    <fileset dir="${lib.dir}">
        <include name="**/*.jar"/>
    </fileset>

    <fileset dir="${common.jar.dir}">
        <include name="**/*.jar"/>
    </fileset>
</path>
```

Introducing cross project dependencies like this is not without risk. If you try to build the webapp sub-project before the common project is built, the build will fail because the dependent JAR won't be present. Of course, most other sub-projects will have dependencies on the common project *by design*—the common project is meant to hold objects that will be shared across all tiers.

Having the webapp sub-project rebuild the common project every time could be an unnecessary step if the common project changes infrequently. If we do not couple the webapp build process to the common build process, webapp developers can informally baseline the common project by only rebuilding it when they make a conscious effort to do so.

Type ant in the webapp top-level directory to build the WAR file. Change to *build/ distribution* and type jar tvf webapp.war to see the contents. Verify that CarDTO is no longer present in the WAR.

The master build

To ensure that each project gets built—in the proper order—we created a master build file. This file doesn't actually compile any code; rather, it calls the appropriate build files of each sub-project in the proper order and then EARs up the results. Any failure of any sub-build will fail the master build, so we can rest assured that a successful master build is predicated on each individual build completing successfully.

To invoke a build script in another directory, we use the <ant> task. Here is what our compile target looks like in the master *build.xml* file in Example 3-3.

Example 3-3. master build.xml

```
<target name="compile" description="Compiles all Java code">
        <echo message="##### Building common #####" />
        <ant dir="${common.dir}" target="all" >
            <property name="jar.name" value="${common.jar.name}"/>
        </ant>

        <echo message="##### Building webapp #####" />
        <ant dir="${webapp.dir}" target="all" >
            <property name="war.name" value="${webapp.war.name}"/>
            <property name="common.jar.dir" value="${basedir}/${common.jar.dir}"/>
        </ant>
    </target>
```

Notice that we also can override properties in the child build process. In both instances, we override the name of the JAR or WAR file specified in the child build. In the case of the webapp build, we can no longer use the same relative path: your base directory is different now, so trying to move up a level and over doesn't work. We pass the webapp build file a fully qualified path to the common output directory.

Ant EAR task

The final step in the process is to EAR up the results of the webapp and common builds. Just as there is a WAR task, Ant also provides us with an EAR task, as in Example 3-4.

Example 3-4. master build.xml

```
<target name="ear" depends="compile">
        <ear destFile="${distribution.dir}/${ear.name}"
            appxml="${meta-inf.dir}/application.xml" >

            <!-- files to be included in / -->
            <fileset dir="${webapp.war.dir}" />
```

Example 3-4. master build.xml (continued)

```
            <fileset dir="${common.jar.dir}" />
        </ear>
    </target>
```

Notice that the EAR task requires us to pass it a well-formed *application.xml* file. Example 3-5 shows what a simple one looks like.

Example 3-5. application.xml

```
<?xml version="1.0" encoding="UTF-8"?>
<application xmlns="http://java.sun.com/xml/ns/j2ee"
             xmlns:xsi="http://www.w3.org/2001/XMLSchema-instance"
             xsi:schemaLocation="http://java.sun.com/xml/ns/j2ee
                 http://java.sun.com/xml/ns/j2ee/application_1_4.xsd"
             version="1.4">
    <display-name>JBossAtWorkEAR</display-name>

    <module>
        <web>
            <web-uri>webapp.war</web-uri>
            <context-root>jaw</context-root>
        </web>
    </module>

    <module>
        <java>common.jar</java>
    </module>

</application>
```

To verify the results of the master build, change to the *build/distribution* directory and type `jar tvf jaw.ear`. You should see *webapp.war, common.jar*, and *application.xml*. We are now ready to deploy the EAR file.

Deploying the EAR

Let's make sure that the WAR files from the previous chapters don't end up conflicting with our EAR file. Delete *jaw.war* from the *deploy* directory before moving on. Now we're ready to drop in our newly created EAR file.

Deploying an EAR by hand is no different than deploying a WAR by hand. Copy *jaw.ear* to *$JBOSS_HOME/server/default/deploy*. Your JBoss console should let you know that it was deployed successfully, as in Example 3-6.

Example 3-6. JBoss console output showing a successful EAR deployment

```
22:37:55,659 INFO  [EARDeployer] Init J2EE application:
    file:/Library/jboss-4.0.1/server/default/deploy/jaw.ear
22:37:55,853 INFO  [TomcatDeployer] deploy, ctxPath=/jaw,
    warUrl=file:/Library/jboss-4.0.1/server/default/tmp/deploy/
```

```
     tmp25111jaw-ear.ear-contents/webapp.war/
22:37:56,159 INFO  [EARDeployer] Started J2EE application:
     file:/Library/jboss-4.0.1/server/default/deploy/jaw-ear.ear
```

Automated Deployments Using Ant

Ant allows you to do far more than simply compile and bundle up your Java application. It has tasks that let you create and delete directories and copy files to a local subdirectory or a remote server by using ftp or scp. Using tasks like exec, rexec, or sshexec, you can even remotely start and stop JBoss.

It's not hard to imagine completely automating the deployment process with an Ant script. But just because you *can* do something doesn't always mean you *should*.

Automating deployment to a test server certainly will help speed up your development iterations. But deployments to a production server should be taken a bit more seriously. Upgrading a production application is something that should be done deliberately, and in our opinion, should be done by hand.

If you provide an Ant task to deploy your application to a production server, you almost certainly guarantee that you will invoke it accidentally at the most inopportune time.

Since we point at a test server for this book, we've provided a convenient couple of Ant targets to deploy your EAR. To do a hot deploy, make sure that you have the $JBOSS_HOME environment variable set, and then simply type ant deploy. The Ant task will copy the EAR file to the correct location for you.

If you want to do a cold deploy, shut down JBoss, type Ant cleandeploy, and then start JBoss back up again. The cleandeploy target will delete the existing EAR file and several temporary directories. Running cleandeploy against a running JBoss instance will cause bad things to happen, so make sure that JBoss is not running before invoking it.

Visit *http://localhost:8080/jaw* to confirm that the application was indeed deployed and still works as expected. Yes, this application doesn't look or behave any differently than the one in the Web chapter. But we added hundreds of lines of new code—isn't that the true measure of a successful J2EE project? (Only kidding....)

In all seriousness, we haven't added any new functionality that the user would notice, but we have set the stage for easy future growth and maximum flexibility. Knowing that the other tiers are coming up soon, these changes will allow you to incorporate the new technology with minimal effort.

Adding a DAO

In that spirit, let's add another component that will pay dividends in future flexibility. Right now, your servlet is creating the car list each time a request comes in. This really isn't optimal. Servlets should deal with the mechanics of the HTTP request/response cycle. They shouldn't perform persistence tier tasks.

We aren't quite ready to install a database (that happens in the next chapter), but we can lay the groundwork by creating a Data Access Object (DAO). A DAO is a layer of abstraction—it hides the actual persistence specifics behind a common interface.

The DAO we create in this chapter still stores the DTO objects in a simple ArrayList. In the next chapter, the DAO will pull car data from a database that uses JDBC. In the chapter after that, it will use Hibernate (an Object/Relational Mapper) to do the same thing. By getting the DAO in place now, however, we'll be able to make these implementation changes without affecting presentation-tier code. Loose coupling and high cohesion comes to the rescue again.

The CarDAO provides a findAll( ) method that returns a List of CarDTOs. The source code in Example 3-7 can be found in the *common* directory in *ch03b-dao*.

Example 3-7. CarDAO.java

```java
package com.jbossatwork.dao;

import java.util.*;
import com.jbossatwork.dto.CarDTO;

public class CarDAO
{
    private List carList;

    public CarDAO()
    {
        carList = new ArrayList();

        carList.add(new CarDTO("Toyota", "Camry", "2005"));
        carList.add(new CarDTO("Toyota", "Corolla", "1999"));
        carList.add(new CarDTO("Ford", "Explorer", "2005"));
    }

    public List findAll()
    {

        return carList;

    }
}
```

The corresponding change in the ControllerServlet calls the newly created DAO in Example 3-8.

Example 3-8. ControllerServlet.java

```
// perform action
      if(VIEW_CAR_LIST_ACTION.equals(actionName))
      {
          CarDAO carDAO = new CarDAO( );
          request.setAttribute("carList", carDAO.findAll( ));

          destinationPage = "/carList.jsp";
      }
```

Not only does this change simplify the code in the servlet, it *feels* more correct as well. The servlet concerns itself solely with web mechanics and delegates the database tasks to a dedicated class. Another pleasant side effect of this is reuse—your data access code can now be called outside of the web tier. If a business tier object needs access to this data, it can make the same call that we make.

Build and deploy the code to verify that we haven't broken your application with this change.

Using XDoclet

The last thing we'll do in this chapter is one more tiny bit of automation.

One of the most important parts of the WAR file is the deployment descriptor—*web. xml*. It lists each servlet and tells the servlet container how to deploy them. By maintaining this file by hand, you almost certainly guarantee that you will forget to update it when you add new components to your application. By using XDoclet in your build process, we can generate it automatically by using nothing but your source code and some well-placed comments.

XDoclet is a collection of custom Ant tasks that generate code during the build process. Sometimes XDoclet can generate the necessary code or deployment descriptor using just the source code. At other times, you'll need to add custom comments to nudge XDoclet along in the right direction.

We have only one servlet right now—ControllerServlet. Example 3-9 shows what your *web.xml* must contain to deploy this servlet correctly.

Example 3-9. web.xml

```
    <!-- servlet definition -->
    <servlet>
        <servlet-name>Controller</servlet-name>
        <servlet-class>com.jbossatwork.ControllerServlet</servlet-class>
    </servlet>

    <!-- servlet mapping -->
    <servlet-mapping>
        <servlet-name>Controller</servlet-name>
```

Example 3-9. web.xml (continued)

```
        <url-pattern>/controller/*</url-pattern>
    </servlet-mapping>
```

Look in *ch03c-xdoclet/src* for the new `ControllerServlet` source code in Example 3-10. Notice the XDoclet comments we've added.

Example 3-10. ControllerServlet.java

```
/**
 * @web.servlet
 *     name="Controller"
 *
 * @web.servlet-mapping
 *     url-pattern="/controller/*"
 */
public class ControllerServlet extends HttpServlet
```

See how they correspond to the *web.xml* elements? Now let's look at *build.xml* to see the newly added XDoclet Ant tasks. We first need to create a couple of new variables, as in Example 3-11.

Example 3-11. Defining XDoclet variables in build.xml

```
<property name="xdoclet.lib.dir" value="${env.XDOCLET_HOME} /lib"/>
<property name="gen.source.dir" value=" ${build.dir}/gensrc"/>
```

`Xdoclet.lib.dir` points to the XDoclet jars. If we have a defined `$XDOCLET_HOME` environment variable, *build.xml* should be automatically pointed in the right direction. (Recall that we installed XDoclet in Chapter 1.)

The second variable defines a new location for our dynamically generated code. By keeping our compiled code and generated source code in the same location (`build.dir`), we can easily delete and recreate it each time we run the Ant tasks. It also gently reminds us that we shouldn't store generated artifacts in source control.

Next, we need to set up a new classpath that includes the XDoclet libraries. We keep XDoclet stuff separate from our regular build process, as in Example 3-12. This ensures that we don't inadvertently create dependencies in our deployed code.

Example 3-12. XDoclet Library Path in build.xml

```
    <path id="xdoclet.lib.path">
        <fileset dir="${xdoclet.lib.dir}">
            <include name="**/*.jar"/>
        </fileset>

        <fileset dir="${compile.lib.dir}">
            <include name="**/*.jar"/>
        </fileset>
    </path>
```

Next we create the generate-web target in Example 3-13.

Example 3-13. generate-web target in build.xml

```
<!-- ====================================== -->
    <target name="generate-web" description="Generate web.xml">
        <taskdef name="webdoclet"
                 classname="xdoclet.modules.web.WebDocletTask"
                 classpathref="xdoclet.lib.path" />

        <mkdir dir="${gen.source.dir}" />

        <webdoclet destdir="${gen.source.dir}">
            <fileset dir="${source.dir}">
                <include name="**/*Servlet.java" />
            </fileset>

            <deploymentdescriptor destdir="${gen.source.dir}"
                                  distributable="false"
                                  servletspec="2.4" />

        </webdoclet>
    </target>
```

Let's step through this:

- To start, we need to define the WebDoclet task. We don't need to use the <taskdef> tag for core Ant tasks, but for third-party tasks, this directive shows Ant where to find the implementation code.
- Next, we create the destination directory for our generated code.
- Finally, we call the <webdoclet> task. As you might guess, it generates web-tier code. In later chapters, we'll see other XDoclet tasks such as <hibernatedoclet> and <ejbdoclet>.
- The <filesetdir> tags tells the <webdoclet> task to look for the source code.
- The <deploymentdescriptor> tag tells <webdoclet> to generate *web.xml*.
- We use the distributable="false" attribute since we are not in a clustered JBoss environment. It adjusts *web.xml* appropriately.

To make sure that our new target gets called at the appropriate time, we add it as a dependency to the war target in Example 3-14.

Example 3-14. war target in build.xml

```
<!-- ====================================== -->
    <target name="war" depends="generate-web,compile"
            description="Packages the Web files into a WAR file">
        <mkdir dir="${distribution.dir}" />

        <war destFile="${distribution.dir}/${war.name}"
             webxml="${gen.source.dir}/web.xml">
```

Example 3-14. war target in build.xml (continued)

```
            <!-- files to be included in / -->
            <fileset dir="${web.dir}"  exclude="WEB-INF/web.xml" />

            <!-- files to be included in /WEB-INF/classes -->
            <classes dir="${classes.dir}" />

            <!-- files to be included in /WEB-INF/lib -->
            <lib dir="${lib.dir}" />

            <!-- files to be included in /WEB-INF -->
            <webinf dir="${web.inf.dir}" excludes="web.xml" />
        </war>
    </target>
```

Notice that we changed the `webxml` attribute in the war task to point to the newly generated *web.xml* file.

Type ant in the *webapp* directory to rebuilt the subproject. You should see console output that looks like this:

```
Buildfile: build.xml

clean:
    [delete] Deleting directory /Users/sdavis/Desktop/jbossatwork/ch03/
            03c-webdoclet/webapp/build

generate-web:
    [mkdir] Created dir: /Users/sdavis/Desktop/jbossatwork/ch03/
            03c-webdoclet/webapp/build/gensrc
[webdoclet] (XDocletMain.start                  47  )
            Running <deploymentdescriptor/>
[webdoclet] Generating web.xml.

compile:
    [mkdir] Created dir: /Users/sdavis/Desktop/jbossatwork/ch03/
            03c-webdoclet/webapp/build/classes
    [javac] Compiling 1 source file to /Users/sdavis/Desktop/jbossatwork/ch03/
            03c-webdoclet/webapp/build/classes

war:
    [mkdir] Created dir: /Users/sdavis/Desktop/jbossatwork/ch03/
             03c-webdoclet/webapp/build/distribution
     [war] Building war: /Users/sdavis/Desktop/jbossatwork/ch03/
            03c-webdoclet/webapp/build/distribution/jaw.war

all:

BUILD SUCCESSFUL
Total time: 6 seconds
```

Look at the newly generated *web.xml* in *build/gensrc*. In addition to the required servlet elements, the comments show the various other parts of *web.xml* that can be generated as required by our application. Clearly, we have just scratched the surface of what the <webdoclet> task brings to the table.

Deploy *jaw.ear* one last time to make sure our application still behaves as expected.

Looking Ahead...

We've covered a lot of ground in these first few chapters. We now have a single EAR file that encapsulates many moving parts of our J2EE application. We have automated the build process where it is appropriate, and set the stage for future growth.

In the next several chapters, we'll leave the web tier and move on to the persistence tier. We've stored our DTOs in an ArrayList for long enough—let's tackle saving them in a true database.

CHAPTER 4

Databases and JBoss

Up to this point, this book has focused on the web tier. Now let's look at the persistence tier. This is where the application data is stored for the long term—for example, between server restarts.

Why use the phrase "persistence tier" instead of simply calling it the "database tier"? We certainly recognize that the probability of information ending up in a database approaches is somewhere close to 100%. J2EE pundits love pointing out that data *could* be stored in any number of manners—as flat files, XML, and even web services to remote servers. These types of storage are mentioned as alternatives, but we have yet to work on an application where they completely usurp the trusty database.

Instead, most modern persistence technologies deal with transforming relational database information into Java objects. These Object/Relational Mappers (ORMs) come in many flavors—commercial and open source—but make the same promise: to free the Java developer from the perils of converting ResultSets to ArrayLists of DTOs.

We continue to use the phrase "persistence tier" to remind us that many supporting services surround the inevitable database.

Persistence Options

You should acknowledge one simple fact up front: if you deal with a relational database, all roads in one form or another lead to JDBC. Whether you write the code yourself or let an ORM write it for you, SQL INSERTs, UPDATEs, and DELETEs are the lingua franca of any database-driven application.

While Sun maintains that JDBC is not an acronym, it looks suspiciously like "Java DataBase Connectivity" to many seasoned programmers. It is the API that allows us to load up database Drivers, make Connections, and create Statements that yield ResultSets upon execution.

While nothing is intrinsically wrong with ResultSets, OO purists bristle at the thought of dealing with a semi-structured collection of strings and primitives. Java programmers are taught from a tender young age that JavaBeans and DTOs are the one true way to represent business objects. So to get from ResultSets to DTOs, we must use hand-code methods that do the transformation for us, one car.setName(resultSet.getString("name")) at a time.

While this isn't terribly difficult, it does get tedious as the number of business objects and database tables grow. Maintaining two separate data schemas, one in Java and the other in SQL, strikes many as a flagrant violation of the DRY principle. The phrase "impedance mismatch" often comes up in JDBC discussions.

One potential way to avoid the problem of marshalling and unmarshalling JavaBeans is to remove the root cause—why not just create a database that deals natively with objects? On paper, object-oriented databases (OODBMS) seem to be the ideal solution to this problem. Sadly, OODBMSes have never gained any serious market share.

If you can't change the root data source—and relational databases are deeply entrenched in most long-term persistence strategies—your only other option is to come up with an API that manages the impedance mismatch: something that allows you to deal with native JavaBeans, and not only hides the JDBC complexity from you, but ideally entirely creates and manages the infrastructure.

One of the earliest attempts at this was the now infamous Entity Bean offering in the EJB specification. Entity beans came in two basic variations: Bean-Managed Persistence (BMPs) and Container-Managed Persistence (CMPs).

BMPs were really nothing more that a fancy way of saying, "I'm going to keep on doing the JDBC wrangling that I've already been doing." Since the Bean was responsible for its own persistence implementation, many programmers fell back on what they knew best—car.setName(resultSet.getString("name")).

CMPs were closer to what we were hoping to achieve—"let me define the business object and then have the container worry about how to persist it." The problem with CMPs ended up being twofold:

- Rather than dealing with a simple POJO, you were forced to create and maintain a complicated variety of interdependent classes and interfaces—Remotes, RemoteHomes, Locals, LocalHomes, and abstract bean classes.
- The resulting tangle of code was tightly coupled to the container and very intrusive—you were forced to inherit from EJBObject and implement specific interfaces rather than following an inheritance tree that more closely modeled your business domain.

While Entity Beans still exist in the EJB specification today, they have largely fallen out of favor in the developer community.

Sun's next attempt at a JavaBean-centric persistence API was Java Data Objects(JDO). The 1.0 specification has been out for several years, but it hasn't captured a lot of mindshare. Some point to a differently but equally complicated API as its main problem. Traditional RDBMS vendors have been slow to support it, although OODBMS vendors have enthusiastically touted it as the Next Big Thing. Regardless, JDO is not an official part of the J2EE specification, so it has gone largely unnoticed by the server-side crowd.

Which leads us to the wild west of independent ORMs. Many solutions—both commercial and open source—have popped up in the absence of an official specification from Sun. All allow you to traffic in unencumbered POJOs—you don't have to inherit from a specific object or implement a specific interface. Some use runtime reflection, and others rely on post-compilation bytecode manipulation to achieve their unobtrusive persistence goals.

JBoss Hibernate is one of the most popular of the bunch, although there are at least half a dozen viable candidates in this category. After we outline a JDBC strategy in this chapter, we'll walk through a simple Hibernate refactoring in the next chapter.

The existence of so many competing persistence solutions demonstrates that this is a complex problem with no one right answer. Any solution you pick will certainly outshine the others in certain circumstances and leave you wanting in others.

Apart from the obvious JBoss tie-in, there is one compelling reason why we chose Hibernate as our second persistence strategy, over any of the others we mentioned. Quite simply, it seems to best represent what next generation persistence APIs will look like.

In 2005, Sun announced the merger of the EJB 3.0 and JDO 2.0 specification teams. Both were working toward—you guessed it—JavaBean-centric persistence APIs. Sun also invited the lead architects from the Hibernate project to sit on the team. Whatever the final name of the specification turns out to be, one thing is certain—it will look and feel like Hibernate or any of the many other ORMs on the market today. By investing a little time in learning an ORM today, you will be that much closer to understanding the official Sun specification when it is released in the future.

But before you can really appreciate what an ORM brings to the table, let's look at a how to solve the persistence problem using nothing but JDBC.

JDBC

JDBC has been around nearly as long as Java itself. The JDBC 1.0 API was released with JDK 1.1. This is the java.sql package. JDBC 2.0 was released with JDK 1.2. It included both the Core package and what was called the Optional Package (javax.sql). The optional package brought with it better enterprise support for database connections, including connection pools and distributed transactions. JDBC 3.0 is the latest release, included with JDK 1.4.

If you've written JDBC code since the good old days, you're probably familiar with using the `DriverManager` to get a database connection, as in Example 4-1.

Example 4-1. Example of the JDBC DriverManager

```
static final String DB_DRIVER_CLASS = "com.mysql.jdbc.Driver";
static final String DB_URL =
            "mysql://localhost:3306/JBossatWorkDB?autoReconnect=true";

Connection connection = null;

try {
    // Load the Driver.
    Class.forName(DB_DRIVER_CLASS).newInstance();

    // Connect to the database.
    connection = DriverManager.getConnection(DB_URL);

} catch (SQLException se) {
    …
} catch (…) {
    …
}
```

While this code certainly works, it has several shortcomings:

- Every time you connect and disconnect from the database, you incur the overhead of creating and destroying a physical database connection.
- You have to manage the database transaction yourself.
- You have a local transaction that's concerned only with database activity. What if you deal with other resources such as JMS Destinations (Queues and Topics)? If there's a problem and you need to roll back database updates, there's no automated way to roll back the work done with these other resources.

One of the main benefits of living in an application server is having the server take care of these sorts of plumbing issues. JBoss, like all other J2EE application servers, deals with the issues listed above on your behalf. However, to facilitate this, we need to slightly change the way you obtain your database connections.

Rather than using a `java.sql.DriverManager`, we need to use a `javax.sql.DataSource` to allow JBoss to manage the details in Example 4-2.

Example 4-2. Example of the JDBC DataSource

```
static final String DATA_SOURCE=
            "java:comp/env/jdbc/JBossAtWorkDS";
```

Example 4-2. Example of the JDBC DataSource (continued)

```
        DataSource dataSource = null;
        Connection conn = null;

        try {
            // Load the Driver.
            dataSource = ServiceLocator.getDataSource(DATA_SOURCE);

            // Connect to the database.
            conn = dataSource.getConnection( );

        } catch (SQLException se) {
            …
        } catch (ServiceLocatorException sle) {
            …
        }
```

A `DataSource` provides the following advantages:

- When you obtain a database connection using a DataSource, you're not creating a new connection. At startup, JBoss creates a database *Connection Pool* managed by a `DataSource`. When you get a database connection from a `DataSource`, you access an already existing connection from the pool. When you "close" the connection, you just return it to the pool so someone else can use it.

- When you use a Container-Managed DataSource, all database access for a particular Transaction Context commits or rolls back automatically. You don't have to manage the transaction yourself anymore.

- If you use Container-Managed Transactions (CMT) *and* your DBMS supports two-phase commit (the XA protocol), then your database transaction can participate in a global transaction. Suppose you have a unit of work that requires database activity and sends JMS messages: if something goes wrong, the JBoss Transaction Manager rolls back everything.

OK, we admit it. We pulled a bit of a fast one on you. Using DataSources brings great power to the table, but it also brings along some added complexity. We should look at a few more moving parts in greater detail.

JNDI

Let's take a moment to parse the DataSource name java:comp/env/jdbc/ JBossAtWorkDS, which is a Java Naming and Directory Interface (JNDI) name. JNDI provides access to a variety of back-end resources in a unified way.

JNDI is to Java Enterprise applications what Domain Name Service (DNS) is to Internet applications. Without DNS, you would be forced to memorize and type IP addresses like *192.168.1.100* into your web browser instead of friendly names like *http://www.jbossatwork.com*. In addition to resolving host names to IP addresses,

DNS facilitates sending email between domains, load-balancing web servers, and other things. Similarly, JNDI maps high-level names to resources like database connections, JavaMail sessions, and pools of EJB objects.

DNS has a naming convention that makes it easy to figure out the organizational structure of a Fully Qualified Domain Name (FQDN). Domain names are dot-delimited and move from the general to the specific as you read them from right-to-left. "com" is a Top-Level Domain (TLD) reserved for commercial businesses. There are a number of other TLDs, including "edu" for educational institutions, "gov" for government entities, and "org" for non-profit organizations.

The domain name reserved for your business or organization is called a Mid-Level Domain (MLD). Jbossatwork.com, apache.org, and whitehouse.gov are all MLDs. You can create any number of subdomains under a MLD, but the left-most element will always be a HostName like "www" or "mail."

Now looking at a domain name like *http://www.parks.state.co.us* or *http://www.npgc. state.ne.us* for a listing of state parks in Colorado or Nebraska begins to make a little more sense. The country/state/department hierarchy in the domain name mirrors the real-life organizational hierarchy.

JNDI organizes its namespace using a naming convention called Environmental Naming Context (ENC). You are not required to use this naming convention, but it is highly recommended. ENC JNDI names always begin with java:comp/env. (Notice that JNDI names are forward slash-delimited instead of dot-delimited and read left-to-right.)

A number of TLD-like top-level names are in the ENC. Each JNDI "TLD" corresponds to a specific resource type, shown in Table 4-1.

Table 4-1. J2EE-style JNDI ENC naming conventions

Resource type	JNDI prefix
Environment Variables	java:comp/env/var
URL	java:comp/env/url
JavaMail Sessions	java:comp/env/mail
JMS Connection Factories and Destinations	java:comp/env/jms
EJB Homes	java:comp/env/ejb
JDBC DataSources	java:comp/env/jdbc

I'm obviously mixing my JNDI and DNS nomenclature, but the JNDI "TLD" for DataSources always should be java:/comp/env/jdbc. In the example DataSource name—java:comp/env/jdbc/JBossAtWorkDS—the "TLD" and "MLD" should be more self-evident now. JBossAtWorkDS is the JNDI "MLD."

DNS names protect us from the perils of hardcoded IP addresses. A change of server or ISP (and the corresponding change in IP address) should remain transparent to the casual end user since their handle to your site is unchanged. Similarly, JNDI gives J2EE components a handle to back-end resources. Since the component uses an alias instead of an actual value (for the database driver, for example) we now have the flexibility to swap out back-end resources without changing the source code.

These JNDI names are local to the EAR. If you deploy multiple EARs to the same JBoss instance, each EAR will get its own JNDI local context. This ensures that your JNDI names are available only to the EAR in which they are set.

In the spirit of encapsulation, we wrap all of the JNDI lookups in class called `ServiceLocator`. It allows us to constrain all of the JNDI semantics to a single class. Here's what our `ServiceLocator` class looks like in Example 4-3.

Example 4-3. ServiceLocator.java

```
package com.jbossatwork.util;

import javax.naming.*;
import javax.sql.*;

public class ServiceLocator {
    private ServiceLocator() { }

    public static DataSource getDataSource(String dataSourceJndiName)
                throws ServiceLocatorException {

        DataSource dataSource = null;
        try {
            Context ctx = new InitialContext();
            dataSource = (DataSource) ctx.lookup(dataSourceJndiName);

        } catch (ClassCastException cce) {
            throw new ServiceLocatorException(cce);
        } catch (NamingException ne) {
            throw new ServiceLocatorException(ne);
        }
        return dataSource;
    }
}
```

All JNDI variables are stored in the `InitialContext`. When you call the `lookup()` method, it returns an `Object` that must be cast to the appropriate type. If you think about it, this is really no different than calling `HashMap.get("JBossAtWorkDS")`.

Now we can see how to get a `DataSource` by doing a JNDI lookup. But this probably brings up the next obvious question: how did our `DataSource` get into the `InitialContext` in the first place? To find out, we need to revisit your favorite deployment descriptor, *web.xml*.

JNDI References in web.xml

In previous chapters, we used the *web.xml* file to describe and deploy servlets. This same file describes and deploys JNDI resources. The new *web.xml* looks like Example 4-4.

Example 4-4. web.xml

```xml
<?xml version="1.0" encoding="UTF-8"?>

<!DOCTYPE web-app PUBLIC
        "-//Sun Microsystems, Inc.//DTD Web Application 2.3//EN"
        "http://java.sun.com/dtd/web-app_2_3.dtd">

<web-app>

    <servlet>
        <servlet-name>Controller</servlet-name>
        <servlet-class>com.jbossatwork.ControllerServlet</servlet-class>
    </servlet>

    <servlet-mapping>
        <servlet-name>Controller</servlet-name>
        <url-pattern>/controller/*</url-pattern>
    </servlet-mapping>

    <resource-ref>
        <res-ref-name>jdbc/JBossAtWorkDS</res-ref-name>
        <res-type>javax.sql.DataSource</res-type>
        <res-auth>Container</res-auth>
    </resource-ref>

</web-app>
```

Let's examine each new element:

- <res-ref-name> is the JNDI resource name. Notice that you don't have to specify "java:comp/env/"—it is assumed, just like "*http://*" is commonly left out of web URLs.

- <res-type> in our case is a DataSource. This must be the fully qualified classname.

- <res-auth> can be either Container or Servlet. Since we use JBoss' DataSource pooling, Container is the appropriate choice here.

OK, so here's where it gets interesting. At first glance, it appears that JBoss doesn't adhere to the ENC naming style when it comes to DataSources. Instead of java:comp/env/jdbc/JBossAtWorkDS, its DataSources are referenced as simply java:/JBossAtWorkDS. So we need a way to map the JBoss name to the ENC name.

The real reason for the mismatch is that JBoss creates a global binding for the DataSource, and we need to create a local reference to it. We mentioned earlier in the chapter that all JNDI references are local to the EAR. Out of courtesy, JBoss doesn't automatically expose global references to us. We need to map the global name to a local name so that we can work with it.

Luckily, a straightforward way to do the cross mapping is available. You can include a JBoss specific deployment descriptor in your WAR named *jboss-web.xml*. Example 4-5 shows what ours should look like.

Example 4-5. jboss-web.xml

```xml
<?xml version="1.0" encoding="UTF-8"?>
<jboss-web>
    <resource-ref>
        <res-ref-name>jdbc/JBossAtWorkDS</res-ref-name>
        <jndi-name>java:/JBossAtWorkDS </jndi-name>
    </resource-ref>
</jboss-web>
```

Since we're already using XDoclet to generate our *web.xml* file, there is no reason not to continue letting it do its thing. Example 4-6 shows the new XDoclet code in ControllerServlet.

Example 4-6. ControllerServlet.java

```java
/**
 * @web.servlet
 *     name="Controller"
 *
 * @web.servlet-mapping
 *     url-pattern="/controller/*"
 *
 * @web.resource-ref
 *     name="jdbc/JBossAtWorkDS"
 *     type="javax.sql.DataSource"
 *     auth="Container"
 *
 * @jboss.resource-ref
 *     res-ref-name="jdbc/JBossAtWorkDS"
 *     jndi-name="java:/JBossAtWorkDS"
 */

public class ControllerServlet extends HttpServlet
```

Chances are good that more than one servlet will end up using the same JNDI resource. While the servlet tags need to be defined in each servlet, the JNDI tags should be specified only once. It doesn't matter which servlet you define them in, but you should come up with a strategy early in the development process for managing it. If you have a central Controller servlet like we do, it is usually a pretty logical candidate for this. (You can also have XDoclet include an XML fragment stored in a file instead of using JavaDoc comments. The choice is yours.)

To generate the *jboss-web.xml* file, we need to add a new XDoclet directive to our build process in Example 4-7—aptly named `<jbosswebxml>`.

Example 4-7. Adding the <jbosswebxml> directive

```
<!-- ======================================= -->
    <target name="generate-web" description="Generate web.xml">
        <taskdef name="webdoclet"
                    classname="xdoclet.modules.web.WebDocletTask"
                    classpathref="xdoclet.lib.path" />

        <mkdir dir="${gen.source.dir}" />

        <webdoclet destdir="${gen.source.dir}">
            <fileset dir="${source.dir}">
                <include name="**/*Servlet.java" />
            </fileset>

            <deploymentdescriptor destdir="${gen.source.dir}"
                                    distributable="false"
                                    servletspec="2.4" />

            <jbosswebxml destdir="${gen.source.dir}" />


        </webdoclet>
    </target>
```

We'll also need to change your `<war>` task in Example 4-8 to include the newly generated JBoss-specific deployment descriptor.

Example 4-8. Including jboss-web.xml in the WAR

```
<!-- ======================================= -->
    <target name="war" depends="generate-web,compile"
            description="Packages the Web files into a WAR file">
        <mkdir dir="${distribution.dir}" />

        <war destFile="${distribution.dir}/${war.name}"
            webxml="${gen.source.dir}/web.xml">
            <!-- files to be included in / -->
            <fileset dir="${web.dir}"  exclude="WEB-INF/web.xml" />

            <!-- files to be included in /WEB-INF/classes -->
            <classes dir="${classes.dir}" />

            <!-- files to be included in /WEB-INF/lib -->
            <lib dir="${lib.dir}" />
```

Example 4-8. Including jboss-web.xml in the WAR (continued)

```
        <!-- files to be included in /WEB-INF -->
        <webinf dir="${web.inf.dir}" excludes="web.xml" />

        <webinf dir="${gen.source.dir}" >
                <include name="jboss-web.xml" />
        </webinf>

    </war>
  </target>
```

OK, so now we know that the JNDI resources are defined in the deployment descriptors. But where do we configure the DataSource itself?

JBoss DataSource Descriptors

Remember in Chapter 1 we dynamically deployed and undeployed a service? We used the Hypersonic database in the example. You can access any database as an MBean by simply including the appropriate *-ds.xml* file in the deploy directory.

Hypersonic is completely implemented in Java and ships standard with JBoss. It is great for playing around with JDBC and not having to worry about installing and configuring an external database. We generally rely on a full-fledged external database for production applications, but we'd be lying if we told you that we didn't use Hypersonic *all the time* for rapid testing and prototyping.

Three types of Hypersonic instances include:

- The default Hypersonic configuration, which gives you a local database whose modifications are saved to disk (and therefore survive between JBoss restarts). We can access this configuration only through a DataSource—it is not accessible to out-of-container clients like Ant or third-party standalone GUIs. It is called an "In-Process Persistent DB".

- As a slight variation, we can configure the "In-Process Persistent DB" to run purely in memory. No files are written to disk, and therefore the database lives only as long as the container is running. This is called an "In-Memory DB."

- If you need to access the database from either a DataSource or an external client, you can configure Hypersonic to listen on a TCP port (1701 by default). This is called a "TCP DB."

The Hypersonic deployment descriptor is *$JBOSS_HOME/server/default/deploy/hsqldb-ds.xml*. Examples of deployment descriptors for all major databases (commercial or open source) are at *$JBOSS_HOME/docs/examples/jca*. The J2EE Connector Architecture (JCA) is a standard way for a J2EE container to connect to external datastores. These example files generally are very well commented. Take a moment to browse the *examples/jca* directory and look through some of the deployment descriptors.

We provide two customized Hypersonic database descriptors in the *ch04/sql* directory. *Jaw-ds.xml* strips out all the comments included in the original *hsqldb-ds.xml* file—sometimes it can be hard to see the forest for the trees. We also included a version that retains the original comments. You might like to compare this version to the default Hypersonic version to see how we've tweaked it.

Let's step through *jaw-ds.xml* line by line.

```
<datasources>

    <local-tx-datasource>
        <jndi-name>JBossAtWorkDS</jndi-name>
```

This is the global/JBoss JNDI name of your `DataSource`. Since this `DataSource` is accessible to all EARs, it only makes sense to bind its name in the global context. (The local ENC name goes with the local EAR in *web.xml*.)

```
<connection-url>jdbc:hsqldb:hsql://localhost:1701</connection-url>
<driver-class>org.hsqldb.jdbcDriver</driver-class>
<user-name>sa</user-name>
<password></password>
```

These values should look familiar to you. They are the standard JDBC parameters that tell you how to connect to the database, which driver to use, and what credentials to supply when connecting.

```
<min-pool-size>5</min-pool-size>
<max-pool-size>20</max-pool-size>
<idle-timeout-minutes>0</idle-timeout-minutes>
<track-statements/>
```

These next settings allow you to optimize the start and peak number of connections in the pool. According to the comments in the default Hypersonic descriptor, `<idle-timeout-minutes>` should be left at 0 as a bug work-around.

```
<metadata>
    <type-mapping>Hypersonic SQL</type-mapping>
</metadata>
<depends>jboss:service=Hypersonic-JAW,database=jawdb</depends>
</local-tx-datasource>
```

The `<metadata>` element is boilerplate for all Hypersonic instances, but the `<depends>` clause should be customized per instance. This is the unique identifier of the MBean defined in the last section of the file.

```
<mbean code="org.jboss.jdbc.HypersonicDatabase"
  name="jboss:service=Hypersonic-JAW,database=jawdb">
  <attribute name="Port">1701</attribute>
  <attribute name="Silent">true</attribute>
  <attribute name="Database">jawdb</attribute>
```

```
        <attribute name="Trace">false</attribute>
        <attribute name="No_system_exit">true</attribute>
    </mbean>

</datasources>
```

The `<local-tx-datasource>` section defines the DataSource. The `<mbean>` section defines the actual database instance. The Database attribute is especially interesting—it tells Hypersonic what to name the physical files stored on disk. (These files are stored in *$JBOSS_HOME/server/default/data/hypersonic*, but they won't show up until you deploy the database. We'll see them in just a moment.)

Now we are ready to deploy the customized JAW datasource. Copy *jaw-ds.xml* to *$JBOSS_HOME/server/default/deploy*. You should see the following code in your server console window:

```
23:06:52,077 INFO  [STDOUT] [Server@d27151]: [Thread[hypersonic-jawdb,5,jboss]]:
checkRunning(false) entered
23:06:52,079 INFO  [STDOUT] [Server@d27151]: [Thread[hypersonic-jawdb,5,jboss]]:
checkRunning(false) exited
23:06:52,080 INFO  [STDOUT] [Server@d27151]: Startup sequence initiated from main( )
method
23:06:52,119 INFO  [STDOUT] [Server@d27151]: Loaded properties from
[/Library/jboss-4.0.1/bin/server.properties]
23:06:52,155 INFO  [STDOUT] [Server@d27151]: Initiating startup sequence...
23:06:52,158 INFO  [STDOUT] [Server@d27151]: Server socket opened successfully in
0 ms.
23:06:52,179 INFO  [STDOUT] [Server@d27151]: Database [index=0, id=2,
db=file:/Library/jboss-4.0.1/server/default/data/hypersonic/jawdb, alias=]
opened sucessfully in 18 ms.
23:06:52,181 INFO  [STDOUT] [Server@d27151]: Startup sequence completed in 23 ms.
23:06:52,263 INFO  [STDOUT] [Server@d27151]: 2005-04-28 23:06:52.263 HSQLDB server
1.7.2 is online
23:06:52,288 INFO  [STDOUT] [Server@d27151]: To close normally, connect and execute
SHUTDOWN SQL
23:06:52,309 INFO  [STDOUT] [Server@d27151]: From command line, use [Ctrl]+[C] to
abort abruptly
23:06:52,569 INFO  [WrapperDataSourceService] Bound connection factory for resource
adapter for ConnectionManager 'jboss.jca:name=JBossAtWorkDS,
service=DataSourceBinding to JNDI name 'java:JBossAtWorkDS'
```

We can glean a couple of interesting nuggets from the console output:

- First, it tells us that the database is now listening on a TCP port (or server socket).

- It also tells us where to look for the physical database files: *$JBOSS_HOME/ server/default/data/hypersonic*. After we add some data to this database, we'll nose around this directory to see the resulting changes.

- Finally, it tells us that our DataSource has been successfully bound to a JNDI name.

We now know that our database has been successfully deployed. We can use a couple of other tricks to confirm this if you'd like.

You can verify the ports that are open on your server by using the netstat command. Type netstat -an on a Windows PC or Mac; or netstat -anp on a Linux box. All platforms should give you a report similar to this:

```
Active Internet connections (including servers)
Proto Recv-Q Send-Q  Local Address          Foreign Address        (state)
tcp46      0      0  *.1701                 *.*                    LISTEN
tcp4       0      0  127.0.0.1.57918        127.0.0.1.631          CLOSE_WAIT
tcp4       0      0  127.0.0.1.57917        127.0.0.1.631          CLOSE_WAIT
tcp46      0      0  *.8008                 *.*                    LISTEN
tcp46      0      0  *.8093                 *.*                    LISTEN
tcp46      0      0  *.8088                 *.*                    LISTEN
tcp46      0      0  *.4445                 *.*                    LISTEN
tcp46      0      0  *.4444                 *.*                    LISTEN
tcp46      0      0  *.8083                 *.*                    LISTEN
tcp46      0      0  *.1099                 *.*                    LISTEN
tcp46      0      0  *.1098                 *.*                    LISTEN
tcp4       0      0  10.11.46.54.56015      207.178.165.2.80       CLOSE_WAIT
tcp4       0      0  127.0.0.1.8005         *.*                    LISTEN
tcp46      0      0  *.8009                 *.*                    LISTEN
tcp46      0      0  *.8080                 *.*                    LISTEN
```

In addition to our Hypersonic instance on port 1701, we can also see our embedded Tomcat instance listening on port 8080.

Since Hypersonic is an MBean, you can also use JBoss' JMX-Console webapp to verify that it is active. Visit *http://localhost:8080/jmx-console* (Figure 4-1). The Hypersonic-JAW MBean should be one of the first links in the list.

Click on the link to our database instance. From here, you can do basic things like start and stop the instance, or modify the port it is listening on. This is nothing you can't also do by hand-editing the configuration files, but some people prefer a GUI like that in Figure 4-2.

Now our database is configured and ready to be tested. To hit it, we'll need to make sure that your application can find the appropriate JDBC driver.

JDBC Driver JARs

A DataSource is a container-managed resource. The JBoss documentation recommends storing the JAR outside of your EAR and in *$JBOSS_HOME/server/default/lib*. (One big reason for this is that JDBC drivers cannot be hot deployed.) For example, the *$JBOSS_HOME/server/default/lib* directory is where you'll find *hsqldb.jar*—the JDBC driver for the Hypersonic database. As an added benefit, if you store the drivers here, you can share them across multiple EARs. With less duplication, there is less of a chance for mismatched drivers and database versions.

JMX Agent View rosencrantz.local

ObjectName Filter (e.g. "jboss:*", "*:service=invoker,*") : [_____] (ApplyFilter)

Catalina

- **type=Server**

JMImplementation

- **name=Default,service=LoaderRepository**
- **type=MBeanRegistry**
- **type=MBeanServerDelegate**

jboss

- **database=jawdb,service=Hypersonic-JAW**
- **database=localDB,service=Hypersonic**
- **name=PropertyEditorManager,type=Service**
- **name=SystemProperties,type=Service**
- **readonly=true,service=invoker,target=Naming,type=http**

Figure 4-1. The JBoss JMX-Console

MBean description:

Management Bean.

List of MBean attributes:

Name	Type	Access	Value	Description
State	int	R	3	MBean Attribute.
ShutdownCommand	java.lang.String	RW	[ ]	MBean Attribute.
User	java.lang.String	RW	sa	MBean Attribute.
Silent	boolean	RW	⊙True ○False	MBean Attribute.
Persist	boolean	RW	⊙True ○False	MBean Attribute.
Port	int	RW	1701	MBean Attribute.
Password	java.lang.String	RW	[ ]	MBean Attribute.
StateString	java.lang.String	R	Started	MBean Attribute.
DatabaseManagerClass	java.lang.String	RW	org.hsqldb.util.DatabaseM	MBean Attribute.
Database	java.lang.String	RW	jawdb	MBean Attribute.
No_system_exit	boolean	RW	⊙True ○False	MBean Attribute.
Trace	boolean	RW	○True ⊙False	MBean Attribute.
InProcessMode	boolean	RW	○True ⊙False	MBean Attribute.
Name	java.lang.String	R	HypersonicDatabase	MBean Attribute.
DatabasePath	java.lang.String	R	/Library/jboss-4.0.1/server/default/data/hypersonic/jawdb	MBean Attribute.

(Apply Changes)

Figure 4-2. MBean configuration

Of course, if you are not going to be hot deploying your EARs you can include your JDBC drivers in your EAR. This gives you the added benefit of allowing each EAR to use potentially different or conflicting versions of the same JDBC driver.

Database Checklist

OK, so here's the checklist of things we've accomplished so far:

- Stored the JDBC driver in *$JBOSS_HOME/server/default/lib* (*hsqldb.jar*)
- Configured the database deployment descriptor in *$JBOSS_HOME/server/ default/deploy* (*hsqldb-ds.xml*) Among other things, this is where we set up the JBoss JNDI name (*java:/JBossAtWorkDS*).
- We created a global JNDI reference to the DataSource in *jboss-web.xml*. This name matches the name in the database deployment descriptor. We also provided a setting that maps the global JNDI name to a local JNDI name using ENC-style naming (*java:comp/env/jdbc/JBossAtWorkDS*).
- We created a local JNDI reference to the DataStore in *web.xml.*.
- We created a ServiceLocator class that encapsulates our JNDI lookup and returns the DataSource.

Because of the way we've set things up, switching databases at this point is relatively easy. For example, if you'd prefer to work against an instance of MySQL, we only need to copy the JDBC drivers to the *$JBOSS_HOME/server/default/lib* directory and copy a new database deployment descriptor into the *deploy* directory. If you use the same JNDI name that we already used, your job is done—all the code upstream will be configured and ready to hit the new database.

We've said it many times before, but it's worth saying again: Hypersonic is a great database for our immediate purposes because it doesn't require configuring an external resource. However, in a production environment, we'd most likely use a more robust database.

We are now ready to create a Car table and insert some sample data.

Accessing the Database Using Ant

Now that we've created the JBossAtWorkDB database instance, we need to create and populate the Car table. Ant has a <sql> task that is ideal for this sort of thing. Keeping these commands in a script allows you to rebuild your database easily and often during the development phase.

The same rules for scripting the deployment of your EAR to a production server apply here as well: Just Say NO! If you create a script that points to a production database, you are only asking for it to be run inadvertently with disastrous results. With great power comes great responsibility—use it wisely.

That said, let's look at the *build.xml* file in the new SQL subproject, shown in Example 4-9. This project doesn't contain any compiled code. It is just a convenient storage location for these SQL scripts.

Example 4-9. SQL subproject build.xml

```
<?xml version="1.0"?>

<project name="sql" default="init" basedir=".">

    <!-- Initialization variables -->
    <property name="database.driver.dir"
            value="${env.JBOSS_HOME}/server/default/lib/"/>
    <property name="database.driver.jar" value="hsqldb.jar"/>

    <path id="sql.classpath">
        <fileset dir="${database.driver.dir}">
            <include name="${database.driver.jar}"/>
        </fileset>
    </path>

    <!-- ======================================== -->
    <target name="init"
            description="Creates test data in the database.">

        <sql driver="org.hsqldb.jdbcDriver"
            url="jdbc:hsqldb:hsql://localhost:1701"
            userid="sa"
            password=""
            print="yes"
            classpathref="sql.classpath">

        DROP TABLE IF EXISTS CAR;

        CREATE TABLE CAR (
            ID BIGINT identity,
            MAKE VARCHAR(50),
            MODEL VARCHAR(50),
            MODEL_YEAR VARCHAR(50)
        );

        INSERT INTO CAR (ID, MAKE, MODEL, MODEL_YEAR)
        VALUES (99, 'Toyota', 'Camry', '2005');

        INSERT INTO CAR (ID, MAKE, MODEL, MODEL_YEAR)
        VALUES (100, 'Toyota', 'Corolla', '1999');

        INSERT INTO CAR (ID, MAKE, MODEL, MODEL_YEAR)
        VALUES (101, 'Ford', 'Explorer', '2005');
```

Example 4-9. SQL subproject build.xml (continued)

```
        SELECT * FROM CAR;
    </sql>
</target>

</project>
```

We provide a classpath to your database driver and set up the connection string. From there, it is straight SQL. Run the script: you should see something like Example 4-10 for console output.

Example 4-10. Ant SQL output

```
Buildfile: build.xml

init:
    [sql] Executing commands
    [sql] 0 rows affected
    [sql] 0 rows affected
    [sql] 1 rows affected
    [sql] 1 rows affected
    [sql] 1 rows affected
    [sql] ID,MAKE,MODEL,MODEL_YEAR
    [sql] 99,Toyota,Camry,2005
    [sql] 100,Toyota,Corolla,1999
    [sql] 101,Ford,Explorer,2005

    [sql] 0 rows affected
    [sql] 6 of 6 SQL statements executed successfully

BUILD SUCCESSFUL
Total time: 3 seconds
```

If you really want to prove to yourself that this worked, look in *$JBOSS_HOME/ server/default/data/hypersonic* one more time. If you open the *jaw-db.log* file in a text editor, you should see the following:

```
/*C1*/CONNECT USER SA
SET AUTOCOMMIT FALSE
 DROP TABLE IF EXISTS CAR
  CREATE TABLE CAR ( ID BIGINT, MAKE VARCHAR(50), MODEL VARCHAR(50),
        MODEL_YEAR VARCHAR(50) )
INSERT INTO CAR VALUES(99,'Toyota','Camry','2005')
INSERT INTO CAR VALUES(100,'Toyota','Corolla','1999')
INSERT INTO CAR VALUES(101,'Ford','Explorer','2005')
COMMIT
DISCONNECT
```

At this point, the stage is set. We have a database table with data in it. All we need to do now is create a new DAO object that will read the information out of the table.

Creating JDBCCarDAO

Our first `CarDAO` was fine to get the project kick-started, but `ArrayLists` aren't the best long-term persistence strategy. Let's create a second DAO that takes advantage of the infrastructure we've just put in place.

Since two classes provide different implementations of the same functionality, we should create a common Interface. In addition to making it trivial to switch back and forth between the two concrete implementations, it will also pave the way for us to add a third DAO implementation for Hibernate in the next chapter.

In the *ch04/common* source tree, notice that we renamed our old DAO class to InMemoryCarDAO. We didn't touch any of the methods, just the name of the class and the corresponding constructor names, as in Example 4-11.

Example 4-11. CarDAO.java

```
package com.jbossatwork.dao;

import java.util.*;
import com.jbossatwork.dto.CarDTO;

public class InMemoryCarDAO implements CarDAO
{
    private List carList;

    public InMemoryCarDAO( )
    {
        carList = new ArrayList( );

        carList.add(new CarDTO("Toyota", "Camry", "2005"));
        carList.add(new CarDTO("Toyota", "Corolla", "1999"));
        carList.add(new CarDTO("Ford", "Explorer", "2005"));
    }

    public List findAll( )
    {
        return carList;
    }
}
```

The CarDAO Interface simply defines the method signature for findAll( ):

```
package com.jbossatwork.dao;

import java.util.*;

public interface CarDAO
{
    public List findAll( );
}
```

The new JDBCCarDAO uses the new DataSource and ServiceLocator class to build the ArrayList of CarDTOs in Example 4-12.

Example 4-12. JDBCCarDAO.java

```java
package com.jbossatwork.dao;

import java.util.*;
import java.sql.*;
import javax.sql.*;
import com.jbossatwork.dto.CarDTO;
import com.jbossatwork.util.*;

public class JDBCCarDAO implements CarDAO
{
    private List carList;
    private static final String DATA_SOURCE="java:comp/env/jdbc/JBossAtWorkDS";

    public JDBCCarDAO( )
    {}

    public List findAll( )
    {
        List carList = new ArrayList( );
        DataSource dataSource = null;
        Connection conn = null;
        Statement stmt = null;
        ResultSet rs = null;

        try
        {
            dataSource = ServiceLocator.getDataSource(DATA_SOURCE);
            conn = dataSource.getConnection( );
            stmt = conn.createStatement( );
            rs = stmt.executeQuery("select * from CAR");

            while(rs.next( ))
            {
                CarDTO car = new CarDTO( );
                car.setMake(rs.getString("MAKE"));
                car.setModel(rs.getString("MODEL"));
                car.setModelYear(rs.getString("MODEL_YEAR"));
                carList.add(car);
            }

        }
        catch (Exception e)
        {
            System.out.println(e);
        }
        finally
        {
            try
```

Example 4-12. JDBCCarDAO.java (continued)

```
        {
            if(rs != null){rs.close();}
            if(stmt != null){stmt.close();}
            if(conn != null){conn.close();}
        }
        catch(Exception e)
        {
            System.out.println(e);
        }
    }

    return carList;
    }
}
```

Finally let's change `ControllerServlet` to instantiate the correct DAO. Notice that courtesy of the new interface we created, switching between implementations is as simple as changing the "new" side of the equation, as shown in Example 4-13.

Example 4-13. ControllerServlet.java

```
// perform action
        if(VIEW_CAR_LIST_ACTION.equals(actionName))
        {
            CarDAO carDAO = new JDBCCarDAO();
            request.setAttribute("carList", carDAO.findAll());

            destinationPage = "/carList.jsp";
        }
```

Now that everything is in place, let's compile and deploy the EAR. Change to *ch04/04a-datasource* and type ant. Copy the *jaw.ear* file to *$JBOSS_HOME/server/default/deploy* and visit *http://localhost:8080/jaw*. (Alternately, you can use the deploy or colddeploy Ant targets.)

Looking Ahead...

Once again, we added hundreds of lines of new code with no visible difference to the application. Hopefully you can appreciate what is transparent to the end user—by layering your application correctly, you can make massive changes to the persistence tier while leaving your presentation tier virtually untouched.

We have one more iteration of the `CarList` example to get through before we move on to more exciting stuff. In the next chapter, we'll create a Hibernate DAO that drastically simplifies the object-relational mapping that we have to do by hand in the JDBC DAO. After that, we'll start adding some new functionality to the application, such as logging in and buying cars.

CHAPTER 5
Hibernate and JBoss

Hibernate is not an official part of the J2EE specification. It is an Object/Relational Mapper that hides the complexity of marshalling and unmarshalling JavaBeans and ResultSets.

Hibernate is unique because it can run either in a J2EE container such as JBoss, or as a standalone service. JBoss 4.0.2 ships standard with Hibernate 3.0.2. This chapter focuses on integrating the two to streamline the persistence tier of your application. (For a more detailed look at installing and running Hibernate, see *Hibernate: A Developer's Notebook* by James Elliott (O'Reilly).)

The Pros and Cons of ORMs

> "Object/Relational mapping is the Vietnam of computer science..."—Ted Neward
> (author, Effective Enterprise Java (Addison-Wesley))

If you've read Neward's work or heard him speak, you know that he is a smart, controversial, and very passionate technologist. We couldn't think of a better sentiment to begin our chapter on ORMs.

His point is that the United States started in Vietnam by sending over a few advisors. Then we began to ship in limited numbers of ground troops. Before too long, things degenerated into a full-blown, messy, unpopular war where we were heavily committed and had a difficult time extricating ourselves.

Working with ORMs (in his mind) is really no different. You start out with simple objects that map neatly to single rows. Then you get brave and begin using composition (classes within classes). Hibernate is smart enough to handle that, but at some point you are going to come up with either a complicated object model or a highly normalized relational database that doesn't map nicely through Hibernate.

Our recommendation is to tread lightly. ORMs like Hibernate are relatively new in the Java world. The related specifications are moving quickly and have yet to really solidify. The degree of mission criticality of your application should be inversely related to the novelty of the technology you choose to implement.

On the other hand, we feel reasonably confident betting on this horse. Hibernate is not currently a J2EE specification—it is a third-party ORM. But as mentioned in the previous chapter, Sun merged the EJB3 and JDO2 specification teams and invited the lead architects of Hibernate to sit on the team as well. It's a safe bet that this future specification, whatever it ends up being called, will bear more than a passing resemblance to Hibernate.

The examples in this chapter were designed to show Hibernate in the best possible light. Keep in mind, though, that the object model is simple and maps neatly to a single database table. We purposely show you the JDBC solution alongside the Hibernate solution to illustrate the fact that they both are viable options.

Bottom line: use common sense. Start with simple objects and see how it goes. You might be able to use Hibernate throughout your application without a hitch. Or you might bump up against a limitation early in the process. Only you can decide how Hibernate fits best into your development strategy.

Hibernate Mapping Files

At the core of Hibernate is the HBM mapping file. This XML file maps your object members to fields in a database table. Some might argue that the clever use of reflection could eliminate the need for this file by simply automatically mapping table fieldnames to class fields. While this is appealing, you might not have complete editorial control over the tables or the classes. By using a file, you have the flexibility to map any table field to any class field, regardless of the name.

Recall that our CarDTO has four fields: id, make, model, and modelYear. See how the *car.hbm.xml* file maps these fields to the Car table in Example 5-1.

Example 5-1. car.hbm.xml

```xml
<?xml version="1.0" encoding="UTF-8"?>

<!DOCTYPE hibernate-mapping PUBLIC
    "-//Hibernate/Hibernate Mapping DTD 3.0//EN"
    "http://hibernate.sourceforge.net/hibernate-mapping-3.0.dtd">

<hibernate-mapping>
    <class
        name="com.jbossatwork.dto.CarDTO"
        table="CAR"   >

        <id
            name="id"
            column="ID"
            type="int" >

            <generator class="native" />
        </id>
```

Example 5-1. car.hbm.xml (continued)

```
    <property
        name="make"
        type="java.lang.String"
        column="MAKE" />

    <property
        name="model"
        type="java.lang.String"
        column="MODEL" />

    <property
        name="modelYear"
        type="java.lang.String"
        column="MODEL_YEAR" />

</class>
</hibernate-mapping>
```

- The <class> element matches POJO to table. It is possible to map a single POJO to multiple tables and vice versa, but we'll stick with the simple use case for this example.

- The <id> element identifies the Primary-Key/Unique Identifier field. The <generator> element tells Hibernate how the PK is created. "Native" tells hibernate to rely on the underlying database to generate the key. There are many different types of generators: "assigned" allows the program to specify the unique value. Use this when the PK has a specific meaning, such as a phone or social security number. Another common generator type is "increment," which lets Hibernate generate its own sequence number. (Recall that you set up an auto-incrementing Primary Key field in Hypersonic by using the "identity" keyword: "CREATE TABLE CAR (ID BIGINT identity, MAKE VARCHAR(50)...);")

- Finally, we see a number of <property> elements, each mapping a class field to a table column.

These mapping files are intentionally simple enough to hand edit and maintain, but as you might have guessed, XDoclet allows us to automate this task by adding comments to your POJO. In the common subproject, look at your newly annotated CarDTO in Example 5-2.

Example 5-2. CarDTO.java with Hibernate/XDoclet annotations

```
package com.jbossatwork.dto;


/**
 * @hibernate.class
 *     table="CAR"
 */
public class CarDTO
{
```

Example 5-2. CarDTO.java with Hibernate/XDoclet annotations (continued)

```java
    private int id;
    private String make;
    private String model;
    private String modelYear;

...

    /**
     * @hibernate.id
     *    generator-class="native"
     *    column="ID"
     */
    public int getId( )
    {
        return id;
    }

...

    /**
     * @hibernate.property
     *    column="MAKE"
     */
    public String getMake( )
    {
        return make;
    }

...

    /**
     * @hibernate.property
     *    column="MODEL"
     */
    public String getModel( )
    {
        return model;
    }

...

    /**
     * @hibernate.property
     *    column="MODEL_YEAR"
     */
    public String getModelYear( )
    {
        return modelYear;
    }

}
```

Can you see the relationship between the XDoclet tags and the HBM file?

Now all we need is an Ant task to create the HBM file in Example 5-3.

Example 5-3. build.xml

```xml
<!-- ======================================= -->
    <target name="generate-hbm" description="Generate Hibernate hbm.xml file">
        <taskdef name="hibernatedoclet"
                    classname="xdoclet.modules.hibernate.HibernateDocletTask"
                    classpathref="xdoclet.lib.path" />

        <mkdir dir="${gen.source.dir}" />

        <hibernatedoclet destdir="${gen.source.dir}">
            <fileset dir="${source.dir}">
                <include name="**/*DTO.java" />
            </fileset>

            <hibernate version="3.0" />

        </hibernatedoclet>
    </target>
```

Not surprisingly, the <hibernatedoclet> tag looks remarkably like the <webdoclet> tag we learned about in the web chapter. It specifies a destination directory for the generated file. The <fileset> limits it only to files that end with DTO. Finally, the <hibernate> tag generates a 3.0 compatible HBM file.

Hibernate MBean Service Descriptor

Now that we have the HBM file in place, we must create an MBean service configuration file for Hibernate. Hibernate is a service, no different than Hypersonic or any of the others. Each MBean needs a service configuration file like Example 5-4 so that JBoss will recognize it and run it on startup.

Example 5-4. hibernate-service.xml

```xml
<server>
    <mbean code="org.jboss.hibernate.jmx.Hibernate"
            name="jboss.har:service=Hibernate">
        <attribute name="DatasourceName">java:/JBossAtWorkDS</attribute>
        <attribute name="Dialect"> org.hibernate.dialect.HSQLDialect</attribute>
        <attribute name="SessionFactoryName">
                    java:/hibernate/SessionFactory</attribute>
        <attribute name="CacheProviderClass">
            org.hibernate.cache.HashtableCacheProvider
        </attribute>
    </mbean>
</server>
```

Let's step through it line by line.

- The <mbean> element names the service and specifies the implementing class.

- The <attribute name="DatasourceName"> element is a link to your Hypersonic datasource using the global JNDI name.

- The <attribute name="Dialect"> element tells Hibernate which type of database it talks to. As much as we'd like to believe the "s" in SQL stands for "standard," the acronym is short for "Structured Query Language." Each database vendor's implementation of SQL varies, and this setting allows Hibernate to generate well-formed SQL for the specific database in question. Other common dialects include org.hibernate.dialect.Oracle9Dialect and org.hibernate.dialect.MySQLDialect.

- The <attribute name="SessionFactoryName"> element is the global JNDI name for this service's SessionFactory. We'll use this name in *jboss-web.xml* (and map it to a local ENC-style name in *web.xml*).

- Finally, the <attribute name="CacheProviderClass"> element tells Hibernate what caching strategy to use. Rather than going round trip to the database for each request, Hibernate caches the results to improve performance. (See the Hibernate documentation for a more in-depth discussion of the different CacheProviders.)

Creating a HAR

Now that we created the HBM files and the Hibernate MBean service deployment descriptor, we are ready to bundle things up and deploy it as a part of the EAR.

Hibernate applications are bundled up in a Hibernate Archive (HAR). We use the standard Ant <jar> task in Example 5-5 to create the HAR.

Example 5-5. build.xml

```
<!-- ========================================= -->
    <target name="har" depends="generate-hbm"
            description="Builds the Hibernate HAR file">
        <mkdir dir="${distribution.dir}" />

        <jar destfile="${distribution.dir}/jaw.har">
            <!-- include the hbm.xml files  -->
            <fileset dir="${gen.source.dir}">
                <include name="**/*.hbm.xml"/>
            </fileset>

            <!-- include hibernate-service.xml -->
            <metainf dir="${hibernate.dir}">
                <include name="hibernate-service.xml"/>
            </metainf>
        </jar>
    </target>
```

Adding the HAR to the EAR

Moving up a level from the common subproject to the master project, we need to make sure that the EAR file includes our newly created HAR. The master build file already handles this step, since the *jaw.har* file is built in the same directory as *common.jar*. (Look in *common/build/distribution* to confirm this.)

But what about our *application.xml* file? This is traditionally where we identify the JARs that are included in the EAR. HARs are not a standard part of a J2EE EAR file, so JBoss looks for a *jboss-app.xml* file to handle container-specific exceptions to the standard. *src/META-INF/* stores this file, right next to your *application.xml* file. Example 5-6 shows what it looks like.

Example 5-6. jboss-app.xml

```
<!DOCTYPE jboss-app PUBLIC "-//JBoss//DTD J2EE Application 1.4//EN"
          "http://www.jboss.org/j2ee/dtd/jboss-app_4_0.dtd">
<jboss-app>
  <module>
    <har>jaw.har</har>
  </module>
</jboss-app>
```

Our `<ear>` task now includes this file along with the traditional *application.xml* in Example 5-7.

Example 5-7. Master build.xml

```
<!-- ======================================= -->
    <target name="ear" depends="compile"
            description="Packages all files into an EAR file">
        <mkdir dir="${build.dir}" />
        <mkdir dir="${distribution.dir}" />

        <echo message="##### Building EAR #####" />
        <ear destFile="${distribution.dir}/${ear.name}"
            appxml="${meta-inf.dir}/application.xml" >
            <!-- files to be included in / -->
            <fileset dir="${webapp.war.dir}" />
            <fileset dir="${common.jar.dir}" />

            <!-- include jboss-app.xml -->
            <metainf dir="${meta-inf.dir}">
                <include name="jboss-app.xml"/>
            </metainf>

        </ear>
    </target>
```

Creating a JNDI Lookup

Hibernate is now ready to use. Let's move to the webapp subproject to create the necessary JNDI lookups.

The first step toward using it is creating a JNDI reference to it in *jboss-web.xml*. Example 5-8 shows what the file looks like now.

Example 5-8. jboss-web.xml

```
<?xml version="1.0" encoding="UTF-8"?>
<!DOCTYPE jboss-web PUBLIC "-//JBoss//DTD Web Application 2.3V2//EN"
 "http://www.jboss.org/j2ee/dtd/jboss-web_3_2.dtd">

<jboss-web>

   <resource-ref>
      <res-ref-name>jdbc/JBossAtWorkDS</res-ref-name>
      <jndi-name>java:/JBossAtWorkDS</jndi-name>
   </resource-ref>

   <resource-ref>
      <res-ref-name>hibernate/SessionFactory</res-ref-name>
      <jndi-name>java:/hibernate/SessionFactory</jndi-name>
   </resource-ref>

</jboss-web>
```

Remember that <res-ref-name> is the local ENC-style name. With the implied java: comp/env/ prefix, the full ENC-style JNDI name for our Hibernate service is java: comp/env/hibernate/SessionFactory.

The global JNDI name (<jndi-name>) matches the setting in *hibernate-service.xml*—java:/hibernate/SessionFactory.

Example 5-9 shows what the *web.xml* file now looks like.

Example 5-9. web.xml

```
<?xml version="1.0" encoding="UTF-8"?>

<web-app  xmlns="http://java.sun.com/xml/ns/j2ee"
          xmlns:xsi="http://www.w3.org/2001/XMLSchema-instance"
          xsi:schemaLocation="http://java.sun.com/xml/ns/j2ee
              http://java.sun.com/xml/ns/j2ee/web-app_2_4.xsd"
          version="2.4">

   <servlet>
      <servlet-name>Controller</servlet-name>
     <servlet-class>com.jbossatwork.ControllerServlet</servlet-class>

   </servlet>
```

Example 5-9. web.xml (continued)

```
    <servlet-mapping>
        <servlet-name>Controller</servlet-name>
        <url-pattern>/controller/*</url-pattern>
    </servlet-mapping>

    <resource-ref >
        <res-ref-name>jdbc/JBossAtWorkDS</res-ref-name>
        <res-type>javax.sql.DataSource</res-type>
        <res-auth>Container</res-auth>
    </resource-ref>

    <resource-ref>
        <res-ref-name>hibernate/SessionFactory</res-ref-name>
        <res-type>net.sf.hibernate.SessionFactory</res-type>
        <res-auth>Container</res-auth>
    </resource-ref>
```

```
</web-app>
```

Of course, our trusty friend XDoclet does all the file generation, courtesy of the tags in ControllerServlet (Example 5-10).

Example 5-10. ControllerServlet.java

```
/**
 * @web.servlet
 *     name="Controller"
 *
 * @web.servlet-mapping
 *     url-pattern="/controller/*"
 *
 * @web.resource-ref
 *     name="jdbc/JBossAtWorkDS"
 *     type="javax.sql.DataSource"
 *     auth="Container"
 *
 * @jboss.resource-ref
 *     res-ref-name="jdbc/JBossAtWorkDS"
 *     jndi-name="java:/JBossAtWorkDS"
 *
 * @web.resource-ref
 *     name="hibernate/SessionFactory"
 *     type="net.sf.hibernate.SessionFactory"
 *     auth="Container"
 *
 * @jboss.resource-ref
 *     res-ref-name="hibernate/SessionFactory"
 *     jndi-name="java:/hibernate/SessionFactory"
 */

public class ControllerServlet extends HttpServle
```

Recall that we perform JNDI lookups via the ServiceLocator class in *common/src/ com/jbossatwork/util*. ServiceLocator.getHibernateSessionFactory() returns a SessionFactory. Realistically, usually we just need to get a Hibernate Session, so a convenience method in Example 5-11 just returns a Session.

Example 5-11. ServiceLocator.java

```
public static SessionFactory getHibernateSessionFactory(
            String jndiSessionFactoryName) throws ServiceLocatorException {

    SessionFactory sessionFactory = null;
    try {
        Context ctx = new InitialContext();
        sessionFactory = (SessionFactory) ctx.lookup(jndiSessionFactoryName);

    } catch (ClassCastException cce) {
        throw new ServiceLocatorException(cce);
    } catch (NamingException ne) {
        throw new ServiceLocatorException(ne);
    }

    return sessionFactory;
}

public static Session getHibernateSession(
            String jndiSessionFactoryName) throws ServiceLocatorException {

    Session session = null;
    try
    {
        session =
          getHibernateSessionFactory(jndiSessionFactoryName).openSession();
    }
    catch (Exception e)
    {
        throw new ServiceLocatorException(e);
    }

    return session;
}
```

For this class to compile, we need to make sure that the Hibernate JARs are on the classpath somewhere. You can either copy the Hibernate jars found in *$JBOSS_ HOME/server/default/lib* to *common/compile-lib*, or refer to them in place as we did in Example 5-12. (Be sure that the environment variable $JBOSS_HOME is defined before you run this.)

Example 5-12. build.xml

```
<property name="hibernate.lib.dir"
  value="${env.JBOSS_HOME}/server/default/lib"/>
```

Example 5-12. build.xml (continued)

```
<!--
  ========================================================
    This builds the classpath used for compilation.
    NOTE: This is independent of your system classpath
  ========================================================
-->
<path id="compile.classpath">
    <fileset dir="${compile.lib.dir}">
        <include name="**/*.jar"/>
    </fileset>
    <fileset dir="${lib.dir}">
        <include name="**/*.jar"/>
    </fileset>
    <fileset dir="${hibernate.lib.dir}">
        <include name="**/*.jar"/>
    </fileset>
</path>
```

Hibernate Checklist

Before we get to the actual `HibernateCarDAO`, let's recap what we've done up to this point. We:

- Added Hibernate tags to the CarDTO and created an Ant task to create the Mapping File (*cardto.hbm.xml*)
- Created a Hibernate MBean service descriptor (*hibernate-service.xml*)
- Bundled these two files up in a HAR (*common/build/distribution/jaw.har*)
- Created a *jboss-app.xml* file so JBoss would know how to deploy the HAR included in the EAR
- Created a global JNDI reference to the Session Factory in *jboss-web.xml* (*java:/hibernate/SessionFactory*)
- Created a local JNDI reference to the Session Factory in *web.xml* conforming to the J2EE ENC naming style (*java:comp/env/hibernate/SessionFactory*)
- Modified the ServiceLocator class that encapsulates all JNDI lookups to return a Hibernate Session

HibernateCarDAO

It's taken a while to get here, but now that the infrastructure is in place, we can get to the whole point of this chapter—seeing Hibernate in action. In `JDBCCarDAO`, we performed the SQL query and manually marshaled the `ResultSet` rows into `CarDTO` objects.

JBoss 4.0.2 and Hibernate 3.0.2 Issues

Bugs are facts of life. Even though JBoss and Hibernate are excellent products, JBoss 4.0.2 and Hibernate 3.0.2 straight out of the box have one significant problem—a core JAR file that inadvertently was left out of the distribution. The Apache Jakarta Commons Collections JAR needs to be downloaded separately and installed for Hibernate to work correctly. Visit the website (http://jakarta.apache.org/site/downloads/downloads_commons-collections.cgi) and download Version 2.1.1 of the JAR. Then copy it to one of the following directories:

- $JBOSS_HOME/server/default/lib
- $JBOSS_HOME/server/default/deploy/jboss-hibernate.deployer

This issue should be resolved in JBoss 4.0.3.

Example 5-13 shows what the JDBC code looks like.

Example 5-13. JDBCCarDAO.java

```java
private static final String DATA_SOURCE="java:comp/env/jdbc/JBossAtWorkDS";

    public List findAll( )
    {
        List carList = new ArrayList( );
        DataSource dataSource = null;
        Connection conn = null;
        Statement stmt = null;
        ResultSet rs = null;

        try
        {
            dataSource = ServiceLocator.getDataSource(DATA_SOURCE);
            conn = dataSource.getConnection( );
            stmt = conn.createStatement( );
            rs = stmt.executeQuery("select * from CAR");

            while(rs.next( ))
            {
                CarDTO car = new CarDTO( );
                car.setId(rs.getInt("ID"));
                car.setMake(rs.getString("MAKE"));
                car.setModel(rs.getString("MODEL"));
                car.setModelYear(rs.getString("MODEL_YEAR"));
                carList.add(car);
            }

        }
        catch (Exception e)
        {
            System.out.println(e);
        }
```

Example 5-13. JDBCCarDAO.java (continued)

```
        finally
        {
            try
            {
                if(rs != null){rs.close();}
                if(stmt != null){stmt.close();}
                if(conn != null){conn.close();}
            }
            catch(Exception e)
            {
                System.out.println(e);
            }
        }

        return carList;
    }
```

It's nearly 50 lines of code, if you include all the exception handling. The point of showing this to you is to remind you that we do all the work by hand.

Now let's see the same method implemented with Hibernate in Example 5-14.

Example 5-14. HibernateCarDAO.java

```
private static final String
 HIBERNATE_SESSION_FACTORY="java:comp/env/hibernate/SessionFactory";

    public List findAll()
    {
        List carList = new ArrayList();
        Session session = null;

        try
        {
            session = ServiceLocator.getHibernateSession(HIBERNATE_SESSION_FACTORY);
            Criteria criteria = session.createCriteria(CarDTO.class);
            carList = criteria.list();
        }
        catch (Exception e)
        {
            System.out.println(e);
        }
        finally
        {
            try
            {
                if (session != null) {session.close();}
            }
            catch (Exception e)
            {
                System.out.println(e);
            }
```

Example 5-14. HibernateCarDAO.java (continued)

```
        }

        return carList;
    }
```

It is far more compact—with a nearly 50% reduction in total lines of code. More importantly, the code doing the real work was reduced to three steps:

1. Acquire a Hibernate session

2. Create a `Criteria` object. This line is the Hibernate equivalent of saying "select * from CAR".

3. Get the resulting `carList` from the query.

The `ResultSet` row marshalling still happens, but the Hibernate API takes care of it behind the scenes. Our code is lean and clean.

We'll explore some more in depth Hibernate examples in just a bit, and will cover the full CRUD spectrum (Create, Read, Update, and Delete). But for now, let's change our `ControllerServlet` and deploy the application.

To begin using `HibernateCarDAO`, all we need to do is change how the `CarDAO` interface is instantiated in `ControllerServlet` (Example 5-15).

Example 5-15. ControllerServlet.java

```
        if(VIEW_CAR_LIST_ACTION.equals(actionName))
        {
            CarDAO carDAO = new HibernateCarDAO();
            request.setAttribute("carList", carDAO.findAll());
            destinationPage = "/carList.jsp";
        }
```

Now that everything is in place, let's build and deploy the application:

1. Type ant in the root directory of *05a-list* to build the project.

2. Shut down JBoss.

3. Type ant `colddeploy`.

4. Start JBoss back up.

5. Visit *http://localhost:8080/jaw* in a web browser.

Click on the View Inventory link to see Figure 5-1.

Make	Model	Model Year
Toyota	Camry	2005
Toyota	Corolla	1999
Ford	Explorer	2005

Figure 5-1. viewCarList using Hibernate

OK, so we've been through at least five distinct iterations that have all given us the same result:

- Using scriptlet code to generate the carList
- Using the ControllerServlet to generate the carList
- Using the InMemoryCarDAO to generate the carList
- Using the JDBCCarDAO to generate the carList
- Using the HibernateCarDAO to generate the carList

In each case, the view remained constant—only the back-end services have gotten progressively more sophisticated. For sticking with us this long, we'll reward you with some new functionality. Let's flesh out this example by allowing the user to add new cars, edit existing cars, and delete cars from the list. This will allow us to run Hibernate through its paces.

Adding a Car

To add a new car, we'll create a new link on the viewCarList page, as in Figure 5-2.

[Add Car]

Make	Model	Model Year
Toyota	Camry	2005
Toyota	Corolla	1999
Ford	Explorer	2005

Figure 5-2. viewCarList with Add Car link

This link will submit an addCar action request to our ControllerServlet (*http://localhost:8080/jaw/controller?action=addCar*).

The ControllerServlet in Example 5-16 places an empty CarDTO in the Request scope and redirects to the *carForm.jsp* page.

Example 5-16. ControllerServlet.java

```
// perform action
    if(VIEW_CAR_LIST_ACTION.equals(actionName))
    {
        CarDAO carDAO = new HibernateCarDAO( );
        request.setAttribute("carList", carDAO.findAll( ));
        destinationPage = "/carList.jsp";
    }
    else if(ADD_CAR_ACTION.equals(actionName))
    {
        request.setAttribute("car", new CarDTO( ));
        destinationPage = "/carForm.jsp";
```

Example 5-16. ControllerServlet.java (continued)

```
    }
    else
    {
        String errorMessage = "[" + actionName + "] is not a valid action.";
        request.setAttribute(ERROR_KEY, errorMessage);
    }
```

The *carForm.jsp* page in Figure 5-3 allows the user to type in the details of a new car and save it.

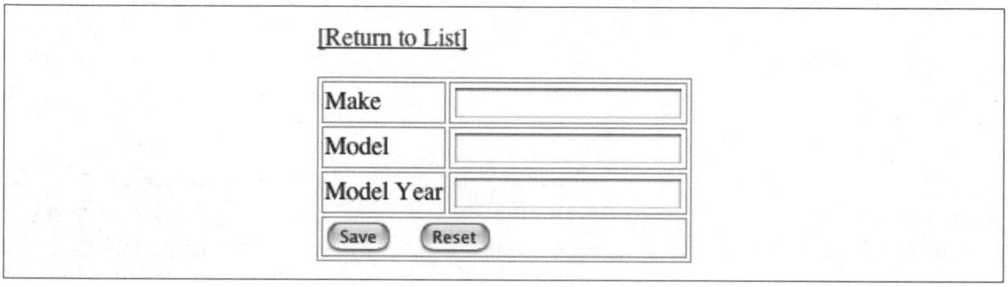

Figure 5-3. carForm.jsp

Example 5-17 shows the JSP code.

Example 5-17. carForm.jsp

```jsp
<%@ taglib prefix="c" uri="http://java.sun.com/jsp/jstl/core" %>

<html>
<head>
  <link rel="stylesheet" type="text/css" href="default.css">
</head>

<body>

  <p><a href="controller?action=viewCarList">[Return to List]</a></p>

  <form method="post" action="controller">
  <input type="hidden" name="action" value="saveCar" />
  <input type="hidden" name="id" value="${car.id}" />
  <table>
    <!-- input fields -->
    <tr>
      <td>Make</td>
      <td><input type="text" name="make" value="${car.make}" /></td>
    </tr>
    <tr>
      <td>Model</td>
      <td><input type="text" name="model" value="${car.model}" /></td>
    </tr>
    <tr>
      <td class="model-year">Model Year</td>
```

Example 5-17. carForm.jsp (continued)

```
      <td><input type="text" name="modelYear" value="${car. modelYear}" /></td>
    </tr>

    <!-- Save/Reset buttons -->
    <tr>
      <td colspan="2">
        <input type="submit" name="save" value="Save" />
          
        <input type="reset" name="reset" value="Reset" />
      </td>
    </tr>
  </table>
  </form>
</body>
</html>
```

The JSP pulls the CarDTO from the Request scope and uses it to populate the HTML form. This is less important right now when the CarDTO is in its initial (empty) state. It will become more important when we reuse this form to edit Car information.

When the user clicks the "Save" button, the data will be sent back up to the ControllerServlet in Example 5-18 through a saveCar action.

Example 5-18. ControllerServlet.java

```java
// perform action
        if(VIEW_CAR_LIST_ACTION.equals(actionName))
        {
            CarDAO carDAO = new HibernateCarDAO( );
            request.setAttribute("carList", carDAO.findAll( ));
            destinationPage = "/carList.jsp";
        }
        else if(ADD_CAR_ACTION.equals(actionName))
        {
            request.setAttribute("car", new CarDTO( ));
            destinationPage = "/carForm.jsp";
        }
        else if(SAVE_CAR_ACTION.equals(actionName))
        {
            //build the car from the request parameters
            CarDTO car = new CarDTO( );
            car.setMake(request.getParameter("make"));
            car.setModel(request.getParameter("model"));
            car.setModelYear(request.getParameter("modelYear"));

            //save the car
            CarDAO carDAO = new HibernateCarDAO( );
            carDAO.create(car);

            //prepare the list
            request.setAttribute("carList", carDAO.findAll( ));
            destinationPage = "/carList.jsp";
```

Example 5-18. ControllerServlet.java (continued)

```
    }
    else
    {
        String errorMessage = "[" + actionName + "] is not a valid action.";
        request.setAttribute(ERROR_KEY, errorMessage);
    }
```

The saveCar action marshals the name/value parameter pairs from the request into a well-formed CarDTO and calls carDAO.create( ) to save it into the database. Just as we delegated object creation to Hibernate when pulling data from the database, all modern MVC web frameworks will marshal name/value pairs into objects on your behalf as well. Our homegrown MVC framework doesn't offer you this convenience, if only to more clearly demonstrate what is going on under the covers.

To give you an idea of what the level of effort would be to use straight JDBC to save your new car to the database, Example 5-19 shows the create( ) method in JDBCCarDAO.

Example 5-19. JDBCCarDAO.java

```
    public void create(CarDTO car)
    {
        DataSource dataSource = null;
        Connection conn = null;
        PreparedStatement pstmt = null;

        String insertSql = "insert into CAR(MAKE, MODEL, MODEL_YEAR) values(?,?,?)";

        try
        {
            dataSource = ServiceLocator.getDataSource(DATA_SOURCE);
            conn = dataSource.getConnection( );
            pstmt = conn.prepareStatement(insertSql);

            pstmt.setString(1, car.getMake( ));
            pstmt.setString(2, car.getModel( ));
            pstmt.setString(3, car.getModelYear( ));
            pstmt.executeUpdate( );
        }
        catch (Exception e)
        {
            System.out.println(e);
        }
        finally
        {
            try
            {
                if(pstmt != null){pstmt.close( );}
                if(conn != null){conn.close( );}
            }
            catch(Exception e)
```

Example 5-19. JDBCCarDAO.java (continued)

```
        {
            System.out.println(e);
        }
    }
}
```

The method accepts a CarDTO, pulls the individual member data out, populates a SQL INSERT statement, and executes the query.

Example 5-20 shows the same functionality using Hibernate.

Example 5-20. HibernateCarDAO.java

```
public void create(CarDTO car)
{
    Session session = null;
    Transaction tx = null;

    try
    {
        session = ServiceLocator.getHibernateSession(HIBERNATE_SESSION_FACTORY);
        tx = session.beginTransaction();
        session.save(car);
        tx.commit();
    }
    catch (Exception e)
    {
        try{tx.rollback();}
        catch(Exception e2){System.out.println(e2);}

        System.out.println(e);
    }
    finally
    {
        try
        {
            if (session != null) {session.close();}
        }
        catch (Exception e)
        {
            System.out.println(e);
        }
    }
}
```

Hibernate handles all the member data wrangling. We simply hand it a CarDTO, and it takes care of the rest.

- Type ant in the root directory of *05b-add* to build the project.
- Shut down JBoss.
- Type ant colddeploy.

- Start JBoss back up.
- Visit *http://localhost:8080/jaw* in a web browser.

Add several cars using the HTML form. Use the Ant script in the SQL directory to query the results outside the container. Prove to yourself that no sneaky stuff is going on—Hibernate is truly inserting the values into the database on our behalf.

Editing a Car

To edit an existing car, we'll add another set of links on the viewCarList page in Figure 5-4.

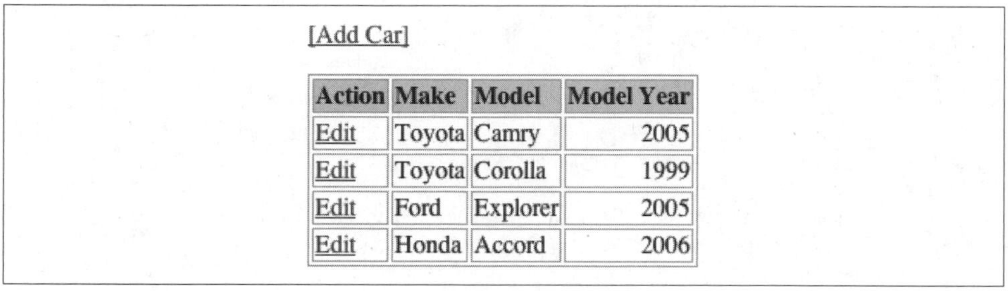

Action	Make	Model	Model Year
Edit	Toyota	Camry	2005
Edit	Toyota	Corolla	1999
Edit	Ford	Explorer	2005
Edit	Honda	Accord	2006

[Add Car]

Figure 5-4. Editing cars

The Edit links each contain the ID of the displayed car. They call the ControllerServlet using the editCar action. Example 5-21 shows the JSP code.

Example 5-21. carList.jsp

```
<%@ taglib prefix="c" uri="http://java.sun.com/jsp/jstl/core" %>
<html>

<head>
  <link rel="stylesheet" type="text/css" href="default.css">
</head>

<body>
  <p><a href="controller?action=addCar">[Add Car]</a></p>

  <table>
      <tr>
          <th>Action</th>
          <th>Make</th>
          <th>Model</th>
          <th class="model-year">Model Year</th>
      </tr>

      <c:forEach items='${carList}' var='car'>
      <tr>
          <td><a href="controller?action=editCar&id=${car.id}">Edit</a></td>
```

Example 5-21. carList.jsp (continued)

```
        <td>${car.make}</td>
        <td>${car.model}</td>
        <td class="model-year">${car.modelYear}</td>
    </tr>
    </c:forEach>

  </table>
</body>

</html>
```

The ControllerServlet in Example 5-22 catches the request, queries the requested CarDTO out of the database using the ID, places it in the Request scope, and finally redirects to the *carForm.jsp*.

Example 5-22. ControllerServlet.java

```
// perform action
    if(VIEW_CAR_LIST_ACTION.equals(actionName))
    {
        CarDAO carDAO = new HibernateCarDAO( );
        request.setAttribute("carList", carDAO.findAll( ));
        destinationPage = "/carList.jsp";
    }
    else if(ADD_CAR_ACTION.equals(actionName))
    {
        request.setAttribute("car", new CarDTO( ));
        destinationPage = "/carForm.jsp";
    }
    else if(EDIT_CAR_ACTION.equals(actionName))
    {
        int id = Integer.parseInt(request.getParameter("id"));
        CarDAO carDAO = new HibernateCarDAO( );
        request.setAttribute("car", carDAO.findById(id));
        destinationPage = "/carForm.jsp";
    }
    else if(SAVE_CAR_ACTION.equals(actionName))
    {
        //build the car from the request parameters
        CarDTO car = new CarDTO( );
        car.setMake(request.getParameter("make"));
        car.setModel(request.getParameter("model"));
        car.setModelYear(request.getParameter("modelYear"));

        //save the car
        CarDAO carDAO = new HibernateCarDAO( );
        carDAO.create(car);

        //prepare the list
        request.setAttribute("carList", carDAO.findAll( ));
        destinationPage = "/carList.jsp";
    }
```

Example 5-22. ControllerServlet.java (continued)

```
    else
    {
        String errorMessage = "[" + actionName + "] is not a valid action.";
        request.setAttribute(ERROR_KEY, errorMessage);
    }
```

This time having a filled-in CarDTO in Request scope allows us to populate the form in Figure 5-5 with the appropriate data.

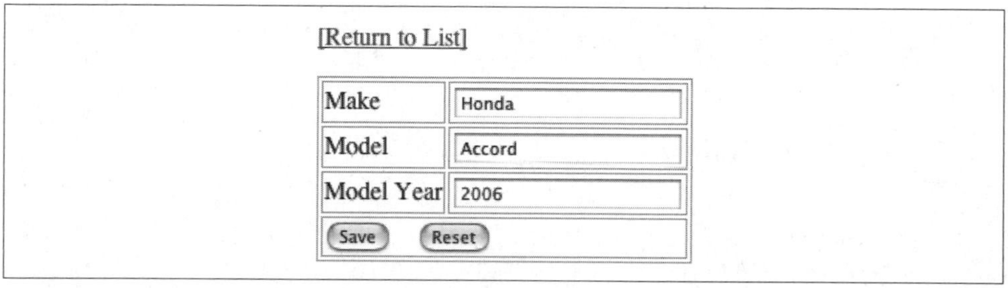

Figure 5-5. carForm.jsp used to edit a CarDTO

The "Save" button still sends the form data back to the ControllerServlet using the saveCar action, only this time the ID value is a positive integer. (Recall that CarDTO.id is initialized to "-1" unless you provide a specific value.) This allows us to reuse the saveCar method for both inserts and updates. Example 5-23 shows the modified method in ControllerServlet.

Example 5-23. ControllerServlet.java

```
// perform action
    if(VIEW_CAR_LIST_ACTION.equals(actionName))
    {
        CarDAO carDAO = new HibernateCarDAO( );
        request.setAttribute("carList", carDAO.findAll( ));
        destinationPage = "/carList.jsp";
    }
    else if(ADD_CAR_ACTION.equals(actionName))
    {
        request.setAttribute("car", new CarDTO( ));
        destinationPage = "/carForm.jsp";
    }
    else if(EDIT_CAR_ACTION.equals(actionName))
    {
        int id = Integer.parseInt(request.getParameter("id"));
        CarDAO carDAO = new HibernateCarDAO( );
        request.setAttribute("car", carDAO.findById(id));
        destinationPage = "/carForm.jsp";
    }
    else if(SAVE_CAR_ACTION.equals(actionName))
    {
        //build the car from the request parameters
```

Example 5-23. ControllerServlet.java (continued)

```
            CarDTO car = new CarDTO( );
            car.setId(Integer.parseInt(request.getParameter("id")));
            car.setMake(request.getParameter("make"));
            car.setModel(request.getParameter("model"));
            car.setModelYear(request.getParameter("modelYear"));

            //save the car
            CarDAO carDAO = new HibernateCarDAO( );
            if(car.getId( ) == -1)
            {
                carDAO.create(car);
            }
            else
            {
                carDAO.update(car);
            }

            //prepare the list
            request.setAttribute("carList", carDAO.findAll( ));
            destinationPage = "/carList.jsp";
        }
        else
        {
            String errorMessage = "[" + actionName + "] is not a valid action.";
            request.setAttribute(ERROR_KEY, errorMessage);
        }
```

Which, of course, brings us back to the DAO. Example 5-24 shows what the update
code looks like in JDBCCarDAO.

Example 5-24. JDBCCarDAO.java

```
public void update(CarDTO car)
    {
        DataSource dataSource = null;
        Connection conn = null;
        PreparedStatement pstmt = null;

        String insertSql =
                "update CAR set MAKE=?, MODEL=?, MODEL_YEAR=? where id=?";

        try
        {
            dataSource = ServiceLocator.getDataSource(DATA_SOURCE);
            conn = dataSource.getConnection( );
            pstmt = conn.prepareStatement(insertSql);

            pstmt.setString(1, car.getMake( ));
            pstmt.setString(2, car.getModel( ));
            pstmt.setString(3, car.getModelYear( ));
            pstmt.setInt(4, car.getId( ));
            pstmt.executeUpdate( );
```

Example 5-24. JDBCCarDAO.java (continued)

```
        }
        catch (Exception e)
        {
            System.out.println(e);
        }
        finally
        {
            try
            {
                if(pstmt != null){pstmt.close( );}
                if(conn != null){conn.close( );}
            }
            catch(Exception e)
            {
                System.out.println(e);
            }
        }


    }
```

And Example 5-25 shows the corresponding reduced code in HibernateCarDAO.

Example 5-25. HibernateCarDAO.java

```
    public void update(CarDTO car)
    {
        Session session = null;
        Transaction tx = null;

        try
        {
            session =
              ServiceLocator.getHibernateSession(HIBERNATE_SESSION_FACTORY);
            tx = session.beginTransaction( );
            session.update(car);
            tx.commit( );
        }
        catch (Exception e)
        {
            try{tx.rollback( );}
            catch(Exception e2){System.out.println(e2);}

            System.out.println(e);
        }
        finally
        {
            try
            {
                if (session != null) {session.close( );}
            }
            catch (Exception e)
```

Example 5-25. HibernateCarDAO.java (continued)

```
        {
            System.out.println(e);
        }
    }
}
```

- Type ant in the root directory of *05c-edit* to build the project.
- Shut down JBoss.
- Type ant colddeploy.
- Start JBoss back up.
- Visit *http://localhost:8080/jaw* in a web browser.

Use the web interface to make changes to the cars in the database.

Deleting a Car

Hopefully, at this point you are getting into a groove. As you incrementally add functionality to the website, you will tend to complete the same steps in order each time:

- Modify the View (JSP pages).
- Modify the Controller (ControllerServlet).
- Modify the Model (CarDTO, CarDAO).

Let's add the final bit of functionality for this chapter—allowing the user to delete cars. First, we'll modify the View in Figure 5-6.

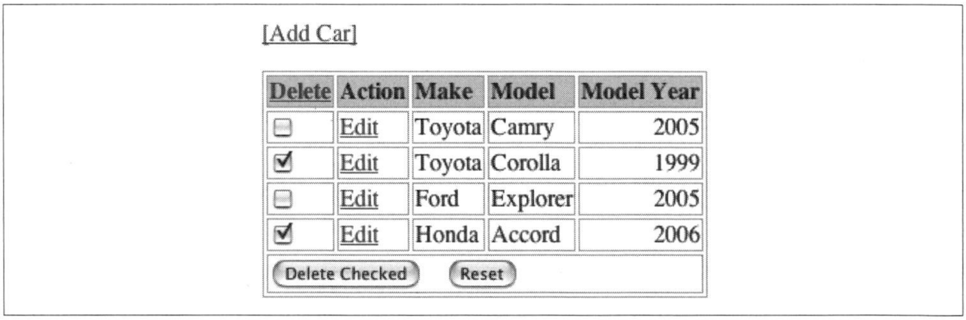

[Add Car]

Delete	Action	Make	Model	Model Year
☐	Edit	Toyota	Camry	2005
☑	Edit	Toyota	Corolla	1999
☐	Edit	Ford	Explorer	2005
☑	Edit	Honda	Accord	2006

(Delete Checked) (Reset)

Figure 5-6. carList.jsp with delete

The final *carList.jsp* in Example 5-26 allows the user to check individual cars and delete them in bulk. Notice that clicking on the Delete column header checks all of the records. Clicking the "Reset" button unchecks all records.

Example 5-26. carList.jsp

```
<%@ taglib prefix="c" uri="http://java.sun.com/jsp/jstl/core" %>
<html>

<head>
  <link rel="stylesheet" type="text/css" href="default.css">

  <script language="JavaScript">
      function checkAll(field)
      {
          for (i=0; i < field.length; i++)
          {
              field[i].checked = true;
          }
      }
  </script>
</head>

<body>
  <p><a href="controller?action=addCar">[Add Car]</a></p>

  <form name="deleteForm" method="post" action="controller">
  <input type="hidden" name="action" value="deleteCar" />
  <table>
    <tr>
      <th><a href="javascript:checkAll(document.deleteForm.id)">Delete</a></th>
      <th>Action</th>
      <th>Make</th>
      <th>Model</th>
      <th class="model-year">Model Year</th>
    </tr>

    <c:forEach items='${carList}' var='car'>
      <tr>
      <td><input type="checkbox" name="id" value="${car.id}"></td>
      <td><a href="controller?action=editCar&id=${car.id}">Edit</a></td>
      <td>${car.make}</td>
      <td>${car.model}</td>
      <td class="model-year">${car.modelYear}</td>
      </tr>
    </c:forEach>

    <tr>
      <td colspan="5">
        <input type="submit" name="Delete Checked" value="Delete Checked" />
          
        <input type="reset" name="Reset" value="Reset" />
      </td>
    </tr>

  </table>
  </form>
</body>
</html>
```

This list is now wrapped in an HTML form. Each record's checkbox field has the same name: ID. This means that if you check multiple records, the IDs will be sent up to the deleteCar action in ControllerServlet as a string array.

The next thing we must do to implement delete functionality is modify the Controller in Example 5-27.

Example 5-27. ControllerServlet.java

```
        else if(DELETE_CAR_ACTION.equals(actionName))
        {
            //get list of ids to delete
            String[] ids = request.getParameterValues("id");

            //delete the list of ids
            CarDAO carDAO = new HibernateCarDAO();
            if(ids != null)
            {
                carDAO.delete(ids);
            }

            //prepare the list
            request.setAttribute("carList", carDAO.findAll());
            destinationPage = "/carList.jsp";
        }
```

Finally, we'll add the delete() method to the DAOs. Example 5-28 shows the JDBCCarDAO implementation.

Example 5-28. JDBCCarDAO.java

```
public void delete(String[] ids)
    {
        DataSource dataSource = null;
        Connection conn = null;
        Statement stmt = null;

        String sql = "delete from CAR where id in(";

        try
        {
            dataSource = ServiceLocator.getDataSource(DATA_SOURCE);
            conn = dataSource.getConnection();
            stmt = conn.createStatement();

            StringBuffer idList = new StringBuffer();
            for(int i = 0; i < ids.length; i++)
            {
                idList.append(ids[i]);

                if(i < (ids.length - 1))
                {
                    idList.append(",");
```

Example 5-28. JDBCCarDAO.java (continued)

```
                    }
            }

            stmt.executeUpdate(sql + idList.toString() + ")");
        }
        catch (Exception e)
        {
            System.out.println(e);
        }
        finally
        {
            try
            {
                if(stmt != null){stmt.close();}
                if(conn != null){conn.close();}
            }
            catch(Exception e)
            {
                System.out.println(e);
            }
        }

    }
```

Example 5-29 shows the greatly simplified code in HibernateCarDAO.

Example 5-29. HibernateCarDAO.java

```
public void delete(String[] ids)
{
    Session session = null;
    Transaction tx = null;

    try
    {
        session =
            ServiceLocator.getHibernateSession(HIBERNATE_SESSION_FACTORY);
        tx = session.beginTransaction();
        for(int i=0; i < ids.length; i++)
        {
            CarDTO car =
                (CarDTO) session.get(CarDTO.class, new Integer(ids[i]));

            session.delete(car);
        }
        tx.commit();
    }
    catch (Exception e)
    {
        try{tx.rollback();}
        catch(Exception e2){System.out.println(e2);}
```

Example 5-29. HibernateCarDAO.java (continued)

```
            System.out.println(e);
        }
        finally
        {
            try
            {
                if (session != null) {session.close( );}
            }
            catch (Exception e)
            {
                System.out.println(e);
            }
        }
    }
}
```

1. Type ant in the root directory of *05d-delete* to build the project.
2. Shut down JBoss.
3. Type ant colddeploy.
4. Start JBoss back up.
5. Visit *http://localhost:8080/jaw* in a web browser.

Remember that you can always run the Ant script in the SQL subproject to repopulate the database.

Looking Ahead...

Hopefully you feel like we're picking up a head of steam here. You should feel comfortable with the Web tier, as well as the Persistence tier, at this point. The next several chapters focus on the middle tier (the Business tier), where you will get comfortable with Stateless Session Beans (SLSBs) and Message-Driven Beans (MDBs).

CHAPTER 6

Stateless Session Beans

Everything we've done up to this point technically could have been done without using JBoss. Our web tier simply uses the embedded Tomcat Servlet container—we could run our WAR unchanged in a standalone Tomcat instance. Our persistence tier used both JDBC and Hibernate. Again, both are available in non-JBoss installations. We simply took advantage of them because they come bundled with JBoss.

We now are firmly in the middle of the business tier. The next several chapters will focus on components that must be run in JBoss. More specifically, we'll look at EJB components that must run inside an EJB container.

Many people would argue that Enterprise JavaBeans are what put the "E" in the Java2 Enterprise Edition. But you also could argue that web-centric applications that use only JSPs and Servlets are still legitimate J2EE applications. These next sections will introduce you to technologies that allow you to build a large-scale, distributed, transaction-based Enterprise application.

Issues with EJBs

Our two biggest complaints about EJBs are that:

- They require a complex set of programming artifacts for deployment.
- Developers tend to overuse them.

The complexity of the EJB programming model has hindered the adoption of J2EE. To deploy an EJB, you are dealing with as many as seven or more files (five Java files and two deployment descriptors). As you'll see later on, the main thrust of J2EE 1.5 (which includes EJB 3.0) is to simplify and lighten J2EE development by eliminating many of the programming artifacts required to deploy components. J2EE 1.5 will still offer core enterprise-class services such as transaction management and security, but it will be much easier to use. This book will not go into much detail about EJB 3. 0 because the specification hasn't been finalized. But it will briefly discuss the improvements you'll see once EJB 3.0 becomes available. This book uses EJB 2.1, and it still has to deal with deployment descriptors and extra Java interfaces. It will show how XDoclet generates most of the code for us so that we can focus on business logic.

As software developers, most of us have the tendency to over-engineer a solution. You may also have heard the old adage, "If all you've got is a hammer, every problem tends to look like a nail." Bruce Tate, author of *Better, Faster, Lighter Java (O'Reilly)*, calls the combination of these two predilections the "Golden Hammer" theory. Developers who know only EJBs tend to use them in wholly inappropriate situations.

Tate's book, as the title might imply, argues against the notion that every application you develop should be "Enterprise-grade," with all the associated complexity and overhead. He recommends the use of other third-party ORMs rather than CMP Entity Beans, and also suggests using a "better, faster, lighter" container to manage transactional applications called the Spring Framework. Like Hibernate, Spring is not J2EE-specification compliant and can run inside either a J2EE container or standalone. Both Hibernate and Spring have had a huge impact on the upcoming EJB 3.0 specification, and due to the influence of these external frameworks, EJB 3.0 will be lighter and simpler to use.

Should I Use EJB or Not?

From their inception, EJBs have been used for the right and wrong reasons. We've seen EJB-based projects that have failed miserably and others that were highly successful. So what made the difference? Here are a couple of key success factors with EJBs:

- Developer knowledge and maturity
- Decision-making

EJB development and deployment is complex with EJB 2.1 and earlier, so even if you have a good reason for using EJBs, your project still could fail if your development team hasn't worked with them before. If you're in this situation, take the same approach with EJBs as you would with any other technology that's new to you—learn how to use it before you build your system. The best way to quickly get up to speed on EJB is to get some training and to augment your team with a few experienced developers who've used them to develop production-quality systems.

But taking classes, hiring experienced developers, and reading books aren't enough. You also should consider some guidelines to help you decide if EJBs are appropriate for your architecture. As we said earlier, there are both good and bad reasons for using EJBs (of all types).

Here are some reasons for not using EJBs:

Your application uses threads
>The EJB specification forbids using threads because the threads your code creates are outside the container's control and could cause unexpected results.

Your application is read-only or read-mostly
>If your application reads data from your database most or all of the time, then transactions aren't important to you. In this case, EJBs are overkill.

Here are some dubious or wrong reasons for developing with EJBs:

You want to use database connection pooling with JDBC `DataSource`*s*
>You don't need an EJB or an EJB container to use a `DataSource`. You can configure a standalone Tomcat container with a database connection pool and use a `DataSource`.

You want to use Entity Beans for persistence
>Other third-party ORMs, such as Hibernate, provide more functionality and better performance.

You think you'll need them later, so you're adding them now
>Don't over-architect. EJBs add complexity, so add them only when they help you solve a problem. Remember that you can always go back and refactor to an EJB solution when the need arises.

You want to group your related business logic together
>You could group order-related functionality into an EJB, but you could also do this with a POJO. The need to group related logic together isn't a strong enough reason to use an EJB. But if your business processes require transactions or if you have external remote clients, you should consider using an EJB—see the good reasons below.

Web tier session caching
>Caching frameworks like JBoss Cache or OSCache (by Open Symphony) provide a powerful, lightweight, and more efficient alternative to the overhead incurred by EJBs.

Here are some good reasons for using EJBs:

Distributed transactions
>Your application may access different types of back-end systems such as databases, messaging systems, or mainframes. If one of these systems has a problem with its part of a transaction, then you want each of the other systems to roll back their unit of work. All parts of the transaction either succeed or fail together.

Asynchronous processing

Message-Driven Beans are designed for consuming JMS messages. It's easier to use an MDB than to create your own infrastructure. The next chapter will talk more about MDBs.

Declarative transactions

Rather than cluttering your code with low-level transaction management logic, you can push transaction settings into deployment descriptors. Container-Managed Transactions (CMT) is one of the most popular reasons for using EJBs. CMT uses the EJB container's transaction services and manages transaction boundaries on behalf of the developer.

Component security

Declarative security enables you to set security levels for EJBs and for individual EJB methods based on user roles. The Security chapter covers EJB security.

Remote access

You may have Java applications spread across multiple servers, or you could have a Swing user interface. In either case, EJBs are a good fit because they're designed to be distributed components. Remote EJB access uses RMI as its communications protocol—RMI is part of the core Java platform and interoperates with CORBA.

If your application requirements match several of the good reasons to use EJBs, then you probably need EJBs. As a rule, if your application doesn't have requirements concerning transactions and/or asynchronous processing, then EJBs probably aren't worth the added complexity and overhead. But if your application has to deal with these issues, EJBs make sense and provide real value. Even if your application requires EJBs, you won't need them everywhere. Consider your needs on a case-by-case basis.

Presumably you've chosen JBoss as your application server because you've already done the analysis and your application truly requires a fully functional EJB container. Even so, the acronym You Ain't Gonna Need It (YAGNI) should never be too far from the forefront of your application design. We take an additive approach when building applications, much like the flow of this book. Don't avoid technologies that clearly solve a problem, but don't add them just because they *might* solve a problem at some point down the road.

Please don't misunderstand us—we don't hate EJBs and we continue to use them on real-world projects. But we encourage you to look at your system-level and business requirements before using EJBs. We use Stateless Session Beans for managing transactions and Message-Driven Beans for asynchronous processing. The next section covers transactions in greater detail.

Business Tier

Let's review the three basic tiers of J2EE development. The Web tier handles the look and feel of the application. It is what the user interacts with. The Persistence tier handles long-term data storage. The Business tier handles coarse-grained business rules.

For example, consider the "Add Car" user story that we implemented in the last chapter. The user clearly has a way to enter new cars into the system—the Web tier provides an HTML form. The new car has a way to be persisted for the long-term— our DAOs in the Persistence tier. But what about the business rules for adding a new car to the JAW inventory?

When a dealer gets a new car on the lot, many actions need to happen. Someone needs to physically receive the car. Someone else needs to affix the dealer logo to the back of the car. Accounting needs to add it to the books as an asset. Marketing needs to add it to the "New Arrivals" listing in the newspaper ads.

While these are actions that would be done by humans in the real world, the same types of things usually need to happen in a J2EE application as well. In a J2EE application, we call a grouping of activities a Transaction. Transactions should be atomic—if one of the steps fails, all grouped activities should roll back to their initial state.

The classic example is a bank transaction—if you transfer money from your checking account to your savings account, the two distinct activities are treated as an atomic transaction. If your SavingsAccountDAO.depositMoney() method fails, you want your CheckingAccountDAO.withdrawMoney() method call to roll back as well. Otherwise, the money you took out will be lost.

Transactions are usually synchronous and represent a series of sequential steps to carry out a business process. Another type of activity occurs over a longer course of time—an asynchronous activity. These types of activities tend to be a series of individual steps that are performed in a specific order, but don't necessarily cause the previous step to roll back. Think "work-flow" instead of "transaction." Think macro-view instead of micro-view. For example, if marketing doesn't get the new car in this week's newspaper ad, we don't need to roll back the dealer logo application and the accounting activities.

The EJB specification provides specific technologies that handle both synchronous and asynchronous activities.

Enterprise JavaBeans

There are three types of EJBs:

Session Beans
> Session Beans allow the developer to group the steps of a business process into a single transaction. The activities contained in a Session Bean are synchronous.

Message-Driven Beans (MDBs)
> MDBs are good for processing business logic asynchronously and/or executing long-running tasks in the background. They listen on Java Messaging Service (JMS) destinations (Queues and Topics) and process incoming messages as they arrive.

Entity Beans
> Entity Beans are a persistence mechanism that encapsulates Create, Read, Update, and Delete (CRUD) operations on database tables.

Although some shops still use entity beans, most of the Java community has moved away from them in favor of other, more flexible third-party ORM solutions. However, the other two types of EJBs still are widely used. We'll talk about Session Beans in this chapter and MDBs in the next.

Our Example

We are going to upgrade the JAW Motors application by adding a "Buy Car" user story that uses a transaction. In addition to marking a record into the CAR table as "Sold", we'll also insert a corresponding record into the ACCOUNTING table. A Session Bean is appropriate because buying a car is an atomic transaction. The update to the CAR table and the insert into the ACCOUNTING table must both succeed—if one database operation fails, the other operation rolls back. We'll take three iterations to move from a web-only application to one that uses a Session Bean for its business logic:

Iteration 1

Introduce a Session Bean. The Controller Servlet uses the InventoryFacadeBean rather than the DAO to list the cars on the web page. All other actions in the Controller Servlet still use the DAO.

Iteration 2

We then move all business logic out of the Controller Servlet into the InventoryFacadeBean (which wraps the DAO).

Iteration 3

Upgrade the web pages, Controller Servlet, and InventoryFacadeBean to buy a car. We'll also create a new AccountingHibernateDAO and AccountingDTO for the ACCOUNTING table.

Iteration 1—Introduce a Session Bean

In this Iteration, we'll take the following steps to introduce a Session Bean to the JAW Motors application and lay the groundwork for the rest of the chapter.

- Modify the Persistence Tier:
  - Add a STATUS column to the CAR table.
  - Make the CarDTO Serializable, and add a status field along with getter and setter methods.
  - Add a filterByStatus() method to the HibernateCarDAO.
- Upgrade the web site:
  - Refactor the Controller Servlet's viewCarList action to use the InventoryFacadeBean for finding all available (unsold) cars.
  - Add a getEjbLocalHome() method to the ServiceLocator to look up an EJB's Local Home Interface using JNDI.

- Add EJB-based JNDI reference settings to the Web deployment descriptors (web.xml and jboss-web.xml).
  - Automate EJB-based JNDI reference settings in the Web deployment descriptors with XDoclet.
- Add a Session Bean:
  - Develop and deploy the InventoryFacadeBean.

Modifying the CAR Table

The CAR table's new STATUS column indicates whether a car is "Sold" or "Available." Example 6-1 shows the new SQL in ch06-a/sql/build.xml used to create the table.

Example 6-1. sql/build.xml

```
CREATE TABLE CAR (
    ID BIGINT identity,
    MAKE VARCHAR(50),
    MODEL VARCHAR(50),
    MODEL_YEAR VARCHAR(50),
    STATUS VARCHAR(10)
);

INSERT INTO CAR (ID, MAKE, MODEL, MODEL_YEAR, STATUS)
VALUES (99, 'Toyota', 'Camry', '2005', 'Available');

INSERT INTO CAR (ID, MAKE, MODEL, MODEL_YEAR, STATUS)
VALUES (100, 'Toyota', 'Corolla', '1999', 'Available');

INSERT INTO CAR (ID, MAKE, MODEL, MODEL_YEAR, STATUS)
VALUES (101, 'Ford', 'Explorer', '2005', 'Available');
```

A car is considered "Available" when you create it. Now let's upgrade the CarDTO.

Upgrading the CarDTO with a Status Field

Here we'll make the CarDTO Serializable and add a new status data member along with corresponding setter and getter methods. Example 6-2 shows the changes.

Example 6-2. CarDTO.java

```
package com.jbossatwork.dto;

import java.io.*;

/**
 * @hibernate.class
 *  table="CAR"
 */
public class CarDTO implements Serializable
```

Example 6-2. CarDTO.java (continued)

```java
{
    public static final String STATUS_AVAILABLE = "Available";
    public static final String STATUS_SOLD = "Sold";
    …
    private String status;

    public CarDTO( )
    {
        …
        this.status = CarDTO.STATUS_AVAILABLE;
    }

    public CarDTO(String make, String model, String modelYear)
    {
        …
        this.status = CarDTO.STATUS_AVAILABLE;
    }

    public CarDTO(int id, String make, String model, String modelYear)
    {
        …
        this.status = CarDTO.STATUS_AVAILABLE;
    }
    …

    /**
     * @hibernate.property
     *   column="STATUS"
     */
    public String getStatus( )
    {
        return status;
    }

    public void setStatus(String status)
    {
        this.status = status;
    }
}
```

Here's a breakdown of the modifications to the CarDTO:

• The CarDTO now implements the java.io.Serializable interface. We do this so that the CarDTO will serialize properly when remote clients call the InventoryFacadeBean. Remote access uses RMI, which requires objects (used as parameters or return values) to be serializable. Since all data members of the CarDTO are serializable, the only thing we need to do to make the DTO serializable is mark it as such. Java's default serialization mechanism takes care of the rest.

• The code that calls the CarDTO will use the STATUS_SOLD and STATUS_AVAILABLE constants to get, set, and check a car's status.

- Each constructor sets the status as "Available" to mark the car as unsold.
- The getStatus() and setStatus() methods get and set the status. The @hibernate.property XDoclet tag for the getStatus() method associates the CarDTO's status data member with the STATUS column in the CAR table.

Now that we've upgraded the database and the CarDTO to hold status information, we'll add a new method to the HibernateCarDAO that looks at the status.

Adding filterByStatus( ) to the HibernateDAO

We've added the filterByStatus() method that returns a List of all cars in the inventory whose status matches the value of the caller-supplied status parameter. Example 6-3 shows the changes to the HibernateCarDAO.

Example 6-3. HibernateCarDAO.java

```
public class HibernateCarDAO implements CarDAO
{
    …

    public List filterByStatus(String status)
    {
        List availableCarList = new ArrayList();
        Session session = null;

        try
        {
            session = ServiceLocator.getHibernateSession(
                            HIBERNATE_SESSION_FACTORY);

            Criteria criteria = session.createCriteria(CarDTO.class)
                    .add( Restrictions.eq("status", status) );

            availableCarList = criteria.list();
        }
        catch (Exception e)
        {
            System.out.println(e);
        }
        finally
        {
            try
            {
                if (session != null) {session.close();}
            }
            catch (Exception e)
            {
                System.out.println(e);
            }
        }
    }
```

Example 6-3. HibernateCarDAO.java (continued)

```
        return availableCarList;
    }
    …
}
```

The new `filterByStatus()` method looks similar to the `findAll()` method from the Hibernate chapter. The only difference is that we use a `Restriction` to limit the result set to those cars whose status matches the value of the `fiterByStatus()` method's status parameter. Think of a Hibernate `Restriction` like a SQL `WHERE` clause.

We've upgraded everything related to the database, and now we're going to modify the Controller Servlet to call the `InventoryFacadeBean`.

Calling the Session Bean from the Controller Servlet

We're now going to introduce the `InventoryFacadeBean` to the JAW Motors application by calling it from the Controller Servlet. We'll modify the Controller Servlet so it uses the `InventoryFacadeBean` rather than the DAO to list the cars on the web page. For now, all other actions in the Controller Servlet still use the DAO. Example 6-4 shows the changes.

Example 6-4. ControllerServlet.java

```
package com.jbossatwork;

…
import com.jbossatwork.ejb.*;
…
import javax.ejb.*;
…
public class ControllerServlet extends HttpServlet
{
    …
    protected void processRequest(HttpServletRequest request,
    HttpServletResponse response) throws ServletException, IOException
    {
        …

        InventoryFacadeLocalHome inventoryHome;

        inventoryHome = (InventoryFacadeLocalHome)
        ServiceLocator.getEjbLocalHome(InventoryFacadeLocalHome.COMP_NAME);

        InventoryFacadeLocal inventory = null;

        try {
            inventory = inventoryHome.create();
        } catch (CreateException ce) {
            throw new RuntimeException(ce.getMessage());
```

Example 6-4. ControllerServlet.java (continued)

```
        }

        // perform action
        if (VIEW_CAR_LIST_ACTION.equals(actionName))
        {
            request.setAttribute("carList", inventory.listAvailableCars( ));
            destinationPage = "/carList.jsp";
        }
        …

    }
}
```

The InventoryFacadeBean is a JNDI-based resource, so we've encapsulated the JNDI lookup with the ServiceLocator—we'll show the look up code in detail in the next section. The ServiceLocator.getEjbLocalHome( ) call does a JNDI lookup on the EJB's Local Home, and creates a Local Home Interface. The viewCarList action now calls the InventoryFacade's listAllAvailableCars( ) method to find all available (unsold) cars in the inventory.

Now that we've shown how to invoke the InventoryFacadeBean, let's take a closer look at the ServiceLocator that wraps the JNDI lookup.

Factoring Out the JNDI Calls

We've used the ServiceLocator throughout this book to wrap JNDI lookup calls— Example 6-5 is the new EJB-related method.

Example 6-5. ServiceLocator.java

```
package com.jbossatwork.util;

…
import javax.ejb.*;
…
import javax.naming.*;
…

public class ServiceLocator {
    …
    public static EJBLocalHome getEjbLocalHome(String localHomeJndiName)
    throws ServiceLocatorException {
        EJBLocalHome localHome = null;

        try {
            Context ctx = new InitialContext( );

            localHome = (EJBLocalHome) ctx.lookup(localHomeJndiName);
        } catch (ClassCastException cce) {
            throw new ServiceLocatorException(cce);
        } catch (NamingException ne) {
```

Example 6-5. ServiceLocator.java (continued)

```
        throw new ServiceLocatorException(ne);
    }

    return localHome;
}
…

}
```

The getEjbLocalHome( ) method encapsulates a JNDI look up for an EJB Local Home object. This method takes the following steps:

1. Create the InitialContext to access the JNDI tree.

2. Perform a JNDI lookup.

3. Cast the object returned from JNDI to the correct type—javax.ejb. EJBLocalHome.

4. Throw a ServiceLocatorException that chains a low-level JNDI-related exception and contains a corresponding error message.

We've written all the necessary code to call an EJB, and now we need to add EJB-based JNDI references to our web deployment descriptors.

EJB-Based JNDI References in Web-Based Deployment Descriptors

In previous chapters we've used the web.xml file to describe and deploy Servlets and JNDI resources. Example 6-6 shows the new EJB-based JNDI references in web.xml so we can use the InventoryFacade EJB from the web tier.

Example 6-6. web.xml

```
<?xml version="1.0" encoding="UTF-8"?>

<web-app xmlns="http://java.sun.com/xml/ns/j2ee"
xmlns:xsi="http://www.w3.org/2001/XMLSchema-instance"
xsi:schemaLocation="http://java.sun.com/xml/ns/j2ee
http://java.sun.com/xml/ns/j2ee/web-app_2_4.xsd" version="2.4">
  …
  <ejb-local-ref>
    <ejb-ref-name>ejb/InventoryFacadeLocal</ejb-ref-name>
    <ejb-ref-type>Session</ejb-ref-type>
    <local-home>InventoryFacadeLocalHome</local-home>
    <local>InventoryFacadeLocal</local>
  </ejb-local-ref>
  …
</web-app>
```

The `<ejb-local-ref>` element enables the web tier to access the `InventoryFacade` EJB through its Local Interface. The `<ejb-ref-name>` is the JNDI name for the EJB—`java:comp/env/ejb/InventoryFacadeLocal`. Notice that you don't have to specify `java:comp/env/`—because it is the assumed prefix. The `<ejb-type>` tells JBoss that this is a Session Bean. The `<local-home>` and `<local>` elements respectively specify the class name of the `InventoryFacade` EJB's Local Home and Local Component Interfaces.

A JNDI resource is linked into an application only if we ask for it. JBoss binds resources under its in-JVM context, `java:/`. The `jboss-web.xml` file provides a mapping between the J2EE-style ENC names and the local JBoss-specific JNDI names that JBoss uses to deploy JNDI-based resources. Example 6-7 shows the EJB-related JNDI references in `jboss-web.xml`.

Example 6-7. jboss-web.xml

```
<?xml version="1.0" encoding="UTF-8"?>
<!DOCTYPE jboss-web PUBLIC "-//JBoss//DTD Web Application 2.4//EN"
"http://www.jboss.org/j2ee/dtd/jboss-web_4_0.dtd">

<jboss-web>
  …
  <ejb-local-ref>
    <ejb-ref-name>ejb/InventoryFacadeLocal</ejb-ref-name>
    <local-jndi-name>InventoryFacadeLocal</local-jndi-name>
  </ejb-local-ref>
  …
</jboss-web>
```

The `jboss-web.xml` descriptor maps the J2EE-style JNDI names to JBoss-specific JNDI names. The `<ejb-local-ref>` element defines a local reference to the `InventoryFacade` Bean. The textual value of each `<ejb-ref-name>` element in `jboss-web.xml` MUST match the value of an `<ejb-ref-name>` in `web.xml`. The JNDI name in `<ejb-ref-name>` is relative to `java:comp/env`, so the full JNDI name is what we want: `java:comp/env/ejb/InventoryFacadeLocal`. The JNDI name in `<local-jndi-name>` is the name JBoss uses internally to reference the EJB for local access.

Automating EJB-Related JNDI Settings in Web-Based Deployment Descriptors

As in previous chapters, we don't want to hardcode our deployment descriptors. Since the JAW Motors application uses EJBs from the web tier, we need to add XDoclet tags to the Controller Servlet so the Ant build process generates the J2EE standard (`web.xml`) and JBoss-specific (`jboss-web.xml`) web deployment descriptors. Example 6-8 shows the new XDoclet tags in the Controller Servlet.

Example 6-8. ControllerServlet.java

```
/**
 * …
 *
 * @web.ejb-local-ref
 *  name="ejb/InventoryFacadeLocal"
 *  type="Session"
 *  home="InventoryFacadeLocalHome"
 *  local="InventoryFacadeLocal"
 *
 * @jboss.ejb-local-ref
 *  ref-name="InventoryFacadeLocal"
 *  jndi-name="InventoryFacadeLocal"
 *
 */
public class ControllerServlet extends HttpServlet
{
    …
}
```

The `@web.ejb-local-ref` XDoclet tag generates the `<ejb-local-ref>` element for the InventoryFacade EJB in `web.xml`, and the `@jboss.ejb-local-ref` XDoclet tag generates the corresponding `<ejb-local-ref>` element in `jboss-web.xml`.

Now that we've created the infrastructure to call the `InventoryFacade` Bean from the web application, we need to choose which type of Session Bean to use.

Session Bean Types

There are two types of Session Beans:

Stateful Session Beans
> Hold on to conversational state and maintain a long-running dialog with a client. A Shopping Cart is an example.

Stateless Session Beans
> Do NOT hold on to conversational state, so the client must pass all data needed by the Stateless Session Bean's business methods.

There is nothing in the example that requires us to maintain state between Session Bean calls. You'll probably find that most transactions will end up being Stateless. Here are some of the differences between Stateful and Stateless Session Beans:

- Stateful Session Beans maintain internal state, which causes significant overhead. Stateless Session Beans are lightweight and do not hold onto application-specific data members.

- A Stateful Session Bean is tied to a single client, so the container creates a new instance for each client that invokes the Bean's create( ) method. A Stateless Session Bean instance is *not* tied to a client, so Stateless Session Beans are more scalable because they are reusable—each instance can service multiple clients concurrently.

- Stateless Session Beans are never passivated (swapped out of the container's memory and into secondary storage) because there is no need to restore internal state, but a container can passivate a Stateful Session Bean, incurring significant I/O overhead.

Due to performance reasons, Stateful Session Beans have fallen into disuse, and we recommend using Stateless Session Beans.

There is really no difference in deploying a Stateful or Stateless Session Bean—you specify the Session Bean type in the ejb-jar.xml deployment descriptor. But before concerning ourselves with deployment, let's look at how to implement a Session Bean.

Session Beans

To add a Session Bean to the JAW Motors application, we need to do the following:

- Define the Local and Remote Interface(s).
- Create the Home Interface(s).
- Develop the Bean Class Code.
- Deploy the Bean with EJB deployment descriptors.
- Automate the Bean deployment with Ant and XDoclet.
- Create the EJB JAR file with Ant.
- Add the EJB JAR file to the EAR.
- Register the EJB JAR file in application.xml.
- Copy the EJB JAR file into the EAR.

Remote Versus Local EJB Calls

Since we're creating a buyCar( ) method, it could be called from any number of clients. We happen to be writing a web application, but the same transaction could conceivably be called from a Swing Application or even a web service.

This method is highly cohesive—it does only one thing—buy a car from our inventory. It is also loosely coupled to the other tiers—there is nothing that returns HTML that would tie it to the web tier, and since it calls a DAO, nothing ties it to a specific database or persistence strategy.

We now need to decide how the other tiers are going to make this buyCar( ) method call. The Servlet container is co-located on the same server in the same JVM as the

EJB container, so we can use the Session Bean's Local interfaces. All objects are in the same memory space, so under the covers, JBoss will pass things around by reference (technically, the memory location of the objects).

As our application grows, we might decide to split out this functionality to physically separate servers. We might move our web tier outside the firewall, move the Persistence tier (or at least the database server) to a box of its own, and leave the EJBs on a third box in the middle. Once we've made this step, we can grow each tier to a cluster of servers—a cluster of Tomcat servers, DB servers, and JBoss servers.

Once we move to separate boxes, we need to start making Remote calls to our EJB instead of local calls. Since our Servlets and EJBs are no longer in the same JVM and memory space, the container can no longer make calls by reference. It now has to make calls by value—this is done by serializing the object, streaming it over the network from one box to the other and reconstituting it on the other side.

Another reason why you might create remote interfaces is if you are writing a Swing client. Since your application is truly distributed, your Swing client will need a way to make method calls on the remote server.

We'll create both local and remote interfaces so you can see what they look like. But remember YAGNI—if you don't have any immediate plans to run on separate boxes, don't do it. We'll just use local calls in our Servlets for this example.

Before we develop a Stateless Session Bean, let's explore the new directory structure we'll use for our EJB development environment

Exploring the New Directory Structure

In previous chapters, we had the following sub-directories:

common
> Contains code and a build.xml file for building the Common JAR.

sql
> Contains a build.xml file for creating the database.

webapp
> Contains code and a build.xml file for building the WAR.

If you change to the ch06/ch06-a directory, you'll see that we've added an ejb sub-directory—this is our EJB development environment. The goal is to keep each portion of the application as autonomous as possible. Granted, most of the application will have dependencies on the common sub-project, but by providing individual Ant scripts we have the opportunity to build each portion of the project separately.

The ejb sub-project

Take a moment to explore the ejb sub-project. It has a single class—InventoryFacadeBean. Notice that we've created a new package structure to store all of our EJBs—com.jbossatwork.ejb.

The Ant build script in the ejb sub-directory generates EJB-specific programming artifacts, compiles the InventoryFacadeBean class, and bundles up everything into an EJB JAR (see the EJB JAR file section for details). Change to the ch06-a root directory and build the project by typing ant. Then, change to the ejb/build/distibution directory and type jar tvf ejb.jar to verify that the Inventory FacadeBean class is indeed stored in ejb.jar.

The main build.xml script in the ch06/ch06-a directory now invokes the ejb sub-directory's build.xml script to build the EJB JAR. Afterwards, the main build adds the EJB JAR file to the EAR. We also changed the webapp's build.xml script to include the EJB JAR in its classpath. Notice that the definition of my.ejb.jar.dir uses a relative path to step up one level from the basedir of the ejb sub-project and down into the ejb sub-project's build/distribution directory.

Now that we've shown the EJB development environment, let's start the EJB development process by showing the Local and Remote Interfaces for the InventoryFacadeBean.

Local and Remote Interfaces

The Local and Remote Interfaces define the business methods that an EJB exposes to its clients. These interfaces are sometimes called an EJB's Component Interfaces in EJB books and other related literature. An EJB's Local and Remote Interface methods serve the same purpose as public methods for a POJO.

Local Interface

The Local Interface defines an EJB's business methods accessed by local, or co-located, clients (Servlets, POJOs, or EJB) that run inside the container. When accessing an EJB though its local interface, there is no overhead for a network call and object serialization because everything runs in the same JVM. A client running outside the container cannot access a Session Bean using local interfaces. All methods in the Local Component Interface throw an EJBException. Our Local Interface, InventoryFacadeLocal, looks like Example 6-9.

Example 6-9. InventoryFacadeLocal.java

```
package com.jbossatwork.ejb;

public interface InventoryFacadeLocal extends javax.ejb.EJBLocalObject
{
```

Example 6-9. InventoryFacadeLocal.java (continued)

```
    public java.util.List listAvailableCars( ) throws javax.ejb.EJBException;
    public CarDTO findCar(int id) throws javax.ejb.EJBException;
    public void deleteCars(String[ ] ids) throws javax.ejb.EJBException;
    public void saveCar(CarDTO car) throws javax.ejb.EJBException;
    public void buyCar(int carId, double price) throws javax.ejb.EJBException;
}
```

Remote Interface

The Remote Interface defines an EJB's business methods accessed by remote clients—applications that run outside the EJB container. All methods in the Remote Component Interface throw a RemoteException. Invoking an EJB though its remote interface incurs overhead for a network call and object serialization because the client and the EJB run in separate JVMs. Example 6-10 is our Remote Interface, InventoryFacadeRemote.

Example 6-10. InventoryFacadeRemote.java

```
package com.jbossatwork.ejb;

public interface InventoryFacadeRemote extends javax.ejb.EJBObject
{
    public java.util.List listAvailableCars( ) throws javax.ejb.RemoteException;
    public CarDTO findCar(int id) throws javax.ejb.RemoteException;
    public void deleteCars(String[ ] ids) throws javax.ejb.RemoteException;
    public void saveCar(CarDTO car) throws javax.ejb.RemoteException;
    public void buyCar(int carId, double price) throws javax.ejb.RemoteException;
}
```

We've shown the Local and Remote Interfaces that define the EJB's business methods, but now we need to talk about the Home Interfaces.

Home Interfaces

An EJB Home Interface is a factory that creates and removes EJB objects in an EJB container. A Session Bean's create( ) method initializes a new Session Bean and returns a proxy object so the client can start using the EJB. An EJB Home is analogous to a POJO's constructor, except that the EJB Home's create method gives you a client-side proxy rather than a concrete object. If you use a Local EJB Home, then you're using a Local Interface to call its business methods. If you look up a Remote EJB Home, then you're working with a Remote Interface to access a Bean's business methods.

Local Home Interface

The Local Home Interface defines an EJB's lifecycle methods—that create and remove bean instances—used by local, or co-located clients (Servlets, POJOs, or EJBs) that run inside the container. Our Local Home Interface, InventoryFacadeLocalHome, looks like Example 6-11.

Example 6-11. InventoryFacadeLocalHome.java

```
package com.jbossatwork.ejb;

public interface InventoryFacadeLocalHome extends javax.ejb.EJBLocalHome
{
    public static final String COMP_NAME="java:comp/env/ejb/InventoryFacadeLocal";
    public static final String JNDI_NAME="InventoryFacadeLocal";

    public com.jbossatwork.ejb.InventoryFacadeLocal create()
        throws javax.ejb.CreateException;
}
```

This is a Session Bean, so you only need a simple create() method with an empty argument list.

Remote Home Interface

The Remote Home Interface defines an EJB's lifecycle methods—that create and remove bean instances—used by applications outside the container. Example 6-12 is our Remote Home Interface, InventoryFacadeRemoteHome.

Example 6-12. InventoryFacadeRemoteHome.java

```
package com.jbossatwork.ejb;

public interface InventoryFacadeRemoteHome extends javax.ejb.EJBHome
{
    public static final String COMP_NAME="java:comp/env/ejb/InventoryFacade";
    public static final String JNDI_NAME="InventoryFacadeRemote";

    public com.jbossatwork.ejb.InventoryFacadeRemote create()
        throws javax.ejb.CreateException,java.rmi.RemoteException;
}
```

The Bean Class

The Bean Class provides the implementation for a Session Bean's business methods. Our Bean Class, InventoryFacadeBean, looks like Example 6-13.

Example 6-13. InventoryFacadeBean.java

```java
package com.jbossatwork.ejb;

import java.util.*;

import javax.ejb.*;

import com.jbossatwork.dao.*;
import com.jbossatwork.dto.CarDTO;

public class InventoryFacadeBean implements SessionBean {

    private SessionContext sessionCtx;

    // EJB 2.1 mandated methods.

    public void setSessionContext(SessionContext sessionCtx) throws EJBException {
        this.sessionCtx = sessionCtx;
    }

    public void ejbCreate() throws CreateException { }
    public void ejbRemove() throws EJBException { }
    public void ejbActivate() throws EJBException { }
    public void ejbPassivate() throws EJBException { }

    // Business methods.

    public List listAvailableCars() throws EJBException {
        CarDAO carDAO = new HibernateCarDAO();

        return carDAO.filterByStatus(CarDTO.STATUS_AVAILABLE);
    }
    …
}
```

Think of the InventoryFacadeBean as an encapsulation of all the inventory-related business functions. Each business method wraps all the activities to implement a User Story or Use Case. Consider each business method as a service that's available to clients, such as a web application, a GUI, or a Web Service client. The listAvailableCars() method tells the CarDAO to return only the cars that are still available (unsold). The DAO is devoid of any real business logic—it's only responsible for CRUD operations on the CAR table in the database.

In addition to business methods, we must implement the following callback methods because a Session Bean implements the javax.ejb.SessionBean interface:

- setSessionContext()
- ejbCreate()
- ejbRemove()
- ejbActivate()
- ejbPassivate()

The EJB container calls these methods during an EJB's lifecycle (from creation, invoking business methods, through removal). With the exception of setSessionContext( ), all these methods are usually empty for Stateless Session Beans. Even though we have only one real business method, we have to add five other methods (four of which are empty) just to comply with the EJB specification. These extra methods are inconvenient because they don't add any real value, but can't deploy our EJB if we don't have them.

We've written the code for the InventoryFacadeBean, and now it's time to deploy the Bean.

EJB Deployment Descriptors

After developing a Session Bean's classes and interfaces, deploy it by adding information about the EJB (meta-data) to the J2EE standard (ejb-jar.xml) and JBoss (jboss.xml) EJB deployment descriptors.

In ejb-jar.xml, the <enterprise-beans> element lists all EJBs in the application. The <session> element describes the bean by telling the container:

- That it's a Session Bean.
- About all the classes that make up the bean.
- That it's Stateless.
- That it uses container-managed transactions (CMT).
- That it uses a Hibernate Session Factory.

Example 6-14 is the ejb-jar.xml file.

Example 6-14. ejb-jar.xml

```
<?xml version="1.0" encoding="UTF-8"?>

<ejb-jar xmlns=http://java.sun.com/xml/ns/j2ee
 xmlns:xsi="http://www.w3.org/2001/XMLSchema-instance"
 xsi:schemaLocation="http://java.sun.com/xml/ns/j2ee
 http://java.sun.com/xml/ns/j2ee/ejb-jar_2_1.xsd" version="2.1">
  <enterprise-beans>
    ...
    <session>
      <display-name>InventoryFacadeSB</display-name>

      <ejb-name>InventoryFacade</ejb-name>

      <home>com.jbossatwork.ejb.InventoryFacadeRemoteHome</home>
      <remote>com.jbossatwork.ejb.InventoryFacadeRemote</remote>
      <local-home>com.jbossatwork.ejb.InventoryFacadeLocalHome</local-home>
      <local>com.jbossatwork.ejb.InventoryFacadeLocal</local>
      <ejb-class>com.jbossatwork.ejb.InventoryFacadeBean</ejb-class>
      <session-type>Stateless</session-type>
      <transaction-type>Container</transaction-type>
```

Example 6-14. ejb-jar.xml (continued)

```
    <resource-ref>
      <res-ref-name>hibernate/SessionFactory</res-ref-name>
      <res-type>org.hibernate.SessionFactory</res-type>
      <res-auth>Container</res-auth>
    </resource-ref>
  </session>
  ...
</enterprise-beans>
...
<assembly-descriptor>
  ...
  <container-transaction>
    <method>
      <ejb-name>InventoryFacade</ejb-name>
      <method-intf>Local</method-intf>
      <method-name>listAvailableCars</method-name>
      <method-params>
      </method-params>
    </method>
    <trans-attribute>Required</trans-attribute>
  </container-transaction>
  <container-transaction>
    <method>
      <ejb-name>InventoryFacade</ejb-name>
      <method-intf>Remote</method-intf>
      <method-name>listAvailableCars</method-name>
      <method-params>
      </method-params>
    </method>
    <trans-attribute>Required</trans-attribute>
  </container-transaction>
  ...
</assembly-descriptor>
</ejb-jar>
```

The <resource-ref> elements specify the JNDI resources available to the InventoryFacadeBean (or any POJO that it calls). The <res-ref-name> is the JNDI name for the resource—java:comp/env/hibernate/SessionFactory. Notice that you don't have to specify java:comp/env/—it is the assumed prefix. The <res-type> for the hibernate/SessionFactory is a Hibernate Session Factory, so org.hibernate. SessionFactory is its fully qualified class name. We want JBoss to manage our resources, so we set <res-auth> to Container.

The <assembly-descriptor> element describes security constraints, and transactions for all EJBs in the application. Each <container-transaction> element describes the transactional environment for every business method for each bean, for both the Remote and Local component interfaces. The read-only listAvailableCars( ) method wouldn't normally require a transaction, but we're using Hibernate 3 and are forced to set the transaction attributed to Required so that the method is guaranteed to run within a transaction. The "EJB Transaction Settings" section covers transactions, and later sections discuss Hibernate 3 and its relationship to EJBs and CMT.

A JNDI resource is linked into an application only if we ask for it. JBoss binds resources under its in-JVM context, java:/. The jboss.xml file provides a mapping between the J2EE-style ENC names and the local JBoss-specific JNDI names that JBoss uses to deploy EJBs and any related JNDI-based resources. Example 6-15 is the jboss.xml descriptor.

Example 6-15. jboss.xml

```
<?xml version="1.0" encoding="UTF-8"?>
<!DOCTYPE jboss PUBLIC "-//JBoss//DTD JBOSS 4.0//EN"
 "http://www.jboss.org/j2ee/dtd/jboss_4_0.dtd">

<jboss>
  …
  <enterprise-beans>
    …
    <session>
      <ejb-name>InventoryFacade</ejb-name>
      <jndi-name>InventoryFacadeRemote</jndi-name>
      <local-jndi-name>InventoryFacadeLocal</local-jndi-name>

      <resource-ref>
        <res-ref-name>hibernate/SessionFactory</res-ref-name>
        <jndi-name>java:/hibernate/SessionFactory</jndi-name>
      </resource-ref>

      <method-attributes>
      </method-attributes>
    </session>
    …
  </enterprise-beans>
  …
  <assembly-descriptor>
  </assembly-descriptor>
  …
  <resource-managers>
  </resource-managers>

</jboss>
```

All EJBs described in jboss.xml must be defined in ejb-jar.xml. Here are the key elements:

<session>

    Provides JBoss-specific deployment information for a session bean, including the JNDI name.

<ejb-name>

    The name of the EJB. This must match the <ejb-name> element for the bean in ejb-jar.xml.

`<jndi-name>`
> The JNDI name that JBoss uses to deploy the EJB. If not specified, JBoss uses the `<ejb-name>` as the JNDI name.

`<local-jndi-name>`
> The JNDI name that JBoss uses to deploy the EJB for local access. If not specified, JBoss uses the `<jndi-name>` as the JNDI name. If the deployer provides the `<local-jndi-name>`, then the `<jndi-name>` specifies the remote JNDI name.

The `<resource-ref>` element enables the InventoryFacadeBean (or any POJO that it calls) to look up resources using JNDI. As before, `<res-ref-name>` is the JNDI name for each resource for which java:comp/env/ is the assumed prefix. The textual value of each `<res-ref-name>` element in jboss.xml MUST match the value of the `<res-ref-name>` in ejb-jar.xml. The `<jndi-name>` is the local JBoss-specific JNDI name that JBoss uses to deploy a Hibernate Session Factory. Since the java:/ ENC is internal to JBoss, the java:/hibernate/SessionFactory JNDI name indicates that the Hibernate Session Factory is available only to applications running inside of JBoss.

Now that we have our classes and interfaces in place, let's take a more detailed look at how EJBs relate to J2EE transactions.

EJB Transaction Settings

The two ways to manage transactions in J2EE are through Container-Managed Transactions (CMT) and Bean-Managed Transactions (BMT). BMT requires extra Java coding to handle transaction logic and forces the developer to manage the transaction and define his own transaction boundaries. In contrast, CMT doesn't require handle transaction logic, pushes transaction settings into deployment descriptors, uses JBoss transaction services, and manages transaction boundaries on behalf of the developer. We'll focus on CMT because it is considered a J2EE best practice and it allows the container to do the work.

A transaction attribute tells the container how to handle CMT transactions for an EJB's business methods. Specify transaction attributes for each Bean in the ejb-jar.xml deployment descriptor. You can set transaction attributes for an entire EJB or for each business method—method-level settings take precedence over bean-level settings. Here are the possible values for EJB transaction settings:

Required
> The EJB method always runs within the scope of a transaction. If a transaction doesn't currently exist, the container starts a new transaction.

RequiresNew
> The container always starts a new transaction before executing the EJB method. If a transaction already exists, the container suspends the current transaction until the new transaction completes.

Supports

> The EJB method runs only within the scope of a transaction if the caller started a transaction before invoking the EJB method. If a transaction does not already exist, the EJB method does not run within a transaction.

Mandatory

> The caller must start a transaction before invoking the EJB method. If there is no current transaction, the container throws a `javax.ejb.TransactionRequiredException`.

NotSupported

> The EJB method does not run within the scope of a transaction. If a transaction already exists, the container suspends the current transaction until the EJB method completes.

Never

> The EJB can not run within the scope of a transaction. If the caller started a transaction before invoking the EJB method, the container throws a `javax.ejb.RemoteException` (for remote calls) or a `javax.ejb.EJBException` (for local calls).

Despite the six possible values for EJB transaction settings, you'll use `Required`, `RequiresNew`, or `Supports` most of the time.

Difficulties Using EJB

At this point, you can deploy the example EJB on JBoss, but the overhead of creating at least one set of Home and Component Interfaces plus two XML deployment descriptors (`ejb-jar.xml` and `jboss.xml`, including transactional attributes) as well as the business code (the Bean Class) is tedious and burdensome. Ideally, we'd only have to write the Bean Class and somehow let deployment take care of itself. Even the Bean Class has issues—we don't care too much about the callback methods yet, but we're forced to implement them because they're part of the Session Bean interface.

It's important to know about the future, but we're still on EJB 2.1 because the specification and the JBoss implementation are complete and we know they'll work in a production environment. For now, we need XDoclet to generate the extra programming artifacts, and we just have to live with writing empty callback implementations in our Session Beans.

The next section shows how XDoclet generates the bean's deployment descriptors and the Home and Component Interfaces, freeing you to concentrate on the EJB's business logic.

Automating Stateless Session Bean Deployment Using XDoclet Tags

Example 6-16 shows the XDoclet tags in `InventoryFacadeBean`.

How Will EJB 3.0 Help?

The main purpose of the EJB 3.0 specification (and J2EE 1.5) is to simplify deployment and make it easier to develop EJBs. EJB 3.0 will use annotations to indicate the runtime behavior of an EJB. A Session Bean will require just a business interface (that declares the EJB's business methods) and a single POJO with EJB 3.0 annotations for deployment. Thus the XML deployment descriptors, along with the Home and Component Interfaces, will become relics of the past. Although XDoclet did a great job of generating these artifacts, won't it be great when we don't have to create them at all? As part of EJB 3.0, you don't have to implement the SessionBean interface anymore. So your annotated POJO will contain only business methods and nothing else—you're no longer forced to implement empty callback methods that you don't care about.

Dependency Injection is a replacement for JNDI lookups and for declaring resource and configuration settings in deployment descriptors. Servlets and EJBs will use annotations to specify their resources and configuration values, and the container "injects" (or uses) these values. Dependency Injection removes the need for JNDI lookup and makes your code simpler.

EJB 3.0 will be a huge leap forward, but the specification won't be final until well after the time of this writing. Although we can't accurately predict the future, we expect EJB 3.0 to be complete by the end of 2005, and that stable, fully functional implementations will be available in the first quarter of 2006.

Example 6-16. InventoryFacadeBean.java

```
/**
 * @ejb.bean
 *   name="InventoryFacade"
 *   display-name="InventoryFacadeSB"
 *   local-jndi-name="InventoryFacadeLocal"
 *   jndi-name="InventoryFacadeRemote"
 *   type="Stateless"
 *   transaction-type="Container"
 *
 * @ejb.resource-ref
 *   res-ref-name="hibernate/SessionFactory"
 *   res-type="org.hibernate.SessionFactory"
 *   res-auth="Container"
 *
 * @jboss.resource-ref
 *   res-ref-name="hibernate/SessionFactory"
 *   jndi-name="java:/hibernate/SessionFactory"
 *
 */
public class InventoryFacadeBean implements SessionBean {
    …

    /**
```

Example 6-16. InventoryFacadeBean.java (continued)

```
     * @ejb.interface-method
     *
     */
    public List listAvailableCars( ) throws EJBException {
        …
    }

    …
}
```

The class-level @ejb.bean XDoclet tag defines the EJB and generates the <session> element in ejb-jar.xml and jboss.xml. The class-level @ejb.resource-ref XDoclet tag generates the <resource-ref> element for the EJB's Hibernate Session Factory in ejb-jar.xml, and the @jboss.resource XDoclet tag generates the corresponding <resource-ref> element in jboss.xml.

Each method-level @ejb.interface-method tag adds a business method to the Remote and Local component Interfaces.

The XDoclet tags appear in class- and method-level Javadoc comments, and you need to run an external program to look at the Java code, interpret the tags, and generate code and deployment descriptors. The next section shows how to run the XDoclet code generator from Ant.

Ant Build Script Using XDoclet

After modifying the EJB to use XDoclet tags, we now use XDoclet's Ant tasks to generate the Home and Component Interfaces, along with the EJB deployment descriptors (ejb-jar.xml and jboss.xml). Example 6-17 shows a portion of the ejb subproject's Ant build script that uses XDoclet to generate deployment artifacts.

Example 6-17. ejb/build.xml

```
    …

<target name="run-ejbdoclet" description="Generate EJB artifacts">
    <taskdef name="ejbdoclet"
        classname="xdoclet.modules.ejb.EjbDocletTask"
        classpathref="xdoclet.lib.path"/>

    <mkdir dir="${gen.source.dir}" />
    <ejbdoclet destdir="${gen.source.dir}" ejbspec="2.1">

        <fileset dir="${source.dir}">
            <include name="**/*Bean.java"/>
        </fileset>

        <remoteinterface pattern="{0}Remote"/>
        <localinterface pattern="{0}Local"/>
```

Example 6-17. ejb/build.xml (continued)

```
        <homeinterface pattern="{0}RemoteHome"/>
        <localhomeinterface pattern="{0}LocalHome"/>

        <deploymentdescriptor destdir="${gen.source.dir}"/>

        <jboss version="4.0" destdir="${gen.source.dir}"/>

    </ejbdoclet>
</target>

...
```

The run-ejbdoclet invokes XDoclet's <ejbdoclet> Ant task to generate the bean interfaces and deployment descriptors. Here are the important attributes and subelements of <ejbdoclet>:

<ejbdoclet>

> This task generates the deployment descriptors, along with the Home and Component Interfaces for all EJBs that contain XDoclet tags. The most important attributes are: destdir (where to output the generated Home and Component Interfaces) and ejbspec (the version of the EJB specification to use—defaults to "2.0").

<fileset>

> Tells XDoclet where to find the Bean Class files to parse.

<remoteinterface>

> Tells XDoclet to generate a Remote Component Interface for all EJBs.

<localinterface>

> Tells XDoclet to generate a Local Component Interface for all EJBs.

<remotehomeinterface>

> Tells XDoclet to generate a Remote Home Interface for all EJBs.

<localhomeinterface>

> Tells XDoclet to generate a Local Home Interface for all EJBs.

<deploymentdescriptor>

> Tells XDoclet to generate the standard J2EE ejb-jar.xml deployment descriptor. The destdir attribute tells where to output ejb-jar.xml.

<jboss>

> Tells XDoclet to generate the JBoss-specifiec jboss.xml deployment descriptor. The most important attributes here are version (the JBoss version we're using) and destdir (where to output jboss.xml).

Now that we have all of the EJB-related pieces in place, let's JAR everything up.

EJB JAR File

An EJB JAR file is the standard deployment unit for the EJB component (EJBs, JMS Destinations, and so on) portion of a J2EE application. It contains ejb-jar.xml (the J2EE standard EJB deployment descriptor), jboss.xml (the JBoss-specific EJB deployment descriptor), the EJB classes, and a JAR manifest. We deploy the example EJB JAR file inside an EAR file alongside the WAR file containing the Controller Servlet that invokes the InventoryFacade EJB. See Figure 6-1 for the structure of the EJB JAR file.

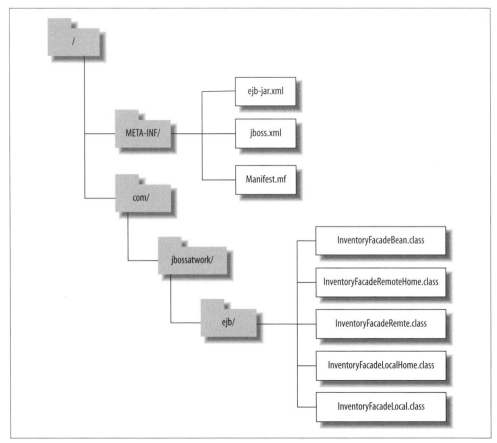

Figure 6-1. EJB JAR file structure

The EJB JAR file above has the following structure:

- The root directory. Some applications may store property files in the root directory.
- The META-INF directory that contains all the metadata: ejb-jar.xml, jboss.xml, and the JAR Manifest file that references external JARS that reside in the

application EAR file. The Deployment Chapter has more information on EAR files, JAR Manifest files, and ClassLoaders.

- The `com/jbossatwork/ejb` directory holds EJB class files.

Now that we know the structure of the EJB JAR file, let's use Ant to create the JAR file.

Ant Task for Creating EJB JAR

Example 6-18 is another portion of the ejb sub-project's Ant build script that creates the EJB JAR file.

Example 6-18. ejb/build.xml

```
...
<target name="build-ejb-jar" depends="run-ejbdoclet, compile"
        description="Packages the EJB files into a EJB JAR file">
    <mkdir dir="${distribution.dir}" />

    <jar destfile="${distribution.dir}/${ejb.jar.name}"
        basedir="${classes.dir}">
        <metainf dir="${gen.source.dir}" includes="*.xml"/>
    </jar>
</target>
...
```

The `<build-ejb-jar>` target depends on the `run-ejbdoclet` (from the previous Ant code example) to generate all the EJB-related programming artifacts and the `compile` target to compile all the code. The `<jar>` task creates the EJB JAR file (`ejb.jar`) and copies the compiled Bean Class, along with the Home and Component Interfaces, into the JAR file (preserving the package directory structure). The `<jar>` task also copies the EJB deployment descriptors (`ejb-jar.xml` and `jboss.xml`) into the JAR's `META-INF` directory. So there's no real "magic" to creating an EJB JAR file—the `<jar>` task above looks similar to something you've seen before. The only real difference between a plain JAR file and the EJB JAR file is that you have deployment descriptors in the `META-INF` directory.

Now that we have our EJB JAR, let's include it in our EAR.

Adding an EJB JAR to the EAR

We've already covered the structure and contents of an EAR file in the Deployment chapter. Here are the steps to add the EJB JAR file to the EAR:

- Register the EJB JAR file in application.xml.
- Copy the EJB JAR file into the EAR.

Example 6-19 is a portion of the application.xml file that now includes the new EJB JAR file, ejb.jar.

Example 6-19. application.xml

```xml
<?xml version="1.0" encoding="UTF-8"?>
<application xmlns="http://java.sun.com/xml/ns/j2ee"
 xmlns:xsi="http://www.w3.org/2001/XMLSchema-instance"
 xsi:schemaLocation="http://java.sun.com/xml/ns/j2ee
 http://java.sun.com/xml/ns/j2ee/application_1_4.xsd"
 version="1.4">
  <display-name>JBossAtWorkEAR</display-name>

  <module>
    <web>
      <web-uri>webapp.war</web-uri>
      <context-root>ch06</context-root>
    </web>
  </module>
  …
  <module>
    <ejb>ejb.jar</ejb>
  </module>
  …
</application>
```

As we've seen in previous chapters, the `<module>` element defines a J2EE module (WAR, EJB JAR, and JAR) contained in the EAR. The `<ejb>` element specifies the EJB JAR file name relative to the EAR file's top-level directory.

Adding the EJB JAR file to the EAR is trivial. Example 6-20 shows a portion of the main Ant build script (ch06-a/build.xml) that creates the EAR.

Example 6-20. build.xml

```xml
…
<ear destFile="${distribution.dir}/${ear.name}"
     appxml="${meta-inf.dir}/application.xml">

    <fileset dir="${ejb.jar.dir}"/>
    <fileset dir="${webapp.war.dir}"/>
    <fileset dir="${common.jar.dir}"/>

    …
</ear>
…
```

We've seen the `<ear>` task before. The only difference is that now we're copying the EJB JAR file into the EAR by adding a `<fileset>` task that includes the EJB JAR file.

Reviewing Iteration 1

It's taken a while to get here, but we now have the core infrastructure in place to use EJBs. The main purpose of Iteration 1 was to introduce an EJB to the JAW Motors application. So, to review:

- We modified the Persistence Tier so that we can tell if a car is available or sold by:
  - Adding a STATUS column to the CAR table.
  - Making the CarDTO Serializable, and adding a status field along with getter and setter methods.
  - Adding a filterByStatus( ) method to the HibernateCarDAO.
- We upgraded the web site by:
  - Refactoring the Controller Servlet's viewCarList action to use the InventoryFacadeBean for finding all available (unsold) cars.
  - Adding a getEjbLocalHome( ) method to the ServiceLocator to look up an EJB's Local Home Interface using JNDI.
  - Adding EJB-based JNDI reference settings to the Web deployment descriptors (web.xml and jboss-web.xml).
  - Automating EJB-based JNDI reference settings in the Web deployment descriptors with XDoclet.
- We added InventoryFacade Session Bean by:
  - Defining the Local and Remote Interface(s).
  - Creating the Home Interface(s).
  - Developing the Bean Class Code.
  - Deploying the Bean with EJB deployment descriptors.
  - Automating the Bean deployment with Ant and XDoclet so that XDoclet created the Remote, Remote Home, Local, and Local Home interfaces for us. We also used XDoclet to create the ejb-jar.xml and jboss.xml deployment descriptors.
- We added EJBs to our EAR file by:
  - Creating the EJB JAR file with Ant.
  - Registering the EJB JAR file in application.xml.
  - Copying the EJB JAR file into the EAR.

As you've just seen, adding EJBs to a J2EE application is non-trivial. But you can mitigate this overhead with Ant and XDoclet.

Testing Iteration 1

Now that we've written and deployed an EJB and called it from the Controller Servlet, let's test the application to ensure that everything still works properly. Here are the steps to build and deploy the application:

- Type ant in the root directory of ch06-a to build the project.
- Shutdown JBoss so that the Ant script can clean up the JBoss deployment area.
- Type ant `colddeploy` to deploy the EAR file (jaw.ear) to the $JBOSS_HOME/server/default/deploy directory.
- Start JBoss back up.
- Go to the ch06-a/sql sub-directory and type ant to modify the database.
- Visit *http://localhost:8080/jaw* in a web browser.

When you click on the "View Inventory" link on the JAW Motors home page, the Controller Servlet takes you to the Inventory page where you can view, add, edit, or delete cars in JAW Motors' Inventory.

We've spent a lot of time in Iteration 1 establishing the core infrastructure for using EJBs in the application, and now we'll move on to Iterations 2 and 3, where we'll move the business logic from the Web Tier to the EJB, and then finally add the ability to buy a car. Since we have all the plumbing in place, these next two Iterations will be much shorter than the first.

Iteration 2—Move Business Logic Out of the Controller

In this Iteration, we're going to move all business logic out of the Controller Servlet into the InventoryFacadeBean (which groups our synchronous activities together and wraps the DAO). We'll take the following steps:

- Move the code from the Controller Servlet's actions into the InventoryFacadeBean.
- Modify the Controller Servlet to call the new methods in the InventoryFacadeBean.
- Modify the HibernateCarDAO to work with CMT.
- Change the ServiceLocator's getHibernateSession( ) method to work with CMT.

Refactoring the Business Logic

If you'll recall from earlier in this chapter, we had modified the Controller Servlet so its viewCarList action used the InventoryFacadeBean to find all available cars. We will now refactor the Controller Servlet by moving all the business logic from its actions into the InventoryFacadeBean. Example 6-21 shows the modifications to the Controller Servlet.

Example 6-21. ControllerServlet.java

```java
package com.jbossatwork;

...

import com.jbossatwork.ejb.*;
...
import javax.ejb.*;
...
public class ControllerServlet extends HttpServlet
{
    ...
    protected void processRequest(HttpServletRequest request,
      HttpServletResponse response) throws ServletException, IOException
    {
        ...
        InventoryFacadeLocalHome inventoryHome;
        inventoryHome = (InventoryFacadeLocalHome)
        ServiceLocator.getEjbLocalHome(InventoryFacadeLocalHome.COMP_NAME);

        InventoryFacadeLocal inventory = null;

        try {
            inventory = inventoryHome.create();
        } catch (CreateException ce) {
            throw new RuntimeException(ce.getMessage());
        }

        // perform action
        if (VIEW_CAR_LIST_ACTION.equals(actionName))
        {
            request.setAttribute("carList", inventory.listAvailableCars());
            destinationPage = "/carList.jsp";
        }
        else if (ADD_CAR_ACTION.equals(actionName))
        {
            request.setAttribute("car", new CarDTO());
            destinationPage = "/carForm.jsp";
        }
        else if (EDIT_CAR_ACTION.equals(actionName))
        {
            int id = Integer.parseInt(request.getParameter("id"));
            request.setAttribute("car", inventory.findCar(id));
            destinationPage = "/carForm.jsp";
        }
        else if (SAVE_CAR_ACTION.equals(actionName))
        {
            // build the car from the request parameters
            CarDTO car = new CarDTO();
            car.setId(Integer.parseInt(request.getParameter("id")));
            car.setMake(request.getParameter("make"));
            car.setModel(request.getParameter("model"));
            car.setModelYear(request.getParameter("modelYear"));
```

Example 6-21. ControllerServlet.java (continued)

```
            // save the car
            inventory.saveCar(car);

            // prepare the list
            request.setAttribute("carList", inventory.listAvailableCars( ));
            destinationPage = "/carList.jsp";
        }
        else if (DELETE_CAR_ACTION.equals(actionName))
        {
            // get list of ids to delete
            String[ ] ids = request.getParameterValues("id");

            // delete the list of ids

            inventory.deleteCars(ids);

            // prepare the list
            request.setAttribute("carList", inventory.listAvailableCars( ));
            destinationPage = "/carList.jsp";
        }
        ...
    }
}
```

So, rather than making DAO calls directly from the Controller Servlet, we're now calling the InventoryFacadeBean to execute the business logic. Let's show the changes in the InventoryFacadeBean(Example 6-22).

Example 6-22. InventoryFacadeBean.java

```
package com.jbossatwork.ejb;

import java.util.*;

import javax.ejb.*;

import com.jbossatwork.dao.*;
import com.jbossatwork.dto.CarDTO;

public class InventoryFacadeBean implements SessionBean {
    ...

    /**
     * @ejb.interface-method
     * @ejb.transaction
     *    type="Required"
     *
     */
    public List listAvailableCars( ) throws EJBException {
        CarDAO carDAO = new HibernateCarDAO( );

        return carDAO.filterByStatus(CarDTO.STATUS_AVAILABLE);
```

Example 6-22. InventoryFacadeBean.java (continued)

```java
    }
    /**
     * @ejb.interface-method
     * @ejb.transaction
     *   type="Required"
     *
     */
    public CarDTO findCar(int id) throws EJBException {
        CarDAO carDAO = new HibernateCarDAO( );

        return carDAO.findById(id);
    }

    /**
     * @ejb.interface-method
     * @ejb.transaction
     *   type="Required"
     *
     */
    public void deleteCars(String[ ] ids) throws EJBException {
        CarDAO carDAO = new HibernateCarDAO( );

        if (ids != null) {
            carDAO.delete(ids);
        }
    }

    /**
     * @ejb.interface-method
     * @ejb.transaction
     *   type="Required"
     *
     */
    public void saveCar(CarDTO car) throws EJBException {
        CarDAO carDAO = new HibernateCarDAO( );

        if (car.getId( ) == -1) {
            carDAO.create(car);
        } else {
            carDAO.update(car);
        }
    }
}
```

Again, there isn't anything too exciting going on here. We've taken all the DAO-related code from the Controller Servlet and created new methods in the InventoryFacadeBean:

findCar( )

Finds a car based on the caller-supplied Car ID.

deleteCars( )

Deletes one or more cars based on the array of caller-supplied Car IDs.

saveCar( )

> Creates the Car if it doesn't exist in the database; updates the Car if it's already in the database.

Notice that even the read-only methods (listAvailableCars( ) and findCar( )) require a transaction. We need run inside a transaction because of how we're getting the Hibernate Session—this is a new wrinkle introduced with Hibernate 3. Each method-level @ejb.transaction tag sets the transaction attribute for an EJB's business method in ejb-jar.xml. We'll cover Hibernate 3 and CMT in the next couple of sections.

You may be wondering why we've taken the trouble to factor our business logic out of the Controller Servlet into a Session Bean. We refactored for a couple of reasons:

- Running our code from within an EJB enables us to use Container-Managed Transactions (CMT), and you'll see in the next section that this greatly reduces the amount of code you have to write.

- We may not always have a web client and we'd like to encapsulate our business logic so other clients can use our services. In the Web Services chapter, we'll expose one of the InventoryFacadeBean's methods as a Web Service.

We could've gone one step further and factored all the business logic in the InventoryFacadeBean into another POJO known as an Application Service, a Core J2EE Pattern. If set up correctly, an Application Service enables you to test your business logic outside of JBoss. But since this isn't a JUnit book, we leave this refactoring to the reader.

Hibernate 3 and CMT

Until now, we've managed Hibernate transactions programmatically. Now that we're inside an EJB and using CMT, we don't have to perform user-managed transactions in Hibernate anymore. Now that the container manages transactions for us, we can remove the Hibernate API calls that set up and tear down our transactions. Example 6-23 contains the original HibernateCarDAO's (first introduced in Chapter 5) read-only findById( ) method that closed its Hibernate Session and the update( ) method that managed its own transaction.

Example 6-23. HibernateCarDAO.java

```
...
public class HibernateCarDAO implements CarDAO
{
    ...

    public CarDTO findById(int id)
    {
        CarDTO car = null;
        Session session = null;
```

Example 6-23. HibernateCarDAO.java (continued)

```
        try
        {
            session = ServiceLocator.getHibernateSession(
                                HIBERNATE_SESSION_FACTORY);

            car = (CarDTO) session.get(CarDTO.class, new Integer(id));
        }
        catch (Exception e)
        {
            System.out.println(e);
        }
        finally
        {
            try
            {
                if (session != null) {session.close();}
            }
            catch (Exception e)
            {
                System.out.println(e);
            }
        }
        return car;
    }

    ...

public void update(CarDTO car)
{
    Session session = null;
    Transaction tx = null;

    try
    {
        session = ServiceLocator.getHibernateSession(
                            HIBERNATE_SESSION_FACTORY);

        tx = session.beginTransaction();
        session.update(car);
        tx.commit();
    }
    catch (Exception e)
    {
        try{tx.rollback();}
        catch(Exception e2){System.out.println(e2);}
        System.out.println(e);
    }
    finally
    {
        try
        {
            if (session != null) {session.close();}
```

Example 6-23. HibernateCarDAO.java (continued)

```
            }
            catch (Exception e)
            {
                System.out.println(e);
            }
        }
    }
    ...
}
```

Most of the code is concerned with transaction and session setup and tear down. Now let's look at the new HibernateCarDAO that uses Container-Managed Transactions in Example 6-24.

Example 6-24. HibernateCarDAO.java

```
...
public class HibernateCarDAO implements CarDAO
{
    private List carList;
    private static final String HIBERNATE_SESSION_FACTORY =
                        "java:comp/env/hibernate/SessionFactory";

    public HibernateCarDAO(){ }

    public List findAll()
    {
        List carList = new ArrayList();
        Session session = null;

        try
        {
            session = ServiceLocator.getHibernateSession(
                            HIBERNATE_SESSION_FACTORY);

            Criteria criteria = session.createCriteria(CarDTO.class);
            carList = criteria.list();
        }
        catch (Exception e)
        {
            System.out.println(e);
        }

        return carList;
    }

    public List filterByStatus(String status)
    {
        List availableCarList = new ArrayList();
        Session session = null;

        try
```

Example 6-24. HibernateCarDAO.java (continued)

```java
    {
        session = ServiceLocator.getHibernateSession(
                          HIBERNATE_SESSION_FACTORY);

        Criteria criteria = session.createCriteria(CarDTO.class)
                .add( Restrictions.eq("status", status));

        availableCarList = criteria.list( );
    }
    catch (Exception e)
    {
        System.out.println(e);
    }

    return availableCarList;
}

public CarDTO findById(int id)
{
    CarDTO car = null;
    Session session = null;

    try
    {
        session = ServiceLocator.getHibernateSession(
                          HIBERNATE_SESSION_FACTORY);

        car = (CarDTO) session.get(CarDTO.class, new Integer(id));
    }
    catch (Exception e)
    {
        System.out.println(e);
    }

    return car;
}

public void create(CarDTO car)
{
    Session session = null;

    try
    {
        session = ServiceLocator.getHibernateSession(
                          HIBERNATE_SESSION_FACTORY);

        session.save(car);
    }
    catch (Exception e)
    {
        System.out.println(e);
    }
```

Example 6-24. HibernateCarDAO.java (continued)

```
    }

    public void update(CarDTO car)
    {
        Session session = null;

        try
        {
            session = ServiceLocator.getHibernateSession(
                            HIBERNATE_SESSION_FACTORY);

            session.update(car);
        }
        catch (Exception e)
        {
            System.out.println(e);
        }
    }

    public void delete(String[ ] ids)
    {
        Session session = null;

        try
        {
            session = ServiceLocator.getHibernateSession(
                            HIBERNATE_SESSION_FACTORY);

            for (int i = 0; i < ids.length; i++)
            {
                CarDTO car = (CarDTO) session.get(CarDTO.class,
                                new Integer(ids[i]));

                session.delete(car);
            }
        }
        catch (Exception e)
        {
            System.out.println(e);
        }
    }
}
```

You should notice the following differences in the new HibernateCarDAO:

- The read-only methods no longer need to close their Session, resulting in a 1/3 reduction in the lines of code.

- The transactional methods no longer use the Hibernate transaction API calls, nor do they close their Session. These changes reduce the code by 50 percent.

The transactional methods don't close the Session anymore because you lose your changes if you perform an update or delete operation and then close the Session.

- Most importantly, the business purpose of the code is clearer.

We've retrofitted the HibernateCarDAO so it works with Container-Managed Transactions, but you're not done yet. We also have to modify how we're getting the Hibernate Session in the ServiceLocator's getHibernateSession( ) method. Previously, we called openSession( ), as in Example 6-25.

Example 6-25. ServiceLocator.java

```
...
public class ServiceLocator {
    ...

    public static Session getHibernateSession(String jndiSessionFactoryName)
    throws ServiceLocatorException {
        Session session = null;
        ...
        session = getHibernateSessionFactory(jndiSessionFactoryName)
        .openSession();
        ...

        return session;
    }
    ...
}
```

To work within a transaction, we had to modify the getHibernateSession( ) method, as in Example 6-26.

Example 6-26. ServiceLocator.java

```
...
public class ServiceLocator {
    ...

    public static Session getHibernateSession(String jndiSessionFactoryName)
    throws ServiceLocatorException {
        Session session = null;
        ...
        session = getHibernateSessionFactory(jndiSessionFactoryName)
        .getCurrentSession();
        ...

        return session;
    }
    ...
}
```

So, rather than using the Session Factory's openSession( ) method to open a new Session, we call the getCurrentSession( ) method to get the Session that's part of the current transactional context managed by the container. Your code *must* run within a transaction, or the Session Factory's getCurrentSession( ) method will throw a NullPointerException—that's why each of the InventoryFacadeBean's methods had a transaction setting of Required.

Reviewing Iteration 2

In Iteration 2, we moved all business logic out of the Controller Servlet into the InventoryFacadeBean (which groups our synchronous activities and wraps the DAO). We took the following steps:

- Moved the business logic from the Controller Servlet's actions into the InventoryFacadeBean.
- Modified the Controller Servlet to call the new methods in the InventoryFacadeBean.
- Modified the HibernateCarDAO to work with CMT by removing the transaction setup and tear down code. We also removed the code that closes Hibernate Sessions.
- Changed the ServiceLocator's getHibernateSession( ) method to work with CMT by calling the SessionFactory's getCurrentSession( ) method.

Testing Iteration 2

Now that we've moved all business logic from Controller Servlet to the InventoryFacadeBean, let's test our application to ensure that everything still works properly. Here are the steps to build and deploy the application:

- Type ant in the root directory of ch06-b to build the project.
- Shut down JBoss so the Ant script can clean up the JBoss deployment area.
- Type ant colddeploy to deploy the EAR file (jaw.ear) to the $JBOSS_HOME/server/ default/deploy directory.
- Start JBoss back up.
- Visit *http://localhost:8080/jaw* in a web browser.

When you click on the "View Inventory" on the JAW Motors home page, the Controller Servlet takes you to the Inventory page where you can view, add, edit, or delete cars in JAW Motors' Inventory.

Now that we have all the infrastructure in place, let's move on to Iteration 3 where we finally add the ability to buy a car.

Iteration 3—Buy a Car

In this Iteration, we're going to enable a user to buy a car from the JAW Motors web site. We'll add a new page to enable the user to buy a car. When the user presses the "Submit" button on the new "Buy Car" page, the business logic changes the car's status to "Sold" and inserts a new row into the ACCOUNTING table.

We'll take the following steps:

- Upgrade the web site:
  - Add a "Buy Car" link to the Car Inventory page (carList.jsp).
  - Add a "Buy Car" action to the Controller Servlet.
- Modify the Persistence Tier:
  - Create an ACCOUNTING table.
  - Write a HibernateAccountingDTO.
  - Develop a HibernateAccountingDAO.
- Change the Session Bean:
  - Add a new buyCar( ) method to the InventoryFacadeBean that encapsulates a Container-Managed Transaction that involves both the CAR and ACCOUNTING tables.

Upgrade the Web Site: Adding a "Buy Car" Link

We've added a "Buy Car" link to the JAW Motors Car Inventory page (carList.jsp) as shown in Figure 6-2.

[Add Car]

Delete	Action	Make	Model	Model Year	Buy Car
☐	Edit	Toyota	Camry	2005	Buy
☐	Edit	Toyota	Corolla	1999	Buy
☐	Edit	Ford	Explorer	2005	Buy
Delete Checked Reset					

Figure 6-2. JAW Motors Inventory Page

When the user clicks on the "Buy" link, the Controller routes them to the Buy Car page as depicted in Figure 6-3 so they can buy the car.

The user enters her price in the form and presses the "Save" button. The Controller Servlet then takes the user back to the Car Inventory page. The purchased car is no longer available, so it won't show up on the Car Inventory page.

Figure 6-3. JAW Motors Buy Car Page

Now that the web pages are done, we have to add actions to the Controller Servlet for buying a car. Example 6-27 shows the changes.

Example 6-27. ControllerServlet.java

```java
public class ControllerServlet extends HttpServlet
{
    ...
    private static final String VIEW_BUY_CAR_FORM_ACTION = "viewBuyCarForm";

    private static final String BUY_CAR_ACTION = "buyCar";
    ...

    protected void processRequest(HttpServletRequest request,
                                  HttpServletResponse response)
    throws ServletException, IOException {
        ...
        else if (VIEW_BUY_CAR_FORM_ACTION.equals(actionName))
        {
            int id = Integer.parseInt(request.getParameter("id"));
            request.setAttribute("car", inventory.findCar(id));
            destinationPage = "/buyCarForm.jsp";
        }
        else if (BUY_CAR_ACTION.equals(actionName))
        {
            int carId = Integer.parseInt(request.getParameter("id"));
            double price;

            // Use $5000.00 as the default price if the user enters bad data.
            try
            {
                price = Double.parseDouble(request.getParameter("price"));
            }
            catch (NumberFormatException nfe)
            {
                price = 5000.00;
            }

            System.out.println("carId = [" + carId + "], price = [" + price + "]");

            // mark the car as sold
            inventory.buyCar(carId, price);

            // prepare the list
            request.setAttribute("carList", inventory.listAvailableCars());
```

Example 6-27. ControllerServlet.java (continued)

```
            destinationPage = "/carList.jsp";
        }
        …
    }
    …
}
```

As shown in the web pages, pressing the "Buy" link on the Car Inventory page invokes the viewBuyCarForm action, and the Controller Servlet routes the user to the "Buy Car" Form. Pressing the "Submit" button from the form invokes the buyCar action, and the Controller Servlet captures the user's price and calls the InventoryFacadeBean's buyCar( ) method to change the car's status to "Sold" and insert a new row into the ACCOUNTING table to record the sale. The Controller then gets the current list of available (unsold) cars and routes the user to the Car Inventory page.

Now that we've upgraded the web site, let's start modifying the Persistence Tier by adding the new ACCOUNTING table.

Creating the ACCOUNTING Table

The new ACCOUNTING table keeps track of the cars we've sold. Example 6-28 is the SQL in ch06-c/sql/build.xml that creates the table:

Example 6-28. sql/build.xml

```
DROP TABLE IF EXISTS ACCOUNTING;

CREATE TABLE ACCOUNTING (
    ID BIGINT identity,
    CAR_ID BIGINT,
    PRICE DOUBLE,
    SALE_DATE DATE
);
```

Due to the CAR_ID column, the ACCOUNTING table depends on the CAR table, but we're not going to complicate things by adding foreign key constraints.

We've created the ACCOUNTING table, so let's add the corresponding AccountingDTO.

The AccountingDTO

The AccountingDTO is an object that Hibernate persists to the ACCOUNTING table. The AccountingDTO has four fields: id, carId, price, and a saleDate. The AccountingDTO has getter and setter methods for each data member, along with XDoclet tags telling the <hibernate> XDoclet task how to generate an HBM mapping file that maps between the AccountingDTO object and the ACCOUNTING table. The AccountingDTO looks very similar to the CarDTO from previous chapters, so we're not showing the code here. If you want to see the AccountingDTO code, you can find it in the com. jbossatwork.dto package under the common sub-directory.

We've created the AccountingDTO, so now we need to develop the HibernateAccountingDAO to persist the AccountingDTO to the ACCOUNTING table.

Developing the HibernateAccountingDAO

The HibernateAccountingDAO looks similar to the HibernateCarDAO, but instead of writing all the CRUD, we only need to insert a row into the ACCOUNTING table. Here, we have only a single create( ) method. Example 6-29 shows the code for the HibernateAccountingDAO.

Example 6-29. HibernateAccountingDAO.java

```java
package com.jbossatwork.dao;

import java.util.*;
import org.hibernate.*;
import org.hibernate.criterion.*;
import com.jbossatwork.dto.AccountingDTO;
import com.jbossatwork.util.*;

public class HibernateAccountingDAO implements AccountingDAO
{
    private static final String HIBERNATE_SESSION_FACTORY =
                            "java:comp/env/hibernate/SessionFactory";

    public HibernateAccountingDAO( ) { }


    public void create(AccountingDTO accountingData)
    {
        Session session = null;

        try
        {
            session = ServiceLocator.getHibernateSession(
                            HIBERNATE_SESSION_FACTORY);

            session.save(accountingData);
        }
        catch (Exception e)
        {
            System.out.println(e);
        }
    }

}
```

The create( ) method calls the ServiceLocator to get the Hibernate Session, and inserts a new row into the ACCOUNTING table by calling the Session's save( ) method for the AccountingDTO. Just like we did before, we let the container manage the transaction, and we're not closing the Session.

We've added all the infrastructure to the web site and the Persistence Tier so we can buy a car. We now wrap up by adding a buyCar( ) method to the InventoryFacadeBean.

Adding buyCar( ) to the InventoryFacadeBean

Example 6-30 is the InventoryFacadeBean's buyCar( ) method.

Example 6-30. InventoryFacadeBean.java

```
...
public class InventoryFacadeBean implements SessionBean {
    ...
    /**
     * @ejb.interface-method
     * @ejb.transaction
     *   type="Required"
     *
     */
    public void buyCar(int carId, double price) throws EJBException {
        CarDAO carDAO = new HibernateCarDAO( );
        CarDTO car;
        AccountingDAO accountingDAO = new HibernateAccountingDAO( );
        AccountingDTO accountingData;

        car = carDAO.findById(carId);
        car.setStatus(CarDTO.STATUS_SOLD);
        carDAO.update(car);

        accountingData = new AccountingDTO(carId, price);
        accountingDAO.create(accountingData);
    }
    ...
}
```

The buyCar( ) method encapsulates a transaction for buying a car. This method takes the carId and price supplied by the caller to mark a car as "Sold" in the CAR table and record the sale in the ACCOUNTING table. If either the update to the CAR table or the ACCOUNTING table fails, the container rolls everything back. If all activities complete successfully, then all changes are committed to the database. After instantiating the DAOs, we use the CarDAO to find the car using the carId. To mark the car as "Sold", we set the CarDTO's status to "Sold" and call the HibernateCarDAO's update( ) method to update the car's status in the CAR table. To record the sale, we instantiate a new

AccountingDTO with the carId and price, and then call the HibernateAccountingDAO's create( ) method to insert a new row in the ACCOUNTING table.

Reviewing Iteration 3

Before moving on to test buying a car, let's recap what we did in Iteration 3:

- Upgraded the web site:
    - Added a "Buy Car" link to the Car Inventory page (carList.jsp).
    - Added a "Buy Car" action to the Controller Servlet.
- Modified the Persistence Tier:
    - Created an ACCOUNTING table.
    - Wrote a HibernateAccountingDTO.
    - Developed a HibernateAccountingDAO.
- Changed the Session Bean:
    - Added a new buyCar( ) method to the InventoryFacadeBean that encapsulated a Container-Managed Transaction that involved the CAR and ACCOUNTING tables.

Testing Iteration 3

Now that we've developed all the code and infrastructure for buying a car, let's test the application to ensure that everything works properly. Here are the steps to build and deploy the application:

- Type ant in the root directory of ch06-c to build the project.
- Shut down JBoss so the Ant script can clean up the JBoss deployment area.
- Type ant colddeploy to deploy the EAR file (jaw.ear) to the $JBOSS_HOME/server/default/deploy directory.
- Start JBoss back up.
- Go to the ch06-c/sql sub-directory and type ant to modify the database.
- Visit *http://localhost:8080/jaw* in a web browser.

When you click on the "View Inventory" on the JAW Motors home page, the Controller Servlet takes you to the Inventory page where you can view, add, edit, delete, or buy cars in JAW Motors' Inventory. Click on one of the "Buy" links and the Controller will route you to the Buy Car page. Enter a price in the form and press the "Save" button. The Controller Servlet then takes you back to the Car Inventory page. The car that was just purchased is no longer available, so it won't show up on the Car Inventory page.

As a final test, we need to ensure that the transaction was recorded properly in the database. Go to the ch06-c/sql sub-directory and type: "ant query". The query target queries the CAR and ACCOUNTING tables. Depending on which car you bought, you should see something like this on the command console:

```
query:
    [echo] Checking the CAR and ACCOUNTING tables ...
    [sql] Executing commands
    [sql] ID,MAKE,MODEL,MODEL_YEAR,STATUS
    [sql] 99,Toyota,Camry,2005,Sold
    [sql] 100,Toyota,Corolla,1999,Available
    [sql] 101,Ford,Explorer,2005,Available

    [sql] 0 rows affected
    [sql] ID,CAR_ID,PRICE,SALE_DATE
    [sql] 0,99,12000.0,2005-06-01

    [sql] 0 rows affected
    [sql] 2 of 2 SQL statements executed successfully
```

Final Thoughts on Session Beans

EJBs are the foundation for the rest of this book, so we took a lot of time to explain when and when not to use them, and how to deploy them. Here are the key take-away points on EJBs.

- Use EJBs when you really need them.
- Know why you're using EJBs.
- We use Stateless Session Beans for managing transactions and Message-Driven Beans for asynchronous processing.
- EJBs require a lot of extra work, but you only have to do the setup once:
    - Adding a new EJB Ant build script that uses XDoclet and creates the EJB JAR file.
    - Referencing the EJB JAR in application.xml.
    - Adding the EJB JAR file to the EAR.
- After the initial setup, things get better. The extra programming artifacts required by EJB 2.1 (Home and Component Interfaces and the deployment descriptors) are tedious and error-prone, but you can generate everything with XDoclet.
- Under EJB 2.1, you still have to implement the callback methods by hand.
- With EJB 3.0, the programming artifacts and callback methods go away. So, you're left with a business interface and a simple POJO that contains only the business methods that you care about. EJB 3.0 will streamline EJB development

and deployment. We hope that a simpler EJB spec will encourage developers and architects to consider EJBs for their future needs when it makes sense to use them.

- We moved our business logic from the Controller Servlet into the InventoryFacade Stateless Bean for the following reasons:
  - Running our code from within an EJB enables us to use Container-Managed Transactions (CMT), which greatly reduces the amount of code you have to write.
  - Since we may not always have a web client, we want other types of clients to use our encapsulated business logic as services. We can expose some of the InventoryFacadeBean's methods as Web Services—we'll show you how to do this in the Web Services chapter.
- When using Hibernate 3 from within an EJB that uses CMT, remember to do the following:
  - Make sure that your EJB method runs within the scope of a transaction.
  - Get a Hibernate Session by using the Session Factory's getCurrentSession( ) method.
  - The Hibernate transaction API calls are no longer needed because the container manages the transactions.
  - Never close your Hibernate Session because doing this loses your changes—let the container do it for you.
- The InventoryFacadeBean's buyCar( ) method encapsulated a Container-Managed Transaction that involved both the CAR and ACCOUNTING tables.

Looking Ahead...

This chapter discussed reasons for and against using EJBs. We added the ability to buy a car on the JAW Motors web site by introducing an InventoryFacade Stateless Session Bean that encapsulates business logic and uses CMT to manage transactions. Along the way, we introduced expected improvements with EJB 3.0, showed the relationship between Hibernate 3 and CMT, and deployed our new Session Bean on JBoss.

In the next chapter, we'll add an MDB to the JAW Motors Application.

CHAPTER 7

Java Message Service (JMS) and Message-Driven Beans

If you've worked through all the previous chapters, you have a fully functional vertical slice of the JAW Motors application that allows you to view, add, edit (update), delete, and buy cars. JAW Motors now wants to run a credit check on potential customers to pre-qualify them for car loans as part of the auto buying process. Like many other businesses, JAW Motors doesn't do its own credit verification and uses an external online service to run a credit check. Once we add a form to the JAW Motors web site to verify someone's credit, what happens when they enter their credit information and press the submit button? Should we make them wait until the external service finishes? This process could take several minutes, hours, or even days. Making the user wait around for the final result is unacceptable. After pressing the submit button, the user should be free to go back to what they were doing— viewing, adding, editing, and deleting cars. We need a way to defer the credit verification process to the background so the user can continue using the web site.

J2EE provides the following mechanisms for deferring work to the background:

- JMS (Java Message Service)
- Message-Driven Beans (MDBs)

The JMS API provides a vendor-neutral standard programming interface for creating, sending, and receiving messages. JMS enables Java applications to asynchronously exchange messages containing data and events. JMS 1.1 is part of the J2EE 1.4 standard.

Message-Driven Beans (MDBs) are EJBs that receive and process JMS messages. MDBs don't maintain state between invocations, so they resemble Stateless Session Beans. But MDBs differ from Stateless Session Beans in that:

- A client is completely decoupled from an MDB—the client sends a JMS message and the MDB picks up the message.
- After sending a JMS asynchronously, the client doesn't wait for the MDB to receive the message. The client continues executing other business logic.

Enterprise-class applications usually defer processing slow, expensive operations to run in the background so clients don't have to wait for completion. A UI sends an asynchronous JMS message, and an MDB receives the message and process it while the client can do other things in the foreground, such as interact with your application's web pages. On completion, the MDB could notify the client with a confirmation email, send another message, or update the database.

This chapter covers JMS and Message-Driven Beans. We'll upgrade the JAW Motors application by adding the ability to run a credit check on a customer by using JMS messaging and an MDB. To set realistic expectations, we won't invoke a real credit verification service, but instead will emulate the credit check as a long-running process. Along the way, we'll show how to deploy these technologies on JBoss.

Let's start by working down through the architecture.

Sending Messages with JMS

To send JMS messages from the JAW Motors application, do the following:

- Upgrade the web site:
  - Add a "Run Credit Check" link and form.
  - Add a "Run Credit Check" action to the Controller Servlet.
- Add JMS:
  - Create an object that holds the user's credit information to send as a JMS message.
  - Write a utility class to encapsulate sending a JMS message.
  - Add JMS-based JNDI reference settings to the Web-based deployment descriptors (web.xml and jboss-web.xml).
  - Automate JMS-based JNDI reference settings with XDoclet.
  - Deploy a JMS Queue on JBoss with an MBean.

Upgrade the Site: Running a Credit Check

We've added a "Run Credit Check" link to the JAW Motors homepage, as shown in Figure 7-1.

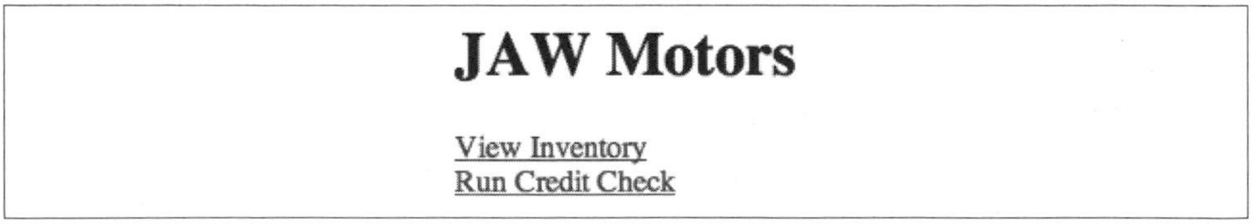

JAW Motors

View Inventory
Run Credit Check

Figure 7-1. JAW Motors homepage

When the user clicks on the "Run Credit Check" link, the Controller routes them to the Run Credit Check page as depicted in Figure 7-2.

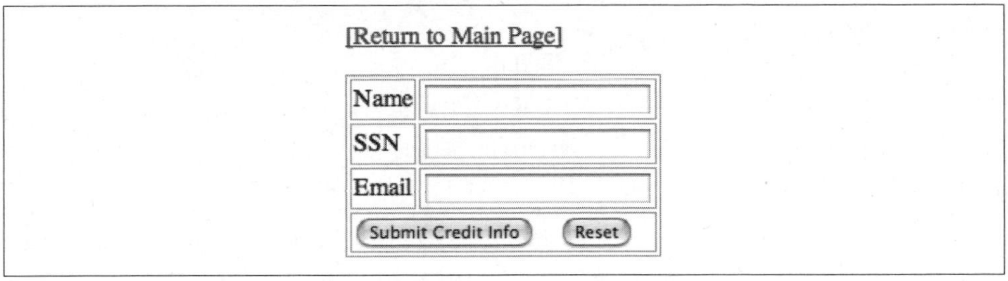

Figure 7-2. JAW Motors Run Credit Check page

The user enters his name, Social Security Number (SSN), and email address in the form and presses the "Submit Credit Info" button. When a customer requests a credit check, he won't have to wait for the external credit verification process to complete. The Controller Servlet sends a JMS message asynchronously to back end components that process business logic for the request. The customer gets routed back to the JAW Motors home page and is then free to continue using the JAW Motors web site while the credit check completes in the background.

Now that the web pages are done, we have to add actions to the Controller Servlet for running the credit check. Example 7-1 shows the changes.

Example 7-1. ControllerServlet.java

```java
public class ControllerServlet extends HttpServlet
{
    …
    private static final String VIEW_CREDIT_CHECK_FORM_ACTION =
                        "viewCreditCheckForm";

    private static final String RUN_CREDIT_CHECK_ACTION = "runCreditCheck";
    …

    protected void processRequest(HttpServletRequest request,
            HttpServletResponse response)
            throws ServletException, IOException {
        …
        else if(VIEW_CREDIT_CHECK_FORM_ACTION.equals(actionName))
        {
            destinationPage = "/creditCheckForm.jsp";
        }
        else if(RUN_CREDIT_CHECK_ACTION.equals(actionName))
        {
            System.out.println("Credit Check:\nName = [" +
                        request.getParameter("name") + "]");
```

Example 7-1. ControllerServlet.java (continued)

```
            System.out.println("SSN = [" + request.getParameter("ssn") + "]");
            System.out.println("Email = [" + request.getParameter("email") + "]");

            destinationPage = "/index.jsp";
        }
        …
    }
    …
}
```

As shown in the web pages, pressing the "Run Credit Check" link on the main page invokes the viewCreditCheckForm action, and the Controller Servlet routes the user to the "Run Credit Check" Form. Pressing the "Submit Credit Info" from the form invokes the runCreditCheck action, and (for now) the Controller Servlet captures the user's credit information and returns them to the main page. Now that we've built the user interface and have the infrastructure in place, we'll keep adding functionality to the runCreditCheck action so we can send a JMS message with the user's credit data.

We now want to wrap the user's credit information in an object and send it as a JMS message. Since the rest of our work depends on JMS, let's take a brief tour through JMS Architecture before we add any more functionality.

JMS Architecture Overview

We need to understand some of the basics of JMS architecture before using JMS in our application. Here are the players:

JMS Provider

> A messaging system that implements the JMS specification. A JMS Provider, also known as a JMS Server, routes messages between clients.

Clients

> Java applications that send or receive JMS messages. A message sender is called the Producer, and the recipient is called a Consumer.

Messages

> Messages contain data or events exchanged between Producers and Consumers.

Destinations

> A Producer sends a message to a JMS Destination (either a Queue or a Topic), and the Consumer(s) listening on the JMS Destination receives the message.

We now will cover messaging models to show how JMS routes messages between Producers and Consumers.

JMS Messaging Models

JMS has two messaging models—*Point-to-Point (P2P)* and *Publish-Subscribe (Pub-Sub)*. P2P is a traditional one-to-one queueing mechanism—although multiple Consumers can listen on a queue, only one Consumer receives a particular message. Producers send messages to a queue, and the JMS Server delivers each message sequentially to a Consumer listening on the queue. Figure 7-3 shows the relationships between Point-to-Point Producers and Consumers.

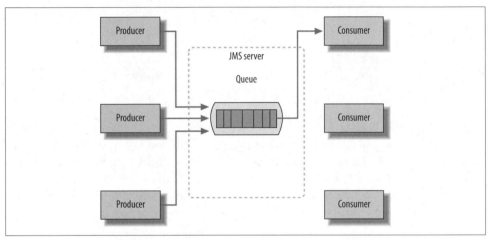

Figure 7-3. JMS Point-to-Point (P2P) Messaging model

Publish-Subscribe is a one-to-many broadcast model, similar to a newsgroup or an RSS newsfeed. Producers publish messages to a topic, and the JMS Server delivers messages sequentially to those Consumers subscribed to that topic. Figure 7-4 shows the relationships between Pub-Sub Producers and Consumers.

Choosing a Messaging Model

Most applications that use the Publish-Subscribe model could use Point-to-Point, and vice versa. How do you choose a messaging model? We'll give the standard consultant's answer—"It depends." Just like other technologies, your application requirements determine how to use JMS messaging. According to Richard Monson-Haefel (author of the best-selling O'Reilly EJB book and co-author of O'Reilly's JMS book), Point-Point JMS messaging is like sending an email message to a single recipient. Point-to-Point is a way to distribute workload because only one consumer receives a particular message. Publish-Subscribe JMS messaging is like sending/broadcasting an email message to a recipient list—many consumers receive the same message.

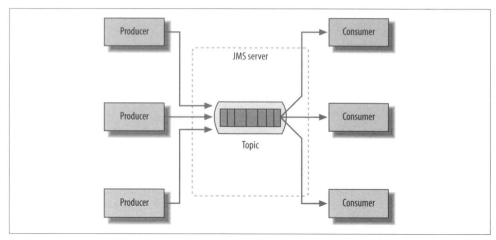

Figure 7-4. JMS Publish-Subscribe (Pub-Sub) Messaging model

The JAW Motors application sends a message when a user requests a credit check, and we want only one consumer to process a particular message just once. So in this chapter, we use the Point-to-Point model. The biggest difference between P2P and Pub-Sub is that in the Publish-Subscribe Model, all Consumers that subscribe to a Topic can receive *all* messages published to that topic, while with Point-to-Point, only one Consumer on a queue receives a particular message.

We've covered the basics of JMS architecture and chosen to use a Queue to hold our message because we selected the Point-to-Point model. Now we need to create a message (that holds the user's credit information) to send to the Queue.

Creating a Message

Now we'll wrap the user's credit data in a `CreditCheckRequestDTO` object so we can send it as a JMS Message. Example 7-2 shows the code.

Example 7-2. CreditCheckRequestDTO.java

```
package com.jbossatwork.dto;

import java.io.*;

public class CreditCheckRequestDTO implements Serializable
{
    private String name;
    private String ssn;
    private String email;

    public CreditCheckRequestDTO() { }

    public CreditCheckRequestDTO(String name, String ssn, String email)
```

Example 7-2. CreditCheckRequestDTO.java (continued)

```java
{
    this.name = name;
    this.ssn = ssn;
    this.email = email;
}

public String getName( )
{
    return name;
}

public void setName(String name)
{
    this.name = name;
}

public String getSsn( )
{
    return ssn;
}

public void setSsn(String ssn)
{
    this.ssn = ssn;
}

public String getEmail( )
{
    return email;
}

public void setEmail(String email)
{
    this.email = email;
}
}
```

The `CreditCheckRequestDTO` is similar to the `CarDTO` that you saw in previous chapters—it has setters and getters for each data member. To send an object as a JMS Message, it must obey the following rules:

- An object must implement `java.io.Serializable`.

- Each data member must be serializable. By default, `String`, the Java primitives (`int`, `float`, and so on) and the Java primitive wrappers (`Integer`, `Float`, and so on) are all serializable.

The `CreditCheckRequestDTO` follows all the rules, so we're done. We've encapsulated the user's credit information, and now we'll send the `CreditCheckRequestDTO` as a JMS Message.

Sending the Message

Example 7-3 shows how to send a JMS Message from the Controller Servlet.

Example 7-3. ControllerServlet.java

```java
public class ControllerServlet extends HttpServlet
{
    …
    private static final String XA_QUEUE_CONNECTION_FACTORY =
                            "java:comp/env/jms/MyXAQueueConnectionFactory";

    private static final String CREDIT_CHECK_QUEUE =
                            "java:comp/env/jms/CreditCheckQueue";

    …

    protected void processRequest(HttpServletRequest request,
            HttpServletResponse response)
            throws ServletException, IOException {

        …
        else if(RUN_CREDIT_CHECK_ACTION.equals(actionName))
        {
            CreditCheckRequestDTO creditCheckReq = null;

            System.out.println("Credit Check:\nName = [" +
                            request.getParameter("name") + "]");

            System.out.println("SSN = [" + request.getParameter("ssn") + "]");
            System.out.println("Email = [" + request.getParameter("email") + "]");


            creditCheckReq = new CreditCheckRequestDTO(
                            request.getParameter("name"),
                            request.getParameter("ssn"),
                            request.getParameter("email"));

            JmsProducer.sendMessage(creditCheckReq, XA_QUEUE_CONNECTION_FACTORY,
                            CREDIT_CHECK_QUEUE);

            destinationPage = "/index.jsp";
        }
        …
    }
    …
}
```

If you'll recall from the "Running a Credit Check" section, pressing the "Submit Credit Info" from the "Run Credit Check" form invokes the Controller Servlet's runCreditCheck action. The Controller Servlet stores the user's credit information in the CreditCheckReqDTO and calls JmsProducer.sendMessage( ) to send the credit data as an asynchronous JMS message. After sending the message, the Controller Servlet returns the user to the main page. The `JmsProducer` is a utility class that hides the details of sending a JMS message—the next few sections cover the JMS API and the `JmsProducer` in greater detail.

We've encapsulated the user's credit information in a `CreditCheckRequestDTO` and shown how to send it as a JMS Message with the `JmsProducer`. After quickly reviewing the core JMS API, we'll see how the `JmsProducer` sends a JMS Message.

Core JMS API

The JMS API resides in the `javax.jms` package. These are the most important classes and interfaces for our purposes:

Message
> Holds business data and routing information. Although you'll find several types of `Messages`, most of the time you'll use either a `TextMessage` (that contains textual data in its body) or an `ObjectMessage` (that holds serializable objects in its body).

Destination
> Holds messages sent by the Producer to be received by the Consumer(s). A Destination is either a `Queue` or a `Topic` that the JMS Server manages on behalf of its clients.

Connection
> Enables a JMS client to send or receive `Messages`. Use a `Connection` to create one or more `Sessions`.

ConnectionFactory
> A `ConnectionFactory` is either a `QueueConnectionFactory` or it is a `TopicConnectionFactory`, depending on the messaging model, and it exists to create `Connections`.

Session
> A `Session` creates Producers, Consumers, and `Messages`. A Publish-Subscribe application uses a `TopicSession`, and a Point-to-Point application uses a `QueueSession`. `Sessions` are single-threaded.

Sending a JMS Message

Now that we know the basics of JMS, we'll take the following steps to send a message:

- Look up a `ConnectionFactory` using JNDI.
- Get a Connection from the `ConnectionFactory`.
- Create a Session associated with the Connection.

- Look up a Destination using JNDI.
- Create a Message Producer tied to the Destination.
- Create a Message.
- Send the Message.
- Tear down the Message Producer, Session, and Connection.

JMS requires a lot of low-level tedious API calls to send a message, so Example 7-4 encapsulates everything into a JmsProducer utility object.

Example 7-4. JmsProducer.java

```java
package com.jbossatwork.util;

import java.io.*;

import javax.jms.*;

/**
 * <code>JmsProducer</code> encapsulates sending a JMS Message.
 *
 */
public class JmsProducer {

    /**
     * Making the default (no arg) constructor private
     * ensures that this class cannnot be instantiated.
     */
    private JmsProducer() {}

    public static void sendMessage(Serializable payload,
            String connectionFactoryJndiName, String destinationJndiName)
            throws JmsProducerException {

        try {
            ConnectionFactory connectionFactory = null;
            Connection connection = null;
            Session session = null;
            Destination destination = null;
            MessageProducer messageProducer = null;
            ObjectMessage message = null;

            connectionFactory = ServiceLocator.getJmsConnectionFactory(
                                                connectionFactoryJndiName);

            connection = connectionFactory.createConnection();
            session = connection.createSession(false, Session.AUTO_ACKNOWLEDGE);
            destination = ServiceLocator.getJmsDestination(destinationJndiName);
            messageProducer = session.createProducer(destination);

            message = session.createObjectMessage(payload);
            messageProducer.send(message);
```

Example 7-4. JmsProducer.java (continued)

```
            messageProducer.close( );
            session.close( );
            connection.close( );
        } catch (JMSException je) {
            throw new JmsProducerException(je);
        } catch (ServiceLocatorException sle) {
            throw new JmsProducerException(sle);
        }
    }

}
```

The JMS ConnectionFactory and Connection are both JNDI-based resources, so we've encapsulated the JNDI lookups with the ServiceLocator—we'll show the look-up code in detail in the "Factoring Out the JNDI Calls" section. The ServiceLocator. getJmsConnectionFactory( ) call finds and instantiates the ConnectionFactory to gain access to the JMS provider. The ConnectionFactory creates a Connection. Use the following parameters in the Connection.createSession( ) call to create the Session:

- The first parameter is a boolean that determines whether the Session is transacted. We've set this value to false because we don't want to manage the transaction programmatically. As you'll see in the later sections on deployment, we use Container-Managed Transactions so that JBoss manages the transaction for us.

- The second parameter sets the acknowledgment mode. Using AUTO_ACKNOWLEDGE means that once the Consumer receives a message, an acknowledgment is sent to the JMS server automatically. Usually, you should use AUTO_ACKNOWLEDGE and let the container do all the work for you.

After we've created the Session, the ServiceLocator.getJmsDestination( ) call finds the Destination, a proxy to the actual destination (a queue, in this case, because of how it's deployed) on the JMS server. The Session's createProducer( ) method creates the MessageProducer, which sends messages to a destination asynchronously. The call to the Session's createObjectMessage( ) method creates an ObjectMessage method that contains the object passed into the JmsProducer's sendMessage( ) method. The MessageProducer's send( ) method sends the message to the destination, and we wrap up by closing the MessageProducer, Session, and Connection.

The code above may look a bit strange to readers experienced with previous releases of JMS (1.0.2 or earlier) and J2EE 1.3. What happened to the QueueConnectionFactory, QueueSender, QueueSession, QueueConnection, and the Queue? We don't need them anymore. Instead, use the JMS Unified Client API.

JMS Unified Client API

As of JMS 1.1, the Unified API is now available and works with both the Publish-Subscribe and Point-to-Point models. The JMS 1.1 specification encourages you to write all your new JMS code by using the Unified API, since the Queue and Topic-based APIs *could* become deprecated in a future version of JMS. However, the model-specific APIs will last for a while because so much production code uses them. Don't get the wrong idea—the physical JMS Queues and Topics are not going away. You'll still use them with the Unified API. The Unified API resembles the Queue and Topic-based APIs because it follows the same calling sequence. The big difference is that your code doesn't really care if you use Queues or Topics. All you need to provide are the JNDI names for Queue/Topic Connection Factory and Queue/Topic.

We recommend using the Unified API because it simplifies development—you don't need the Queue or Topic APIs anymore. You'll still send messages to a Queue or Topic (depending on the JNDI name you use), but this is now just a configuration issue. Your code becomes much more generic because it no longer uses queue or topic-specific API calls. With the Unified API, you always access JMS-based resources in the same way, regardless of your JMS messaging model.

We've wrapped the JMS API calls in the `JmsProducer` utility to make it easy to send a JMS message from the Controller Servlet. The `JmsProducer` used the `ServiceLocator` utility to find the `ConnectionFactory` and the JMS `Destination` using JNDI. Let's take a closer look at the `ServiceLocator`.

Factoring Out the JNDI Calls

We used the `ServiceLocator` throughout this book to wrap JNDI lookup calls—Example 7-5 shows the new JMS-related methods.

Example 7-5. ServiceLocator.java

```
package com.jbossatwork.util;

…

import javax.jms.ConnectionFactory;
import javax.jms.Destination;
import javax.naming.*;
…

public class ServiceLocator {
    …

    public static ConnectionFactory getJmsConnectionFactory(
        String jmsConnectionFactoryJndiName) throws ServiceLocatorException {

        ConnectionFactory jmsConnectionFactory = null;
```

Example 7-5. ServiceLocator.java (continued)

```
        try {
            Context ctx = new InitialContext();

            jmsConnectionFactory = (ConnectionFactory)
                    ctx.lookup(jmsConnectionFactoryJndiName);

        } catch (ClassCastException cce) {
            throw new ServiceLocatorException(cce);
        } catch (NamingException ne) {
            throw new ServiceLocatorException(ne);
        }

        return jmsConnectionFactory;
    }

    ...

    public static Destination getJmsDestination(String jmsDestinationJndiName)
    throws ServiceLocatorException {
        Destination jmsDestination = null;

        try {
            Context ctx = new InitialContext();

            jmsDestination = (Destination) ctx.lookup(jmsDestinationJndiName);
        } catch (ClassCastException cce) {
            throw new ServiceLocatorException(cce);
        } catch (NamingException ne) {
            throw new ServiceLocatorException(ne);
        }

        return jmsDestination;
    }
}
```

The `getJmsConnectionFactory()` and `getJmsDestination()` methods, respectively, encapsulate a JNDI lookup for a JMS `ConnectionFactory` or JMS `Destination`. Both methods have the following steps in common:

- Create the `InitialContext` to access the JNDI tree.

- Perform a JNDI lookup.

- Cast the object returned from JNDI to the correct JMS object type (`ConnectionFactory` or `Destination`) .

- Throw a `ServiceLocatorException` that chains a low-level JNDI-related exception and contains a corresponding error message.

We've written all the code necessary to send a JMS message, and now we need to add JMS to our deployment. We'll start by adding JMS-based JNDI references to our web deployment descriptors.

JMS-Based JNDI References in Web-Based Deployment Descriptors

In previous chapters, we've used the `web.xml` file to describe and deploy Servlets and JNDI resources. Example 7-6 shows the new JMS-based JNDI references in `web.xml`, so that we can use the JMS `ConnectionFactory` and the `CreditCheckQueue`.

Example 7-6. web.xml

```
<?xml version="1.0" encoding="UTF-8"?>

<web-app  xmlns="http://java.sun.com/xml/ns/j2ee"
xmlns:xsi="http://www.w3.org/2001/XMLSchema-instance"
xsi:schemaLocation="http://java.sun.com/xml/ns/j2ee
http://java.sun.com/xml/ns/j2ee/web-app_2_4.xsd" version="2.4">
    …
    <resource-ref >
        <res-ref-name>jms/CreditCheckQueue</res-ref-name>
        <res-type>javax.jms.Queue</res-type>
        <res-auth>Container</res-auth>
    </resource-ref>

    <resource-ref >
        <res-ref-name>jms/MyXAQueueConnectionFactory</res-ref-name>
        <res-type>javax.jms.QueueConnectionFactory</res-type>
        <res-auth>Container</res-auth>
    </resource-ref>
    …
</web-app>
```

`<res-ref-name>` is the JNDI name for each resource—java:comp/env/jms/ CreditCheckQueue and java:comp/env/jms/MyXAQueueConnectionFactory. Notice that you don't have to specify java:comp/env/—because it is the assumed prefix. The `<res-type>` for the `CreditCheckQueue` is a JMS Queue, and `javax.jms.Queue` is its fully qualified class name. The `<res-type>` for the Connection Factory is a JMS Queue Connection Factory—`javax.jms.QueueConnectionFactory`. We want JBoss to manage our JMS resources, so you set `<res-auth>` to `Container`.

A JNDI resource links into an application only if we ask for it. JBoss binds resources under its in-JVM context, java:/. The `jboss-web.xml` file provides a mapping between the J2EE-style ENC names and the local JBoss-specific JNDI names that JBoss uses to deploy JNDI-based resources. Example 7-7 shows the JMS-related JNDI references in `jboss-web.xml`.

Example 7-7. jboss-web.xml

```
<?xml version="1.0" encoding="UTF-8"?>
<!DOCTYPE jboss-web PUBLIC "-//JBoss//DTD Web Application 2.4//EN"
"http://www.jboss.org/j2ee/dtd/jboss-web_4_0.dtd">
```

Example 7-7. jboss-web.xml (continued)

```
<jboss-web>
   …
   <resource-ref>
       <res-ref-name>jms/CreditCheckQueue</res-ref-name>
       <jndi-name>queue/CreditCheckQueue</jndi-name>
   </resource-ref>

   <resource-ref>
       <res-ref-name>jms/MyXAQueueConnectionFactory</res-ref-name>
       <jndi-name>java:/JmsXA</jndi-name>
   </resource-ref>
   …
</jboss-web>
```

`<res-ref-name>` is the JNDI name for each resource wherein java:comp/env/ is the assumed prefix. The textual value of each `<res-ref-name>` element in jboss-web.xml MUST match the value of the `<res-ref-name>` in web.xml. The Queue's `<jndi-name>` is the local JBoss-specific JNDI name that JBoss uses to deploy a JMS Queue. You'll usually prefix queue JNDI names with queue/ and topic JNDI names with topic/. The Queue Connection Factory's `<jndi-name>` is the local JBoss-specific JNDI name that JBoss uses to deploy a JMS QueueConnectionFactory, and the value java:/JmsXA indicates that this QueueConnectionFactory participates in distributed transactions. Let's take a more detailed look at JMS and its relationship to J2EE transactions.

JMS and Its Relationship to J2EE Transactions

When you use JMS, you can participate in either distributed or local transactions:

Local transaction
> A local JMS transaction uses programmatic transaction management and only includes JMS messages in its transaction context. If any of the message send operations fail, then the transaction manager rolls back all JMS messages so they're not delivered to the JMS destination. Other resources (such as JDBC, EJB, and JCA) are not considered part of the transaction context. In this case, you'll use the JMS Session to manage the transaction, so you set the transaction flag to true, and then call the Session's commit( ) or rollback( ) method to manage the transaction yourself. You can use a local transaction from both external and in-container clients. However, container-managed transactions are one of a J2EE container's core services, and you normally wouldn't use a local transaction within a J2EE component.

Distributed transaction
> A distributed transaction (or two-phase commit) uses the JTA for container-managed transactions that include JMS and other resources, including JDBC, EJBs, and JCA in its transaction context. Any failure causes JMS messages and database updates to be rolled back. The transaction manager commits only if

access to all resources was successful. Set the transaction flag to false, and use a `ConnectionFactory` that participates in a distributed transaction. You can use a distributed transaction only from within a J2EE container. When you get a `ConnectionFactory` that participates in a distributed transaction, you're actually getting an `XAConnectionFactory` that uses the XA two-phase commit transaction protocol.

Automating JMS-Related JNDI Settings in Web-Based Deployment Descriptors

As in previous chapters, we don't want to hardcode your deployment descriptors. Since the JAW Motors application uses JMS from the web tier, we need to add XDoclet tags to the Controller Servlet so that the Ant build process generates the J2EE standard (`web.xml`) and JBoss-specific (`jboss-web.xml`) web deployment descriptors, as in Example 7-8.

Example 7-8. ControllerServlet.java

```
/**
 *  …
 *
 * @web.resource-ref
 *  name="jms/CreditCheckQueue"
 *  type="javax.jms.Queue"
 *  auth="Container"
 *
 * @jboss.resource-ref
 *  res-ref-name="jms/CreditCheckQueue"
 *  jndi-name="queue/CreditCheckQueue"
 *
 * @web.resource-ref
 *  name="jms/MyXAQueueConnectionFactory"
 *  type="javax.jms.QueueConnectionFactory"
 *  auth="Container"
 *
 * @jboss.resource-ref
 *  res-ref-name="jms/MyXAQueueConnectionFactory"
 *  jndi-name="java:/JmsXA"
 *
 */
public class ControllerServlet extends HttpServlet
{
    …
}
```

The `@web.resource-ref` XDoclet tags generate the `<resource-ref>` elements for the `CreditCheckQueue` and `MyXAQueueConnectionFactory` in `web.xml`, and the `@jboss.resource` XDoclet tags generate the corresponding `<resource-ref>` elements in `jboss-web.xml`.

At this point, we've written code to send a JMS message and added JMS-based JNDI references to your web deployment descriptors. To complete the deployment, we'll deploy our Queue on JBoss.

Deploying JMS Destinations on JBoss

JBoss implements and manages JMS Queues and Topics as JMX MBeans that create the Destination and register its JNDI name. Here are a few options for creating an MBean for our Queue:

The JMX console
> Go to the JMX Console by visiting the following URL—*http://localhost:8080/jmx-console*. Click on the `service=DestinationManager` link (under the `jboss.mq` heading) to see the JBossMQ DestinationManager MBean page. Look for the `createQueue( )` operation and enter `jms/CreditCheckQueue` for the first parameter (the J2EE JNDI name would then be `java:comp/env/jms/CreditCheckQueue`), and `queue/CreditCheckQueue` for the second parameter (the JBoss-specific JNDI name). Using the JMX console is easy and provides a dynamic way to specify JMS resources, but your settings will be lost once you shut down JBoss.

Add an `<mbean>` element for the queue to `$JBOSS_HOME/server/default/deploy/jms/jbossmq-destinations-service.xml` *file.*
> This file is part of the core JBoss deployment and contains JBoss-specific default test Queues and Topics.

Create your own service descriptor file (post-fixed with `-service.xml`*) that resides in* `$JBOSS_HOME/server/default/deploy` *and add an* `<mbean>` *element for the queue.*
> This is a custom file that you create either by hand or with an automated tool as part of your build and deployment process.

We created our own service file because we wanted your JMS destination settings to survive JBoss startup/shutdown, and we didn't want to co-mingle your application-specific JMS Destinations with JBoss-internal Destinations. Co-mingling destinations is bad because each time you upgrade to a new version of JBoss, you have to re-add the `<mbean>` elements to your service descriptor to make things work again. Example 7-9 shows the `jaw-jms-destinations.xml` file that creates an MBean for the `CreditCheckQueue`.

Example 7-9. jaw-jms-destinations.xml

```
<?xml version="1.0" encoding="UTF-8"?>

<server>
    <mbean code="org.jboss.mq.server.jmx.Queue"
           name="jboss.mq.destination:service=Queue,name=CreditCheckQueue">
```

Example 7-9. jaw-jms-destinations.xml (continued)

```
    <depends optional-attribute-name="DestinationManager">
       jboss.mq:service=DestinationManager
    </depends>
  </mbean>
</server>
```

To deploy our Queue to JBoss, the Ant build script copies the `jaw-jms-destinations-service.xml` file from the `ch07/src/META-INF` directory to the JBoss deployment directory—`$JBOSS_HOME/server/default/deploy`.

JMS Checklist

Before moving on to Message-Driven Beans, let's recap what we've done so far:

- Upgraded the web site:
  - Added a "Run Credit Check" link and form.
  - Added a "Run Credit Check" action to the Controller Servlet.
- Added JMS:
  - Created a `CreditCheckReqDTO` object that holds the user's credit information to send as a JMS message.
  - Wrote the `JmsProducer` utility class to encapsulate sending a JMS message.
  - Added JMS-based JNDI reference settings to the Web-based deployment descriptors (`web.xml` and `jboss-web.xml`).
  - Automated JMS-based JNDI reference settings with XDoclet.
  - Deployed the JMS `CreditCheckQueue` on JBoss with an MBean.

We developed the code to send a JMS message, and completely deployed your JMS Queue on JBoss. We now need to add a Message-Driven Bean that consumes and processes the credit check JMS message.

Message-Driven Beans (MDBs)

It's taken a while to get here, but we now have the core infrastructure in place to send a JMS message. To consume JMS messages with an MDB, we'll do the following:

- Write the MDB.
- Deploy the MDB.
- Automate MDB deployment with XDoclet.

A Message-Driven Bean (MDB) is an EJB whose sole purpose is to consume JMS messages. When a JMS producer sends a message to a JMS destination, the MDB listening on that destination receives the message and processes it. MDBs are pooled, stateless, and do not have a Home or Component interface. An MDB implements the JMS MessageListener interface; its onMessage( ) method processes the message received from the JMS destination and implements business logic. Pooling enables concurrent behavior, so several instances of an MDB would run in parallel if multiple messages are in the queue or topic.

Writing an MDB

In the JAW Motors application, the CreditCheckProcessor MDB:

- Consumes a JMS ObjectMessage that contains a CreditCheckRequestDTO
- Invokes an emulated external credit verification service

Example 7-10 is the code for the MDB.

Example 7-10. CreditCheckProcessorBean.java

```
package com.jbossatwork.ejb;

import javax.ejb.*;
import javax.jms.*;

import com.jbossatwork.dto.*;
import com.jbossatwork.util.*;

public class CreditCheckProcessorBean implements MessageDrivenBean, MessageListener
{

    private MessageDrivenContext ctx = null;

    public CreditCheckProcessorBean( ) {}

    public void setMessageDrivenContext(MessageDrivenContext ctx)
    throws EJBException {
        this.ctx = ctx;
    }

    /**
     * Required creation method for message-driven beans.
     */
    public void ejbCreate( ) {
        // no specific action required for message-driven beans
    }

     /** Required removal method for message-driven beans. */
    public void ejbRemove( ) {
        ctx = null;
    }
```

Example 7-10. CreditCheckProcessorBean.java (continued)

```java
    /**
     * Implements the business logic for the MDB.
     *
     * @param message The JMS message to be processed.
     */
    public void onMessage(Message message) {
        System.out.println(
            "CreditCheckProcessorBean.onMessage(): Received message.");

        try {
            if (message instanceof ObjectMessage) {
                ObjectMessage objMessage = (ObjectMessage) message;
                Object obj = objMessage.getObject();

                if (obj instanceof CreditCheckRequestDTO) {
                    String result = null;
                    CreditCheckRequestDTO creditCheckReq =
                                            (CreditCheckRequestDTO) obj;

                    System.out.println("Credit Check:");
                    System.out.println("Name = [" + creditCheckReq.getName() +
                                        "]");

                    System.out.println("SSN = [" + creditCheckReq.getSsn() + "]");
                    System.out.println("Email = [" + creditCheckReq.getEmail() +
                                        "]");

                    System.out.println("Verifying Credit ...");
                    result = CreditVerificationService.verifyCredit(
                                                creditCheckReq);

                    System.out.println("Credit Check Result = {" + result + "]");
                } else {
                    System.err.println(
                                "Expecting CreditCheckRequestDTO in Message");
                }
            } else {
                System.err.println("Expecting Object Message");
            }
        } catch (Throwable t) {
            t.printStackTrace();
        }
    }
}
```

The onMessage() method consumes a JMS message that contains the user's credit information, but we have to pull the CreditCheckRequestDTO out of the message before using it. Compare this process to peeling the layers of an onion. We first cast the Message we received into an ObjectMessage, call its getObject() method to get the Object out, and then cast it into a CreditCheckRequestDTO. Now that we have the original data entered by the user, we pass the CreditCheckRequestDTO to our emulated external credit verification service. The CreditVerificationService.verifyCredit( ) simulates a long-running process and returns a String value that tells whether the credit check passed or failed. The code for verifyCredit( ) isn't that interesting, so we're not showing it here in the book. If you're dying of curiosity, you can find the CreditVerificationService class in the JAW Motors application common sub-project.

You may have noticed that in the onMessage( ) method we're catching and logging all exceptions rather than re-throwing them. Exceptions thrown from an MDB have no real calling code to catch them, so they roll all the way back to the application server. Then, the JMS provider re-delivers the message to the MDB and the cycle repeats itself. To avoid this "poison message" problem, your code needs to catch any exceptions so the JMS server considers the message delivered/consumed and will not attempt to re-deliver the message. In addition to logging exceptions, you'll probably want to save them in some sort of "dead letter" queue and send an email or pager message so that system personnel can look into the problem.

Now that we've written an MDB, let's take a more detailed look at how Message-Driven Beans relate to J2EE transactions.

MDB Transaction Settings

Like the other EJB types, a Message-Driven Bean has two ways to manage transactions: Container-Managed Transactions (CMT) and Bean-Managed Transactions (BMT). BMT requires extra Java coding to handle transaction logic and forces the developer to manage the transaction and define his own transaction boundaries. In contrast, CMT doesn't require you to handle transaction logic, pushes transaction settings into deployment descriptors, uses JBoss transaction services, and manages transaction boundaries on behalf of the developer. We'll focus on CMT because it is considered a J2EE best practice and allows the container to do the work.

A transaction attribute tells the container how to handle CMT transactions for an MDB's onMessage( ) method. Specify transaction attributes for each Bean in the ejb-jar.xml deployment descriptor. Here are the possible transaction settings for an MDB:

Required
> The onMessage( ) method always runs within the scope of a transaction. If a transaction doesn't currently exist, the container starts a new transaction.

NotSupported
> The onMessage( ) method does not run within the scope of a transaction.

A Message-Driven Bean does not run in the transaction context of the client that sent the JMS message to the queue or topic because an MDB isn't tied to a caller. The

JMS message producer doesn't know if the transaction in the Message-Driven Bean's onMessage( ) method committed or rolled back.

There's no need to specify a transaction setting in the CreditCheckProcessor MDB because it doesn't participate in a transaction. The Bean's onMessage( ) method only sends an email message and doesn't do anything transactional (like updating a database).

We've written a Message-Driven Bean and discussed transactions, and now we need to deploy our MDB.

Deploying an MDB

After developing the code for a Message-Driven Bean (MDB), deploy it by adding information about the EJB (meta-data) to the J2EE standard (ejb-jar.xml) and JBoss (jboss.xml) EJB deployment descriptors. The new <message-driven> element describes the MDB by telling the container:

- That it's a Message-Driven Bean.
- About the bean class.
- That it uses container-managed transactions (CMT).
- That its Acknowledgment mode is Auto-acknowledge.
- That it listens on a non-durable Queue.

Example 7-11 shows the changes to ejb-jar.xml.

Example 7-11. ejb-jar.xml

```
<?xml version="1.0" encoding="UTF-8"?>

<ejb-jar xmlns=http://java.sun.com/xml/ns/j2ee
         xmlns:xsi="http://www.w3.org/2001/XMLSchema-instance"
         xsi:schemaLocation="http://java.sun.com/xml/ns/j2ee
         http://java.sun.com/xml/ns/j2ee/ejb-jar_2_1.xsd" version="2.1">

  <enterprise-beans>
    ...
    <message-driven>
      <display-name>CreditCheckProcessorMDB</display-name>
      <ejb-name>CreditCheckProcessor</ejb-name>
      <ejb-class>com.jbossatwork.ejb.CreditCheckProcessorBean</ejb-class>

      <messaging-type>javax.jms.MessageListener</messaging-type>
      <transaction-type>Container</transaction-type>
      <message-destination-type>javax.jms.Queue</message-destination-type>
      <activation-config>
        <activation-config-property>
          <activation-config-property-name>
            destinationType
          </activation-config-property-name>
```

Example 7-11. ejb-jar.xml (continued)

```
            <activation-config-property-value>
               javax.jms.Queue
            </activation-config-property-value>
         </activation-config-property>

         <activation-config-property>
            <activation-config-property-name>
               acknowledgeMode
            </activation-config-property-name>
            <activation-config-property-value>
               Auto-acknowledge
            </activation-config-property-value>
         </activation-config-property>

         <activation-config-property>
            <activation-config-property-name>
               subscriptionDurability
            </activation-config-property-name>
            <activation-config-property-value>
               NonDurable
             </activation-config-property-value>
         </activation-config-property>
       </activation-config>

    </message-driven>
    …
  </enterprise-beans>
  …
</ejb-jar>
```

In the `ejb-jar.xml` file you can only indicate that your MDB listens on a `Queue`, but there are no elements that associate the `CreditCheckProcessor` MDB with the `CreditCheckQueue`. Since specifying the Queue name isn't part of the EJB specification, we use the jboss.xml descriptor to associate an MDB with a JMS Destination. The `<message-driven>` element's `<destination-jndi-name>` sub-element tells JBoss that the `CreditCheckProcessor` MDB listens on and receives messages from the `CreditCheckQueue` in Example 7-12.

Example 7-12. jboss.xml

```
<?xml version="1.0" encoding="UTF-8"?>
<!DOCTYPE jboss PUBLIC "-//JBoss//DTD JBOSS 4.0//EN"
                    "http://www.jboss.org/j2ee/dtd/jboss_4_0.dtd">

<jboss>

  <enterprise-beans>
    …
    <message-driven>
      <ejb-name>CreditCheckProcessor</ejb-name>
      <destination-jndi-name>queue/CreditCheckQueue</destination-jndi-name>
```

Example 7-12. jboss.xml (continued)

```
    </message-driven>
    ...
  </enterprise-beans>
  ...
</jboss>
```

Automating MDB Deployment with XDoclet

As in previous chapters, we don't want to hardcode your deployment descriptors. We need to add XDoclet tags to the CreditCheckProcessor MDB in Example 7-13 so that the Ant build process adds it to the J2EE standard (ejb-jar.xml) and JBoss-specific (jboss.xml) EJB deployment descriptors.

Example 7-13. CreditCheckProcessorBean.java

```
/**
 * @ejb.bean name="CreditCheckProcessor"
 *   display-name="CreditCheckProcessorMDB"
 *   acknowledge-mode="Auto-acknowledge"
 *   destination-type="javax.jms.Queue"
 *   subscription-durability="NonDurable"
 *   transaction-type="Container"
 *
 * @jboss.destination-jndi-name
 *   name="queue/CreditCheckQueue"
 *
 */
public class CreditCheckProcessorBean implements MessageDrivenBean, MessageListener
{
    ...
}
```

The @ejb.bean XDoclet tag generates the CreditCheckProcessor MDB's <message-driven> element and all its subelements in ejb-jar.xml. The @jboss.destination-jndi-name XDoclet tag generates the corresponding <message-driven> element in jboss.xml that indicates that the CreditCheckProcessor MDB listens for messages on the CreditCheckQueue.

MDB Checklist

We took the following steps to add an MDB to the JAW Motors Application:

- Wrote the CreditCheckProcessor MDB.
- Deployed the CreditCheckProcessor MDB in ejb-jar.xml and jboss.xml.
- Automated deployment of the CreditCheckProcessor MDB with XDoclet.

Testing the Credit Check

Now that we've deployed the JMS Queue and an MDB to run the credit check, let's test our application to ensure that everything still works properly. Here are the steps for building and deploying the application:

- Type ant in the root directory of ch07 to build the project.
- Shut down JBoss so the Ant script can clean up the JBoss deployment area.
- Type ant colddeploy to deploy the EAR file (jaw.ear) to the $JBOSS_HOME/server/default/deploy directory. Notice that the Ant build script also deploys the jaw-jms-destinations.xml JMS Destination service file to JBoss.
- Start JBoss back up.
- Visit *http://localhost:8080/jaw* in a web browser.

Click on the "Run Credit Check" link on the JAW Motors home page, enter data on the "Run Credit Check" form, and press the "Submit Credit Info" button. You should be routed back to the main page and see the following output on your JBoss console:

```
...
17:05:55,707 INFO  [STDOUT] CreditCheckProcessorBean.onMessage(): Received message.
17:05:55,707 INFO  [STDOUT] Credit Check:
17:05:55,707 INFO  [STDOUT] Name = [Fred]
17:05:55,707 INFO  [STDOUT] SSN = [999999999999999]
17:05:55,707 INFO  [STDOUT] Email = [fred@acme.org]
17:05:55,707 INFO  [STDOUT] Verifying Credit ...
17:05:59,703 INFO  [STDOUT] Credit Check Result = [Fail Credit Check]
```

Looking Ahead...

This chapter covered JMS and Message-Driven Beans. We upgraded the JAW Motors application by adding the ability to run a credit check on a customer by using JMS messaging and an MDB. Along the way, we showed how to deploy these technologies on JBoss.

The JBoss console output proves that the Controller Servlet sent the credit check JMS message and that the CreditCheckProcessor MDB consumed and processed the message. However, it isn't completely satisfying because the web site user doesn't know the final result of the credit verification process. In the next chapter, we'll upgrade the MDB to use the JavaMail API when sending the user an email notification message.

CHAPTER 8

JavaMail

In the previous chapter, we upgraded the JAW Motors application by adding the ability to run a credit check on a customer using JMS messaging and an MDB. We didn't want to make the user wait a long time for the credit verification to complete, so we deferred this process to the background. As you'll recall, the `CreditCheckProcessor` MDB received the credit check message, invoked a simulated external credit verification service, and printed the result. But this wasn't completely satisfying because the user on the web site didn't know the final result of the credit verification process. In this chapter, we'll upgrade the MDB to use the JavaMail API for sending an email notification message to the user. Along the way we'll show how to deploy and configure JavaMail on JBoss.

JavaMail 1.2 is a J2EE API that enables Java programs to send and receive email messages. With JavaMail, you can send text or HTML messages, and you have the option to include Multipurpose Internet Mail Extensions (MIME) attachments. To keep things simple, we'll send text messages without attachments.

Let's start by briefly reviewing where we left off in the last chapter.

Running a Credit Check

If you'll recall, we added a "Run Credit Check" link to the JAW Motors homepage as shown in Figure 8-1.

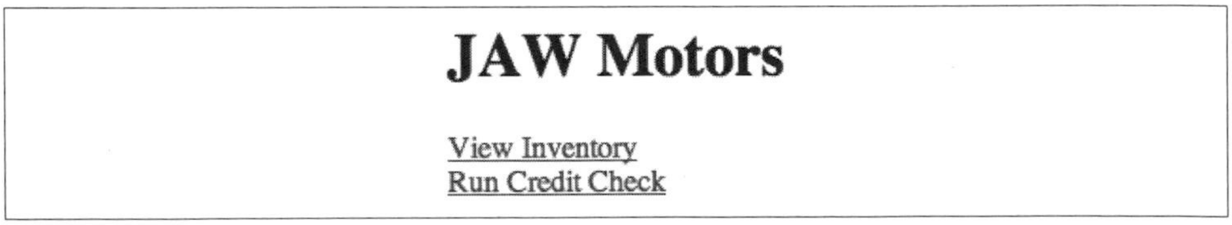

Figure 8-1. JAW Motors homepage

When the user clicks on the "Run Credit Check" link, the Controller routes them to the Run Credit Check page as depicted in Figure 8-2.

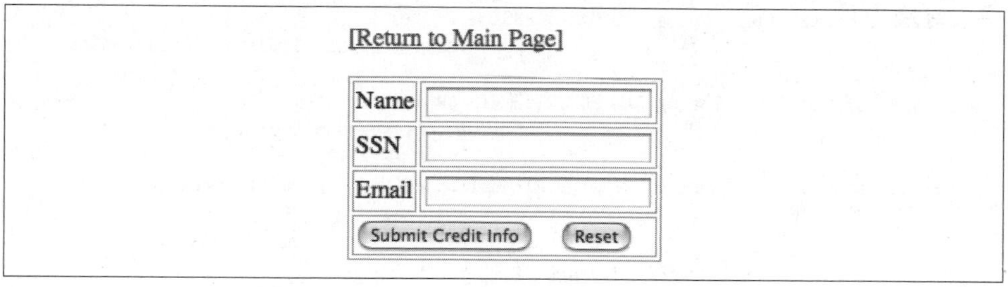

Figure 8-2. JAW Motors Run Credit Check page

The user enters his name, Social Security Number (SSN), and email address in the form, and presses the "Submit Credit Info" button. When a customer requests a credit check, he won't have to wait while for the external credit verification process to complete. The Controller Servlet sends a JMS message asynchronously to back end components that process business logic for the request. The customer gets routed back to the JAW Motors home page and then is free to continue using the JAW Motors web site while the credit check completes in the background.

Sending Email Messages with JavaMail

To upgrade the JAW Motors application to send email messages using JavaMail, we need to do the following:

- Add Java Code:
  - Call the JavaMail utility class from the MDB.
  - Write a utility class to encapsulate sending an email message with JavaMail.
  - Factor out JNDI calls into the ServiceLocator.
- Upgrade deployment:
  - Add JavaMail-based JNDI reference settings to the EJB-based deployment descriptors (ejb-jar.xml and jboss.xml).
  - Automate JavaMail-based JNDI reference settings with XDoclet.
  - Configure JavaMail on JBoss with an MBean.

Upgrading the MDB to Send an Email Message

If you'll recall from the JMS and MDB chapter, the CreditCheckProcessor MDB's onMessage( ) method consumes the message and invokes a simulated external credit verification service. Example 8-1 shows the changes necessary to send an email message with JavaMail.

Example 8-1. CreditCheckProcessorBean.java

```java
public class CreditCheckProcessorBean implements MessageDrivenBean, MessageListener
{
    private static final String JAVAMAIL_SESSION =
                                    "java:comp/env/mail/JawJavaMailSession";

    private static final String JAW_MOTORS_EMAIL_ADDRESS =
                                    "credit.check@jbossatwork.com";

    private static final String CREDIT_VERIFICATION_RESULT = "Credit Check Result";
    ...

    public void onMessage(Message message) {
        System.out.println(
            "CreditCheckProcessorBean.onMessage( ): Received message.");

        try {
            if (message instanceof ObjectMessage) {
                ObjectMessage objMessage = (ObjectMessage) message;
                Object obj = objMessage.getObject( );

                if (obj instanceof CreditCheckRequestDTO) {
                    String result = null;
                        CreditCheckRequestDTO creditCheckReq =
                                            (CreditCheckRequestDTO) obj;

                    System.out.println("Verifying Credit ...");
                    result = CreditVerificationService.verifyCredit(
                                            creditCheckReq);

                    System.out.println("Credit Check Result = [" + result + "]");
                    sendNotificationEmail(creditCheckReq, result);
                } else {
                    System.err.println(
                                "Expecting CreditCheckRequestDTO in Message");
                }
            } else {
                System.err.println("Expecting Object Message");
            }
        } catch (Throwable t) {
            t.printStackTrace( );
        }
    }

    private void sendNotificationEmail(CreditCheckRequestDTO creditCheckReq,
                                    String result) {
        javax.mail.Session javaMailSession = null;

        try {
            javaMailSession =
                        ServiceLocator.getJavaMailSession(JAVAMAIL_SESSION);

            TextEmail email = new TextEmail(javaMailSession);
```

Example 8-1. CreditCheckProcessorBean.java (continued)

```
        email.setBody(result);
        email.setSender(JAW_MOTORS_EMAIL_ADDRESS);
        email.setSubject(CREDIT_VERIFICATION_RESULT);
        email.addRecipient(creditCheckReq.getEmail());
        System.out.println("Sending Email to [" + creditCheckReq.getEmail() +
                              "] ...");

        email.send();

    } catch (ServiceLocatorException sle) {
        System.err.println("Error Looking up JavaMail Session: " + sle);
        sle.printStackTrace();
    }
  }
}
```

The onMessage( ) method consumes a JMS message that contains the user's credit information. After pulling the CreditCheckRequestDTO out of the JMS message, we pass it to our emulated external credit verification service. The CreditVerificationService.verifyCredit( ) method simulates a long-running process and returns a String result value that indicates whether the credit check passed or failed. The sendNotificationEmail( ) method takes the CreditCheckRequestDTO and credit check result as parameters and sends a notification email to the customer. The sendNotificationEmail( ) method uses the ServiceLocator to look up a JavaMail Session by using JNDI, and then invokes the TextEmail utility class to send the email message. Some readers may not be familiar with using JNDI to look up a JavaMail Session—we'll cover this in the "JavaMail Sessions" section. The "Factoring out JNDI Calls" section shows the new ServiceLocator method used to find the Java-Mail Session.

Let's take a closer look at the TextEmail utility to see how it uses the JavaMail API calls to send an email message.

Sending an Email Message

Creating and sending an email message with JavaMail requires the following steps:

- Get a JavaMail Session (which we did in the MDB's sendEmailNotification( ) method).
- Create the message.
- Set the "From" email address.
- Set the recipients' email addresses.
- Set the subject.
- Create the body and add it to the message.
- Send the message.

JavaMail requires a lot of low-level tedious API calls to send an email message, so we've encapsulated everything into the TextEmail utility object in Example 8-2.

Example 8-2. TextEmail.java

```java
package com.jbossatwork.util;

import javax.mail.*;
import javax.mail.internet.*;

import java.util.*;

/**
 * TextEmail defines utility methods for the JavaMail API, which provides
 * a platform independent and protocol independent framework to build Java
 * technology-based mail and messaging applications.
 *
 */
public class TextEmail {
    …

    private Session session;
    private InternetAddress sender = new InternetAddress();
    private String subject = new String();
    private StringBuffer body = new StringBuffer();
    private List recipients = new ArrayList();
    …

    public TextEmail(Session session) throws EmailException {
        setSession(session);
    }

    …

    public void setSession(Session session) {
        this.session = session;
    }

    …

    public void send() throws EmailException {

        try {
            …
            InternetAddress[] recipientsArr = (InternetAddress[])
                        recipients.toArray(new InternetAddress[0]);

            // Create a New message.

            MimeMessage msg = new MimeMessage(session);

            // Set the "From" address.

            msg.setFrom(sender);
```

Example 8-2. TextEmail.java (continued)

```
            // Set the "To recipients" addresses.

            msg.setRecipients(Message.RecipientType.TO, recipientsArr);

            …

            // Set the Subject.

            msg.setSubject(subject);

            // Set the Text.

            msg.setText(body.toString());

            // Set the sent date.

            msg.setSentDate(getSentDate());

            // Send the message.

            Transport.send(msg);
        } catch (MessagingException me) {
            throw new EmailException(me);
        }
    }
}
```

We left out the getter and setter methods for the sender, subject, body, and recipients data members to shorten the code example above, but you can look at the full TextEmail class in the book's code distribution.

The send() method first converts the list of recipients from Strings to InternetAddresses that represent email addresses in the standard RFC822 format—something like *name@host.domain* is a common syntax. The MimeMessage constructor takes a JavaMail Session and instantiates the JavaMail message. We'll talk more about JavaMail Sessions in the next section. The message's setFrom() method sets the sender's email address, and the message's setRecipients() call sets the required recipients list. The message's setSubject() method sets the email message's subject line and the MimeMessage's setText() method sets the email message's body text. The message's setSentDate() method sets the email message's sent date, and the Transport.send() call sends the message.

JavaMail Sessions

A JavaMail Session represents a connection to a JavaMail provider that enables an application to send or receive email messages. After looking at the TextEmail code above, you may be thinking, "I already know JavaMail, so how is this different from what I've done before?" You may be familiar with setting JavaMail properties and using the Session.getDefaultInstance( ) method to get a JavaMail Session. You've probably written code that looks like Example 8-3.

Example 8-3. TextEmail.java

```
private Session getDefaultSession( ) {
    Properties props = new Properties( );

    props.setProperty("mail.store.protocol", "pop3");
    props.setProperty("mail.pop3.host", "mail.isp.host.name");

    props.setProperty("mail.transport.protocol", "smtp");
    props.setProperty("mail.smtp.host", "smtp.isp.host.name");
    props.setProperty("mail.smtp.port", "25");

    // Get the default Session using Properties.
    Session session = Session.getDefaultInstance(props);

    return session;
}
```

In the example above, we use Sun's default JavaMail provider and supply an email server's Simple Mail Transfer Protocol (SMTP) and Post Office Protocol (POP) properties to get a JavaMail Session. Your email service provider also may require a user ID and password.

When creating a JavaMail Session, you can use either Sun's default JavaMail provider (as shown in the above getDefaultSession( ) method) or the JavaMail provider that comes with JBoss (using JNDI, as shown in the CreditCheckProcessorBean's sendNotificationEmail( ) method). If your code runs inside the JBoss application server, we recommend using the JBoss JavaMail provider because:

- Using the container's JavaMail provider is a standard practice, and all J2EE application servers must implement a JavaMail provider. In other words, if you're already working with JBoss, then use its services.

- You can use the container's JavaMail provider without adding application-specific setup information to your code. Your code thus remains portable across J2EE application servers. Each server defines JavaMail setup in its own way, but they usually have an external XML-based descriptor that configures a JavaMail Session.

The JAW Motors application uses JBoss' JavaMail provider by using a JNDI lookup to find the JavaMail Session associated with the JBoss server instance. We've wrapped the JavaMail API calls in the TextEmail utility to make it easy to send an email message with the JavaMail API. The CreditCheckProcessorBean used the ServiceLocator utility to find the JavaMail Session that uses JNDI. Let's take a closer look at the ServiceLocator.

Factoring out the JNDI Calls

We've used the ServiceLocator throughout this book to wrap JNDI lookup calls—Example 8-4 shows the new JavaMail-related method.

Example 8-1. ServiceLocator.java

```java
package com.jbossatwork.util;

...

import javax.naming.*;

...

public class ServiceLocator {
    ...

    public static javax.mail.Session getJavaMailSession(
                String javaMailSessionJndiName) throws ServiceLocatorException {

        javax.mail.Session javaMailSession = null;

        try {
            Context ctx = new InitialContext();

            javaMailSession = (javax.mail.Session)
                        ctx.lookup(javaMailSessionJndiName);

        } catch (ClassCastException cce) {
            throw new ServiceLocatorException(cce);
        } catch (NamingException ne) {
            throw new ServiceLocatorException(ne);
        }

        return javaMailSession;
    }

    ...
}
```

The getJavaMailSession( ) method encapsulates a JNDI lookup for JavaMail Session by taking the following steps:

- Create the InitialContext to access the JNDI tree.
- Perform a JNDI lookup.
- Cast the object returned from JNDI to the correct type—javax.mail.Session
- Throw a ServiceLocatorException that chains a low-level JNDI-related exception and contains a corresponding error message.

We've written all the necessary code to send an email message with the JavaMail API, and now we need to add JavaMail to our deployment. We'll start by adding JavaMail-based JNDI references to our EJB deployment descriptors.

JavaMail-Based JNDI References in EJB Deployment Descriptors

In previous chapters we've used the `ejb-jar.xml` and `jboss.xml` file to describe and deploy EJBs and JNDI resources. Here are the new JavaMail -based JNDI references in `ejb-jar.xml` that enable the `CreditCheckProcessor` MDB to use a JavaMail Session, as in Example 8-5.

Example 8-5. ejb-jar.xml

```xml
<?xml version="1.0" encoding="UTF-8"?>

<ejb-jar xmlns=http://java.sun.com/xml/ns/j2ee
         xmlns:xsi="http://www.w3.org/2001/XMLSchema-instance"
         xsi:schemaLocation="http://java.sun.com/xml/ns/j2ee
         http://java.sun.com/xml/ns/j2ee/ejb-jar_2_1.xsd" version="2.1">

  <enterprise-beans>
    …
    <message-driven>
      <display-name>CreditCheckProcessorMDB</display-name>
      <ejb-name>CreditCheckProcessor</ejb-name>
      …
      <resource-ref>
        <res-ref-name>mail/JawJavaMailSession</res-ref-name>
        <res-type>javax.mail.Session</res-type>
        <res-auth>Container</res-auth>
      </resource-ref>
      …
    </message-driven>
    …
</ejb-jar>
```

The `<resource-ref>` elements specify the JNDI resources available to the `CreditCheckProcessorMDB` (or any POJO that it calls). `<res-ref-name>` is the JNDI name for the resource—java:comp/env/mail/JawJavaMailSession. Notice that you don't have to specify java:comp/env/—because it is the assumed prefix. The `<res-type>` for the `mail/JawJavaMailSession` is a JavaMail Session, and `javax.jms.Session` is its fully qualified class name. We want JBoss to manage our JavaMail resources, so we set `<res-auth>` to `Container`.

A JNDI resource is linked into an application only if we ask for it. JBoss binds resources under its in-JVM context, java:/. The `jboss.xml` file provides a mapping from the J2EE-style ENC names and the local JBoss-specific JNDI names that JBoss uses to deploy a JavaMail Session. Example 8-6 shows the JavaMail-related JNDI references for the `CreditCheckProcessor` MDB in `jboss.xml`.

Example 8-6. jboss.xml

```xml
<?xml version="1.0" encoding="UTF-8"?>
<!DOCTYPE jboss PUBLIC "-//JBoss//DTD JBOSS 4.0//EN"
                    "http://www.jboss.org/j2ee/dtd/jboss_4_0.dtd">

<jboss>

  <enterprise-beans>
    ...
    <message-driven>
      <ejb-name>CreditCheckProcessor</ejb-name>
      <destination-jndi-name>queue/CreditCheckQueue</destination-jndi-name>

      <resource-ref>
        <res-ref-name>mail/JawJavaMailSession</res-ref-name>
        <jndi-name>java:/Mail</jndi-name>
      </resource-ref>
    </message-driven>
    ...
  </enterprise-beans>
  ...
</jboss>
```

As you'll see in the "Deploying JavaMail on JBoss" section, the java:/Mail name is the local JNDI name that JBoss uses to deploy its JavaMail Session.

Automating JavaMail-Based JNDI References with XDoclet

As in previous chapters, we don't want to hardcode our deployment descriptors. We need to add XDoclet tags to the `CreditCheckProcessor` MDB so the Ant build process can add the JavaMail JNDI settings to the J2EE standard (`ejb-jar.xml`) and JBoss-specific (`jboss.xml`) EJB deployment descriptors in Example 8-7.

Example 8-7. CreditCheckProcessorBean.java

```java
/**
 * ...
 *
 * @ejb.resource-ref
 *   res-ref-name="mail/JawJavaMailSession"
 *   res-type="javax.mail.Session"
 *   res-auth="Container"
 *
 * @jboss.resource-ref
 *   res-ref-name="mail/JawJavaMailSession"
 *   jndi-name="java:/Mail"
```

Example 8-7. CreditCheckProcessorBean.java (continued)

```
 *
 */
public class CreditCheckProcessorBean implements MessageDrivenBean, MessageListener
{
    ...
}
```

The @ejb.resource-ref XDoclet tag generates the <resource-ref> element for the JawJavaMailSession in ejb-jar.xml, and the @jboss.resource XDoclet tag generates the corresponding <resource-ref> element in jboss.xml.

At this point, we've written code to send an email message with JavaMail and added JavaMail-based JNDI references to our EJB deployment descriptors. To complete the deployment, we'll deploy JavaMail on JBoss.

Deploying JavaMail on JBoss

We now need to configure JBoss so we can use it as a JavaMail provider. JBoss manages a JavaMail Session as a JMX MBean that creates the Session and registers its JNDI name. The JBoss JavaMail XML descriptor, $JBOSS_HOME/server/jbossatwork/deploy/mail-service.xml, sets up a JMX MBean that configures a JNDI-based Java-Mail Session in Example 8-8.

Example 8-8. mail-service.xml

```xml
<?xml version="1.0" encoding="UTF-8"?>
<!DOCTYPE server>

<server>

  <mbean code="org.jboss.mail.MailService"
         name="jboss:service=Mail">
    <attribute name="JNDIName">java:/Mail</attribute>
    <attribute name="User">yourUserId</attribute>
    <attribute name="Password">yourPassword</attribute>
    <attribute name="Configuration">
       <configuration>
          <!-- Set the protocol for your mail server -->
          <property name="mail.store.protocol" value="pop3"/>
          <property name="mail.transport.protocol" value="smtp"/>

          <!-- Configure the POP3 Server  -->
          <property name="mail.pop3.host" value="yourIsp.pop3.host"/>

          <!-- Configure the SMTP gateway server -->
          <property name="mail.smtp.host" value="yourIsp.smtp.host "/>
          <property name="mail.smtp.port" value="25"/>

          <property name="mail.debug" value="true"/>
       </configuration>
```

Example 8-8. mail-service.xml (continued)

```
    </attribute>
  </mbean>

</server>
```

The `mail-service.xml` file configures a JavaMail `Session` with the email account properties that you use to connect with your email service provider:

- Mail Store Protocol
- Mail Transport Protocol
- SMTP server name
- POP server name
- An email account user ID
- An email account password

These are standard JavaMail properties, and you can find a complete listing of them in Appendix A of the JavaMail Design Specification at: *http://java.sun.com/products/javamail/JavaMail-1.2.pdf*.

The example above uses bogus values for its ISP settings, so you'll need to edit the `$JBOSS_HOME/server/jbossatwork/deploy/mail-service.xml` file and fill in the protocol and account settings you use to access your ISP's mail server. You could change the JNDI name to something other than `java:/Mail`, but every JBoss installation we've seen uses this value to deploy its JavaMail `Session`. Therefore we recommend sticking with the default value to be consistent with the way most people use JBoss.

JavaMail Checklist

Before we move on to test the JAW Motors application's new email functionality, let's recap what we've done to implement JavaMail:

- Added Java Code:
    - Called the `TextEmail` JavaMail utility class from the `CreditCheckProcessor` MDB
    - Wrote a `TextEmail` utility class to encapsulate sending an email message with JavaMail
    - Factored out JNDI calls into the `ServiceLocator`
- Upgraded deployment:
    - Added JavaMail-based JNDI reference settings to the EJB-based deployment descriptors (`ejb-jar.xml` and `jboss.xml`)
    - Automated JavaMail-based JNDI reference settings in the `CreditCheckProcessor` MDB with XDoclet
    - Configured JavaMail on JBoss with an MBean

Testing the Credit Check Notification Email

Now that we've developed and deployed JavaMail code to send an email notification message to the user, let's test our application to ensure that everything still works properly. Here are the steps to build and deploy the application:

- Type ant in the root directory of ch08 to build the project.
- Shut down JBoss so the Ant script can clean up the JBoss deployment area.
- Type ant colddeploy to deploy the EAR file (jaw.ear) to the *$JBOSS_HOME/ server/default/deploy* directory.
- Start JBoss back up.
- Visit *http://localhost:8080/jaw* in a web browser.

Click on the "Run Credit Check" link on the JAW Motors home page, enter data on the "Run Credit Check" form, and press the "Submit Credit Info" button. You should be routed back to the main page, and in a minute or two you should see a message that looks like this in your email client's Inbox:

```
From:    credit.check@jbossatwork.com
To:      yourName@host.domain
Subject: Credit Check Result

Pass Credit Check
```

The credit check randomly passes or fails, so you could also see "Fail Credit Check" in the email message body.

Looking Ahead...

This chapter covered JavaMail. We upgraded the JAW Motors application by using JavaMail to send an email notification to the customer after running a credit check. Along the way, we showed how to deploy and configure JavaMail on JBoss.

For our purposes, we're now finished with core functionality for the JAW Motors application. In the next chapter, we'll show how to secure the application.

CHAPTER 9

Security

If you've worked through all the previous chapters, you have a fully functional vertical slice of the JAW Motors application that allows you to run a credit check and view, add, edit (update), delete, and buy cars. Although this works, there's a gaping hole—anyone with a browser who knows the application's URL can modify JAW Motors' inventory. So we need to add security to the application. In this chapter, we'll secure the "Car Inventory" and "Add/Edit Car" pages so that only authorized users can modify cars in the inventory. We won't secure the "Buy Car" or "Run Credit Check" pages (and their underlying functionality) because we still want all users to be able to buy a car or run a credit check without having to log in. We'll discuss J2EE web-based security, Java Authentication & Authorization Service (JAAS), and EJB security. Along the way we'll show how to deploy these security mechanisms on JBoss.

J2EE Security

Security is an important part of J2EE application architecture because the J2EE components and tiers used in a system's architecture determine the choice of security technologies. If an application uses only web-based technologies, then it only needs to restrict access to JSPs, Servlets, and so on. But EJBs are now part of the JAW Motors architecture, so they must be protected as well. The system must create a security context that encompasses the entire J2EE stack from frontend web pages to backend business logic and data. We need a unified security mechanism that propagates the user's credentials to all components in the application.

The two fundamental concepts in J2EE security are:

Authentication
> Answers the following questions:
>> • Who is attempting to access the system?
>>
>> • Is this person allowed to access the system?

Authorization
> Determines what an authenticated user can access in an application.

Authentication is an important aspect of a J2EE application's architecture and security strategy, and ensures that only valid users or entities can use the system's resources. Authentication is the front line of defense in protecting sensitive business logic and data from users. Authentication identifies a user in the system, and requires the user to log on just as they would log on to an operating system or database. Users identify themselves to the system by supplying credentials, which could be in the form of passwords, certificates, or keys. If the user enters a valid username and password, the user can access sensitive portions of the web site; otherwise, access is denied.

Although restricting access on internal business functions and web pages to known users of the JAW Motors is a good first step in securing the system, it still isn't enough. We know who the user is, but what can they do in the system? What are they not allowed to do? How can we ensure that users see only what they're allowed to access? Authorization answers these questions and strengthens security by adding the concept of roles to our security realm. Each role represents different types of users, and the JAW Motors application has the following roles:

Manager
    A manager is an administrative user who can modify the JAW Motors inventory.

Guest
    A guest is a user who can only view the JAW Motors inventory.

Although there is no need to protect public pages and their underlying business logic, we must prevent unauthenticated/unauthorized users from accessing protected web pages and business functions.

Let's start by securing the web tier and working our way down through the architecture.

Web-Based Security

To secure the web site, we need to do the following:

- Protect the administrative pages:
    - Restrict access based on the URL pattern.
    - Associate security roles with the URL.
    - Create security roles for the JAW Motors application.
- Choose an Authentication mechanism and implement it.
- Automate extra web.xml settings with XDoclet.
- Create a security realm that associates a user with the roles he plays in the system.
- Configure a JAAS LoginModule that's tied to the security realm.
- Deploy the JAAS-based security realm with the JBoss container.

- Protect MVC administrative actions:
  - Restrict access based on the URL pattern.
- Propagate the correct user credentials from the web tier:
  - Establish a default user identity for non-secure web access.
  - Use the right user identity for secure web access.

Protecting the Administrative Pages

J2EE provides Declarative Security, so rather than writing code to protect our resources, we can accomplish this through URL patterns and deployment descriptors. If you'll recall, the Car Inventory page (carList.jsp), as shown in Figure 9-1, enables you to view and modify the JAW Motors inventory.

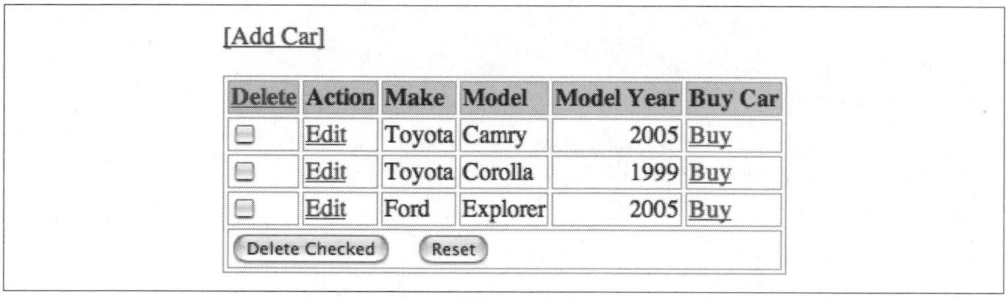

[Add Car]

Delete	Action	Make	Model	Model Year	Buy Car
☐	Edit	Toyota	Camry	2005	Buy
☐	Edit	Toyota	Corolla	1999	Buy
☐	Edit	Ford	Explorer	2005	Buy

[Delete Checked]   [Reset]

Figure 9-1. JAW Motors Car Inventory page

We also must protect the Add/Edit Car page (carForm.jsp—you see this page when you press the "Add Car" or "Edit" link on the Car Inventory page) (Figure 9-2).

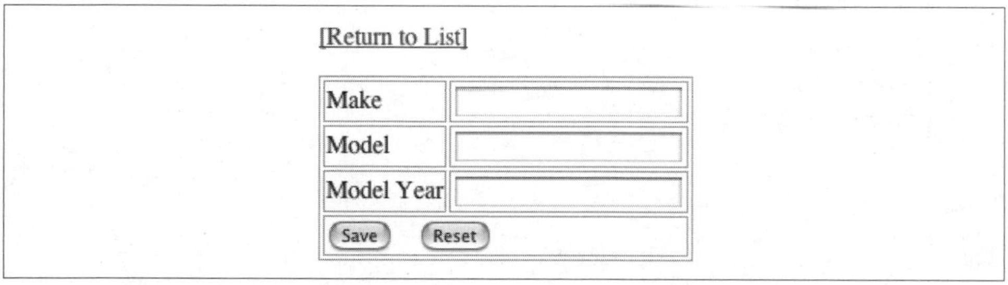

[Return to List]

Make	
Model	
Model Year	

[Save]   [Reset]

Figure 9-2. JAW Motors Add/Edit Car page

We first move carList.jsp and carForm.jsp to a sub-directory under WEB-INF (in the WAR file) called admin to differentiate these protected pages from the public pages. Now our pages in the WAR file look like this:

WEB-INF/
> All public non-protected pages, including index.jsp, go here.

WEB-INF/admin/
> All administrative protected pages, including carList.jsp and carForm.jsp, go here.

To access these pages, you would now use this URL as a prefix: *http://localhost:8080/ ch09/admin/*

But we still need to restrict access to the administrative pages by creating security roles and associating them with these URL patterns in web.xml.

Restricting Access with web.xml

We restrict access to the administrative page URLs in web.xml as in Example 9-1.

Example 9-1. web.xml

```
...

<security-constraint>

  <web-resource-collection>
    <web-resource-name>
      JAW Application protected Admin pages.
    </web-resource-name>
    <description>Require users to authenticate.</description>
    <url-pattern>/admin/*</url-pattern>
  </web-resource-collection>

  <auth-constraint>
    <description>
      Allow Manager role to access Admin pages.
    </description>
    <role-name>Manager</role-name>
  </auth-constraint>

</security-constraint>

<security-role>
  <description>JAW Managers</description>
  <role-name>Manager</role-name>
</security-role>

...
```

The <security-constraint> element protects the administrative pages by specifying:

- A protected URL pattern for the admin pages, /admin/* —the protected JSPs reside in the web application's /admin directory.
- That only users who are in the Manager role can access the administrative page. This role must be specified in a separate <security-role> element.

To be complete, we've also modified the Controller Servlet in Example 9-2 to prefix all administrative pages with the admin/ URL.

Example 9-2. ControllerServlet.java

```java
public class ControllerServlet extends HttpServlet
{
    …

    protected void processRequest(HttpServletRequest request,
      HttpServletResponse response) throws ServletException, IOException {

        …
        // perform action
        …
        else if(MODIFY_CAR_LIST_ACTION.equals(actionName))
        {
            …
            destinationPage = "/admin/carList.jsp";
        }
        …

    }
}
```

What About Web-Based Programmatic Security?

The Servlet API enables you to go farther with security and add more fine-grained control to resources by using the following methods on HttpServletRequest:

- getRemoteUser( )
- isUserInRole( )
- getUserPrincipal( )

These methods determine the user's identity, or whether they play a particular role in the system. You also could write Servlet Filters that protect access to resources and determine if a user has logged in. Many developers write a LoginAction that checks the user's ID and password from a custom form.

Programmatic security is declining in popularity because it clutters your application with security-related calls. Declarative security handles the above scenarios on your behalf so you don't have to write so much code. Before using these API calls, see if J2EE Declarative Security can meet all or most of your needs.

But declarative security isn't a silver bullet that solves all your problems. What if you have a loan application in which loan officer X can approve loans up to only a certain amount? In this case, you'll have to add some code to enforce this business policy. Even if you really do need to use some form of programmatic security, starting with declarative security will reduce the complexity and the amount of code you write. But in practice, we've seen that declarative security usually satisfies our security needs.

We've protected the administrative pages' URLs so that only authenticated users can access these pages. We now have to choose an authentication method.

Web-Based Authentication

Authentication establishes the user's identity in the system. There are four methods of authentication:

HTTP Basic Authentication
> With HTTP Basic Authentication, the container asks for the user's name and password from a pop-up dialog box. The user information sent back to the server is not encrypted.

HTTP Digest Authentication
> HTTP Digest Authentication also uses a pop-up dialog, but the username and password are encrypted when sent to the HTTP server. Digest Authentication isn't widely used, and the Servlet 2.4 Specification doesn't require Servlet containers to implement it.

HTTPS Client (or Client-Cert) Authentication
> Client-Cert Authentication uses Secure Sockets Layer (SSL) Certificates, and the server determines whether the certificate from the client is valid.

Form-based Authentication
> When the user clicks on a protected page, she is redirected to an application-specific login page. If the user enters a valid user ID and password, she's allowed to access the protected resource(s). Otherwise, the user is redirected to a custom login error page.

What About Configuring SSL on JBoss?

Since JBoss uses Tomcat as its Servlet container, you are going to do the same type of setup that you have always done before. Go into the Tomcat SAR subdirectory of your server configuration's deployment directory—*$JBOSS_HOME/server/default/deploy/jbossweb-tomcat55.sar*. Edit the *server.xml* file and uncomment the <Connector> element for SSL that listens on port 8443. Then, use the Java keytool program to generate a certificate and copy it to your server configuration's conf directory—*$JBOSS_HOME/server/default/conf*.

Form-Based Authentication

We're using Form-based authentication because it is the most commonly used authentication technique and we want to use our own login page. Example 9-3 shows how we configure Form-based authentication in `web.xml`.

Example 9-3. web.xml

```
...
<login-config>
    <auth-method>FORM</auth-method>
```

Example 9-3. web.xml (continued)

```
    <realm-name>JawJaasDbRealm</realm-name>
    <form-login-config>
      <form-login-page>/login.jsp</form-login-page>
      <form-error-page>/loginError.jsp</form-error-page>
    </form-login-config>
  </login-config>
  …
```

The <realm-name> element specifies the name of our security realm, and its textual value, JawJaasDbRealm, *must* match the name of the security realm specified in the JBoss JAAS login configuration file. We'll see the login.jsp and loginerror.jsp pages in action in the "Testing Secure JSPs" section. For now, let's take a closer look at the login page.

The Login Form

Example 9-4 is an excerpt from the form in the login.jsp page.

Example 9-4. login.jsp

```
<form method="POST" action="j_security_check">
  <input type="text" name="j_username">
  <input type="password" name="j_password">
</form>
```

Form-based Authentication requires the following naming conventions on the login form:

- The user ID and password fields must be named j_username and j_password, respectively.

- The form must post the user login information to j_security_check.

- Everything else (the appearance and location of the login and error page) is under our control.

Automating Declarative Authentication and Authorization in web.xml

In web.xml, we had to add the <security-constraint>, <security-role>, and <login-config> elements to set up Form-based authentication, but XDoclet doesn't provide a way to generate these elements. We could've hardcoded these elements, but this wouldn't fit with our Ant-based build process. So we created an XDoclet merge file called web-security.xml that XDoclet merged in as it generated web.xml. You can find web-security.xml in the xdoclet/merge directory in the ch09-a project's webapp subproject that comes with the JAW Motors code distribution.

Creating a Security Realm

We're now going to create a security realm using database tables that associates a user with the roles he plays in the system. Table 9-1 shows the Users from the USER table.

Table 9-1. JAW Motors USER table

USER_ID	USER_NAME	PASSWORD
1	Fsmith	fred
2	Jjones	john

Table 9-2 shows the JAW Motors application's Roles in the ROLE table.

Table 9-2. JAW Motors ROLE table

ROLE_ID	ROLE_NAME
1	Manager

Now we need to specify the roles for each user in the system. Table 9-3 shows the USER_ROLE table that shows which roles a user has by joining the USER and ROLE tables.

Table 9-3. JAW Motors USER_ROLE table

USER_ID	ROLE_ID
1	1
2	1

When joined with the USER and ROLE tables, the data in the USER_ROLE table indicates that both users have the Manager role. You can find these new security-related tables in the ch09-a project's sql/build.xml file.

Now that we've set up declarative security and created a security realm, we need to deploy the security realm on JBoss. Before we can discuss web-based security any further, we need to cover core JAAS concepts because the JBoss security manager, JBoss Security Extension (JBossSX), is based on JAAS. After discussing the core JAAS API, we'll then get to the heart of JAAS-based security—the LoginModule.

JAAS

The Java Authentication & Authorization Service (JAAS) enables an application to protect its resources by restricting access to only those users with proper credentials and permissions. JAAS provides a layer of abstraction between an application and its underlying security mechanisms, making it easier to change security technologies and realms without impacting the rest of the system. JAAS is a standard Java extension in J2SE 1.4, and provides pluggable authentication to give application designers a wide choice of security realms:

- DBMS
- Application Server
- LDAP
- Operating System (UNIX or Windows NT/2000)
- File System
- JNDI
- Biometrics

JAAS supports single sign-on for an application. Rather than forcing the user to log in to a web site, and then log in again to a forum or a backend legacy system used by the application, JAAS wraps all of this in one central login event to make it easier to coordinate access to all systems that the user needs. We chose JAAS as the basis for our security strategy because:

- It provides a security context that covers the entire J2EE architecture from the web tier to the EJB tier.
- It is application server neutral.
- It integrates with the Java 2 security model.
- It is part of the J2SE 1.4 extension API.
- It is more sophisticated than the other authentication mechanisms and provides more functionality.
- It supports single sign-on by coordinating multiple security realms.
- It addresses authorization in addition to authentication.
- It provides good encapsulation for authentication and authorization, enabling an application to be independent of the underlying security mechanisms used.
- JBoss bases its security mechanism on JAAS.

Although this isn't a JAAS book, we've added more detailed information on JAAS in Appendix C—JAAS Tutorial.

LoginModule

The LoginModule logs a user/Subject into a security realm based on their username and password. A LoginModule could interact with an operating system, a database, JNDI, LDAP, or a biometric device like a retinal scanner or touch pad. Application developers normally don't need to know very much about LoginModules because the LoginContext invokes them on behalf of an application. So your code never interacts with LoginModules. To add or remove a LoginModule used by your application, you need to modify only the LoginModule Configuration file—your code remains unchanged. This indirection enables an application to be independent of the underlying security mechanisms used

Although you could write your own `LoginModule`, it is usually unnecessary because of the abundance of quality third-party Open Source implementations available. You only need to know how to configure (in the `LoginModule` Configuration file) and deploy them for your particular runtime environment. If the Open Source `LoginModule` implementations don't provide all the functionality you need, you can either modify the code from that library or write your own `LoginModule`. Since this topic is outside the scope of this book, please see the JAAS `LoginModule` Developers' Guide (*http://java.sun. com/j2se/1.4.2/docs/guide/security/jaas/JAASLMDevGuide.html*) for further details. Here are some freely available `LoginModules`:

Tagish

Tagish has a set of Open Source JAAS `LoginModules` released under the GNU LGPL (Lesser GNU Public License) that can be found at *http://free.tagish.net/ jaas*. The Tagish collection has the following `LoginModules`:

- DBMS
- File System
- Windows NT/2000 domain

Sun Microsystems

Sun bundles several `LoginModules` with J2SE 1.4. However, they are in the `com. sun.security.auth.module` package and not officially part of J2SE 1.4 because they're Sun's implementation of the JAAS interfaces. Sun provides the following `LoginModules`:

- Kerberos
- Key Store
- JNDI
- Windows NT
- UNIX

JBoss

JBoss provides several `LoginModules` with its distribution, including:

- DBMS
- File-based
- Key Store
- LDAP
- External Client

We could easily configure the Tagish, Sun, or JBoss `LoginModules` and use them with the JAW Motors application. We chose the JBoss `LoginModules` because they're already bundled with JBoss and we don't need to configure any third party JARs.

Even though we're using `LoginModules` provided by JBoss, the application code remains vendor-neutral because:

- The `LoginModules` are configured in an external configuration file.
- The application code doesn't change if you use different `LoginModules`.

Deploying a JAAS-Based Security Realm on JBoss

There is no standard for integrating JAAS deployment with a J2EE application server, so each server has its own way to set up `LoginModule` configuration and domain names. So, we need to:

- Configure the `LoginModule`.
- Add the `LoginModule`'s security domain name to `jboss-web.xml`.

JBoss LoginModule Configuration

To Configure a `LoginModule` in JBoss, you have a couple of options.

- Add the `LoginModule` configuration data to the JBoss default `$JBOSS_DIST/server/default/conf/login-config.xml`.
- Create your own custom `LoginModule` configuration file in `$JBOSS_DIST/server/default/conf` that has the same structure as `login-config.xml` and conforms to the `security_config.dtd`.

Custom LoginModule Configuration

We chose to create our own separate LoginModule Configuration file, `jaw-login-config.xml`, because we didn't want to co-mingle our application-specific JAAS LoginModule configuration with JBoss-internal `LoginModule` settings. Co-mingling `LoginModule` settings is bad because each time you upgrade to a new version of JBoss, you have to re-add your `<application-policy>` elements to the default `login-config.xml` file to make things work again. To deploy the LoginModule configuration file to JBoss, the Ant build script copies the `jaw-login-config.xml` file from the `ch09-a/src/META-INF` directory to the JBoss configuration directory—`$JBOSS_HOME/server/default/conf`. The `jaw-login-config.xml` file in Example 9-5 looks just like the JBoss default `login-config.xml`, but our file contains only application-specific `<application-policy>` elements.

Example 9-5. jaw-login-config.xml

```
<?xml version='1.0'?>
<!DOCTYPE policy PUBLIC
        "-//JBoss//DTD JBOSS Security Config 3.0//EN"
        "http://www.jboss.org/j2ee/dtd/security_config.dtd">
```

Example 9-5. jaw-login-config.xml (continued)

```
<policy>

  <application-policy name = "JawJaasDbRealm">
    <authentication>
      <login-module code = "org.jboss.security.auth.spi.DatabaseServerLoginModule"
                     flag = "required">
        <module-option name="unauthenticatedIdentity">guest</module-option>
        <module-option name="password-stacking">useFirstPass</module-option>
        <module-option name="dsJndiName">java:/JBossAtWorkDS</module-option>
        <module-option name="principalsQuery">SELECT PASSWORD FROM USER WHERE NAME=?
        </module-option>
        <module-option name="rolesQuery">SELECT ROLE.NAME, 'Roles' FROM ROLE,
USER_ROLE, USER WHERE USER.NAME=? AND USER.ID=USER_ROLE.USER_ID AND ROLE.ID =
USER_ROLE.USER_ID</module-option>
      </login-module>
    </authentication>
  </application-policy>

</policy>
```

JBoss uses an MBean that reads the *$JBOSS_HOME/server/default/conf/jaw-login-config.xml* file at startup time to configure its security domains. Each <application-policy> element configures a LoginModule for a security realm. The name attribute sets the JAAS application name to "JawJaasDbRealm". The <login-module> element configures the JBoss-specific DatabaseServerLoginModule to query the USER and ROLE tables in the JAW Motors database to authenticate the user. The <login-module> element's flag attribute is set to required because we don't want to allow the user to access sensitive portions of the JAW Motors application unless she successfully logs on to all the security realms.

The <module-option> elements for the DatabaseServerLoginModule specify LoginModule options (JAAS-speak for initialization parameters):

unauthenticatedIdentity
> The default username assigned when no authentication information is supplied. A common use for this option is when you access an unsecured EJB or an EJB method that isn't associated with a security role. We'll see how it works when we add in EJB-based security toward the end of the chapter.

password-stacking
> If this value is set to useFirstPass, and a previous LoginModule has already established the user ID and password, then the DatabaseServerLoginModule does nothing. Otherwise, the DatabaseServerLoginModule looks in the database to find the user ID and password.

dsJndiName
> The JBoss-specific JNDI name for a database's DataSource.

principalsQuery

> This is a SQL query that selects a user's password from the JAW Motors database.

rolesQuery

> This is a SQL query that selects a user's roles from the JAW Motors database. The second column, set to the constant string "Roles," is mandatory—if it's not part of the query, the DatabaseServerLoginModule fails. The LoginModule uses the "Roles" column internally.

Since the JAW Motor's application-specific LoginModule configuration file is not part of the default JBoss setup anymore, we need to tell JBoss to load this file at startup time. To do this, we create a JMX MBean defined in a service file—jaw-login-config-service.xml (see Example 9-6).

Example 9-6. jaw-login-config-service.xml

```
<?xml version="1.0" encoding="UTF-8"?>
<!DOCTYPE server>

<server>
   <mbean code="org.jboss.security.auth.login.DynamicLoginConfig"
          name="jboss:service=DynamicLoginConfig">
      <attribute name="AuthConfig">jaw-login-config.xml</attribute>
      <depends optional-attribute-name="LoginConfigService">
         jboss.security:service=XMLLoginConfig
      </depends>
      <depends optional-attribute-name="SecurityManagerService">
         jboss.security:service=JaasSecurityManager
      </depends>
   </mbean>
</server>
```

This service file, courtesy of the JBoss Wiki, configures the DynamicLoginConfig MBean so it uses the JBoss XMLLoginConfig MBean to read the application-specific jaw-login-config.xml and configure our LoginModule. If the DynamicLoginConfig MBean is stopped, the JaasSecurityManager MBean logs out all the LoginModule's users by cleaning out all Subjects (users) and Principals (roles) set by the LoginModule(s) configured in our LoginModule configuration file. For more information on the DynamicLoginConfig MBean, visit the JBoss Wiki at: *http://wiki.jboss.org/wiki/Wiki.jsp?page=DynamicLoginConfig*.

To deploy the MBean service file to JBoss, the Ant build script copies the *jaw-login-config-service.xml* file from the *ch09-a/src/META-INF* directory to the JBoss deployment directory—*$JBOSS_HOME/server/default/deploy*.

JAAS Domain Settings in jboss-web.xml

The security domain in jboss-web.xml defines a security domain used by all web components in the application. Later in the chapter we'll extend the security domain to protect the entire application by including EJBs, but we don't have to worry about that right now. The ‹security-domain› element used in the JBoss-specific jboss-web.xml deployment descriptor must match the "JawJaasDbRealm" JAAS application name from login-config.xml. The ‹security-domain› element comes before the elements that define the JNDI-based resources. Here's the ‹security-domain› element in jboss-web.xml (Example 9-7).

Example 9-7. jboss-web.xml

```
<jboss-web>
    <security-domain>java:/jaas/JawJaasDbRealm</security-domain>
    …
</jboss-web>
```

The ‹security-domain› uses java:/jaas/JawJaasDbRealm because it is the JBoss-specific JNDI name used in jaw-login-config.xml when JBoss deploys the LoginModule as a managed service. The pattern here is that JBoss prefixes its JAAS JNDI names with java:/jaas.

Automating JAAS Domain Settings in jboss-web.xml

If you'll recall from the Web chapter, we used XDoclet's Ant ‹webdoclet› task and its ‹jbosswebxml› subtask to respectively generate the J2EE standard web.xml and jboss-web.xml JBoss-specific EJB deployment descriptors. We now add a securitydomain attribute to the ‹jbosswebxml› subtask in the webapp sub-project's build.xml (Example 9-8) to generate the ‹security-domain› element in jboss-web.xml.

Example 9-8. webapp/build.xml

```
    …
    <webdoclet>
        …
        <jbosswebxml version="4.0" destdir="${gen.source.dir}"
                    securitydomain="java:/jaas/JawJaasDbRealm"/>

    </webdoclet>
    …
```

Testing Secure JSPs

We've taken a lot of steps to get here, but we're now ready to take our new secure web site for a test drive. First, let's try to access one of the protected JSPs directly. Here are the steps to build and deploy the application:

- Type ant in the root directory of ch09-a to build the project.
- Shut down JBoss so the Ant script can clean up the JBoss deployment area.

- Type ant colddeploy to deploy the EAR file (jaw.ear) to the *$JBOSS_HOME/server/default/deploy* directory. The Ant build script also deploys:
  - The MBean service file (jaw-login-config-service.xml, which tells JBoss that we're using our own LoginModule Configuration file) to the *$JBOSS_HOME/server/default/deploy* directory.
  - The LoginModule Configuration file (jaw-login-config.xml) to the *$JBOSS_HOME/server/default/conf* directory.
- Start JBoss back up.
- Go to the *ch09-a/sql* sub-directory and type ant to modify the database.
- Visit *http://localhost:8080/jaw/admin/carList.jsp* in a web browser.

The Servlet container should re-direct you to the login page and you'll see the login page, /login.jsp, as shown in Figure 9-3.

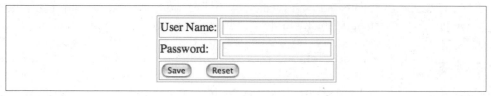

Figure 9-3. JAW Motors Login page

When the user presses the "Save" button, the browser sends the user ID and password to the Servlet Container, which validates the user's credentials against a security realm. If the user logs in successfully, the Servlet container takes him to the "Car Inventory" page. You'll notice that no cars are displayed because we bypassed the Controller Servlet that pulls the cars from the database before rendering the page. Otherwise, the container sends the user to the login error page, /loginError.jsp as depicted in Figure 9-4.

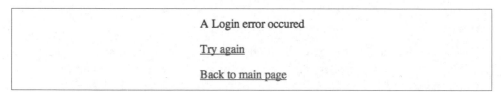

Figure 9-4. JAW Motors Login Error page

The user can either return to the login page to try another user I and password or go back to the JAW Motors home page.

We have now successfully locked down the administrative pages, but this isn't good enough. Now exit the browser (to end your session) and re-start your browser. Try to use the JAW Motors web site by visiting the home page: *http://localhost:8080/jaw*, as shown in Figure 9-5.

JAW Motors

Modify Inventory
View Inventory
Run Credit Check

Figure 9-5. JAW Motors Home page

The "View Inventory" link is new and takes you to a read-only version of the JAW Motors Inventory page. Think of the new link and page as you would a control group for an experiment. We want to make sure that the non-secure pages remain accessible without logging in, and that the secure pages require you to log in before reaching them.

Use the site like you normally would, and don't circumvent the Controller with direct URLs to the protected pages. Click on the "Modify Inventory" link from the home page, and you'll go directly to the Car Inventory page where you can add, edit, or delete cars in the inventory. You've just bypassed all the security we've added. At this point, you may wonder why we bothered with the extra infrastructure if we're still unprotected. What went wrong? The JAW Motors web site doesn't only consist of raw JSPs—it uses an MVC framework to control page flow. We have more work to do—we need to protect the URLs for administrative actions that enable the user to add, edit, or delete cars.

Protecting the Administrative Actions

We can continue to use J2EE Declarative Security, as shown earlier, to protect the administrative actions like modifyCarList, addCar. To lock down the administrative actions, we'll take steps similar to those we used to protect the JSPs:

- Associate the administrative actions with an URL pattern.
- Protect the new administrative action URL pattern.

To associate the admin actions with an URL pattern, we prefix them with admin/ in the JSPs and in the Controller Servlet. For example, index.jsp (the main page) now invokes the modifyCarList action through the Controller Servlet, as in Example 9-9.

Example 9-9. index.jsp

```
<html>
  <head>
    …
  </head>
  <body>
    <h1>JAW Motors</h1>
    <a href="controller/admin/modifyCarList">Modify Inventory</a><br/>
    <a href="controller/viewCarList">View Inventory</a><br/>
```

Example 9-9. index.jsp (continued)

```
    <a href="controller/viewCreditCheckForm">Run Credit Check</a>
  </body>
</html>
```

The viewCarList action takes you to a read-only page, so it doesn't need any extra security. To fully protect the administrative action URLs, we add a new <url-pattern> to web.xml so that it now looks like Example 9-10.

Example 9-10. web.xml

```
    <security-constraint>
    <web-resource-collection>
      <web-resource-name>
        JAW Application protected Admin pages and actions.
      </web-resource-name>
      <description>Require users to authenticate.</description>
      <url-pattern>/admin/*</url-pattern>
      <url-pattern>/controller/admin/*</url-pattern>
    </web-resource-collection>

    <auth-constraint>
      <description>
        Allow Manager role to access Admin pages.
      </description>
      <role-name>Manager</role-name>
    </auth-constraint>

  </security-constraint>
  <security-role>
    <description>JAW Managers</description>
    <role-name>Manager</role-name>
  </security-role>

  …
```

The new /controller/admin/* <url-pattern> (a sub-element of <web-resource-collection>) finally gives us what we want—it forces the user to log in before accessing secure actions. As before, we add this new <url-pattern> element to the webapp/xdoclet/merge/web-security.xml file, and XDoclet adds the new security to web.xml on our behalf.

Are We Done with Web Security Yet?

At this point, we've secured the web tier and could start testing. But as you'll see in the next section, we need to associate security roles with both secure and non-secure action URL patterns to propagate security credentials from the web tier to the EJB tier. We could have added these modifications later, but we wanted to finish configuring web security before dealing with EJBs.

Propagating Security Credentials from the Web Tier

Specifying an identity for an URL pattern ensures that the Servlet container automatically propagates the correct role to the EJB container when accessing EJB methods. The EJB Security section covers security roles and EJB methods in greater detail. The J2EE specification does not state what happens if the web tier does not establish a user's credentials before calling an EJB, so the JBoss `LoginModules` enable you to provide a default user identity so calls to unsecured EJB methods succeed if the user hasn't logged in. Recall from the `login-config.xml` section that we've set up the JBoss `LoginModules` with an unauthenticated identity called "guest". Example 9-11 shows the changes we made to `web.xml`.

Example 9-11. web.xml

```
<servlet>
  <servlet-name>SecureController</servlet-name>
  <servlet-class>com.jbossatwork.ControllerServlet</servlet-class>
</servlet>

<servlet>
  <servlet-name>NonsecureController</servlet-name>
  <servlet-class>com.jbossatwork.ControllerServlet</servlet-class>

  <run-as>
    <role-name>guest</role-name>
  </run-as>
</servlet>

<servlet-mapping>
  <servlet-name>NonsecureController</servlet-name>
  <url-pattern>/controller/*</url-pattern>
</servlet-mapping>

<servlet-mapping>
  <servlet-name>SecureController</servlet-name>
    <url-pattern>/controller/admin/*</url-pattern>
</servlet-mapping>

...
```

The new `<servlet-mapping>` elements for the Controller Servlet ensure that:

- Any secure page or action (under the `/controller/admin/*` URL pattern) runs as an authorized user role—`Manager`.

- Any non-secure page or action (under the `/controller/*` URL pattern) runs as the unauthenticated guest user identity.

Automating Security Credential Propagation in web.xml

In web.xml, we had to modify the <servlet> and <servlet-mapping> elements to propagate the correct credentials from the Controller Servlet. Thus we modified the XDoclet tags in the Controller Servlet (Example 9-12) to generate the mapping for the SecureController and /controller/admin/* <url-pattern>.

Example 9-12. ControllerServlet.java

```
/**
 * @web.servlet
 *   name="SecureController"
 *
 * @web.servlet-mapping
 *   url-pattern="/controller/admin/*"
 *
 * …
 */
public class ControllerServlet extends HttpServlet {
    …
}
```

We also added a new <servlet-mapping> element to web.xml for non-secure URL action patterns (NonSecureServlet). However, XDoclet doesn't provide a way to generate more than one set of these elements for a Servlet. We could have hardcoded these elements in web.xml, but this wouldn't fit with our Ant-based build process. So we created XDoclet merge files called servlets.xml and servlet-mappings.xml files that contain the extra settings, and XDoclet merges them in as it generates web.xml. You can find these files in the xdoclet/merge directory in the ch09-b project's webapp sub-project.

Testing Web Security

Now that we've locked down the administrative portions of the web site, let's test our application to ensure that everything still works properly. Here are the steps to build and deploy the application:

- Type ant in the root directory of ch09-b to build the project.
- Shut down JBoss so the Ant script can clean up the JBoss deployment area.
    - Type ant colddeploy to deploy the EAR file (jaw.ear) to the *$JBOSS_HOME/ server/default/deploy* directory.
- Start JBoss back up.
- Visit *http://localhost:8080/jaw* in a web browser.

As advertised, clinking on the "View Inventory" link on the JAW Motors home page takes you to a read-only version of the JAW Motors Inventory page that doesn't require you to log in first. Clicking on the "Modify Inventory" link now takes you to the login page, and you have to enter a valid user ID and password to gain access. After you log in successfully, the Servlet container takes you to the Modify Inventory page. JBoss remembers your security credentials, so once you've logged in, you don't have to re-login each time you try to access a secure action or page. Go ahead and try to add, edit, or delete a car, and you'll see that everything works properly. The big difference is that now you can access these pages and actions only *after* you've logged into the system.

Web Security Checklist

Before we move on to securing the EJB tier, let's recap what we've done so far:

- Protected the administrative pages by:
  - Restricting access based on the /admin/* URL pattern in web.xml
  - Associating security roles with the /admin/* URL pattern in web.xml
  - Moving the administrative pages beneath the /admin sub-directory in WEB INF
  - Creating security roles for the JAW Motors application in web.xml
- Implemented FORM-based Authentication by:
  - Adding a <login-config> element to web.xml and tying it to a security realm
  - Creating a login page, login.jsp with a form that follows FORM-based Authentication naming conventions
  - Developing a login error page—loginerror.jsp
- Automated extra web.xml settings with the servlets.xml, servlet-mappings.xml, and web-security.xml XDoclet merge files
- Created a security realm in the JAW Motors database that associates a user with the roles they play in the system
- Deployed the JAAS-based security realm with the JBoss container by:
  - Configuring a JAAS LoginModule that's tied to the database security realm using $JBOSS_HOME/server/default/conf/jaw-login-config.xml and $JBOSS_HOME/server/default/deploy/jaw-login-config-service.xml
  - Adding the JAAS domain settings to jboss-web.xml
- Added a read-only page and MVC action to ensure that we can still access non-secure resources without logging in
- Protected MV administrative actions by:
  - Modifying JSPs and the Controller Servlet to prefix all administrative action URLs with /admin/
  - Modifying web.xml with the new /controller/admin/* <url-pattern> element to lock down the administrative action URLs

- Propagated the correct user credentials from the web tier:
  - Established a default guest user identity for non-secure actions and pages in web.xml
  - Used the Manager identity for secure actions and pages in web.xml

Integrating Web Tier and EJB Tier Security

It's taken a while to get here, but now that we've secured the web tier, we have the core infrastructure in place to secure the rest of the JAW Motors application. Although we've protected access to the InventoryFacadeBean EJB through the Controller Servlet in the web application, the EJB is still vulnerable. Unauthenticated/ unauthorized external applications could look up the InventoryFacadeBean and access its administrative methods—saveCars( ) and deleteCars( ). We must protect the EJB tier by securing the administrative methods on the InventoryFacadeBean, yet still allow non-secure access to the non-administrative methods— listAvailableCars( ), findCar( ), and buyCar( ). We'll show how the JBoss security manager, in keeping with the J2EE specification, propagates the user's credentials from the web tier to the EJB container. We now discuss EJB security in greater detail.

EJB Security

To secure the EJB tier, we need to do the following:

- Deploy the JAAS-based security realm with the JBoss container.
- Protect the EJB:
  - Allow access to non-secure methods.
  - Configure access to administrative methods.
  - Add security roles.
- Automate extra ejb-jar.xml settings with XDoclet.

JAAS Domain in jboss.xml

The security domain in jboss.xml defines a security domain used by all EJBs in the application. To join the global security domain for the entire JAW Motors application, the security domain must match the "JawJaasDbRealm" JAAS application name from login-config.xml and the <security-domain> element in jboss-web.xml. The <security-domain> element defines a single security domain used by all EJBs in the application. The <security-domain> element comes before the elements that define the JNDI-based resources. Example 9-13 shows the <security-domain> element in jboss.xml.

Example 9-13. jboss.xml

```
<jboss>
    <security-domain>java:/jaas/JawJaasDbRealm</security-domain>
    …
</jboss>
```

The `<security-domain>` uses `java:/jaas/JawJaasDbRealm` because it is the JBoss-specific JNDI name used when JBoss deploys the `LoginModule` as a managed service. The pattern here is that JBoss prefixes its JAAS JNDI names with `java:/jaas`.

Automating JAAS Domain Settings in jboss.xml

If you recall from the Session Bean chapter, we used XDoclet's Ant `<ejbdoclet>` task and its `<jboss>` subtask to generate the J2EE standard `ejb-jar.xml` and `jboss.xml` JBoss-specific EJB deployment descriptors, respectively. We now add a securitydomain attribute to the `<jboss>` subtask in the ejb sub-project's `build.xml` (Example 9-14) to generate the `<security-domain>` element in `jboss.xml`.

Example 9-14. ejb/build.xml

```
    …
    <ejbdoclet>
        …
        <jboss version="4.0" destdir="${gen.source.dir}"
               securitydomain="java:/jaas/JawJaasDbRealm"/>

    </ejbdoclet>
    …
```

Protecting EJBs with ejb-jar.xml

J2EE provides Declarative Security, so we modify `ejb-jar.xml` in Example 9-15 to configure EJB security.

Example 9-15. ejb-jar.xml

```
<enterprise-beans>

    <session>
        …
        <ejb-name>InventoryFacade</ejb-name>
        …
    </session>
    …
</enterprise-beans>
…
 <!-- Assembly Descriptor -->
   <assembly-descriptor>

    <security-role>
      <role-name>Manager</role-name>
    </security-role>
```

Example 9-15. ejb-jar.xml (continued)

```
<security-role>
  <role-name>guest</role-name>
</security-role>

...

<method-permission>
  <role-name>guest</role-name>
  <role-name>Manager</role-name>
  <method>
    <ejb-name>InventoryFacade</ejb-name>
    <method-intf>Local</method-intf>
    <method-name>create</method-name>
    <method-params>
    </method-params>
  </method>
</method-permission>

<method-permission>
  <role-name>guest</role-name>
  <role-name>Manager</role-name>
  <method>
    <ejb-name>InventoryFacade</ejb-name>
    <method-intf>Remote</method-intf>
    <method-name>create</method-name>
    <method-params>
    </method-params>
  </method>
</method-permission>

<method-permission>
  <role name>guest</role-name>
  <role-name>Manager</role-name>
  <method>
    <ejb-name>InventoryFacade</ejb-name>
    <method-intf>Local</method-intf>
    <method-name>listAvailableCars</method-name>
    <method-params>
    </method-params>
  </method>
</method-permission>

<method-permission>
  <role-name>guest</role-name>
  <role-name>Manager</role-name>
  <method>
    <ejb-name>InventoryFacade</ejb-name>
    <method-intf>Remote</method-intf>
    <method-name>listAvailableCars</method-name>
    <method-params>
    </method-params>
  </method>
</method-permission>
```

Example 9-15. ejb-jar.xml (continued)

```
    <method-permission>
      <role-name>guest</role-name>
      <role-name>Manager</role-name>
      <method>
        <ejb-name>InventoryFacade</ejb-name>
        <method-intf>Local</method-intf>
        <method-name>findCar</method-name>
        <method-params>
            <method-param>int</method-param>
        </method-params>
      </method>
    </method-permission>

    <method-permission>
      <role-name>guest</role-name>
      <role-name>Manager</role-name>
      <method>
        <ejb-name>InventoryFacade</ejb-name>
        <method-intf>Remote</method-intf>
        <method-name>findCar</method-name>
        <method-params>
            <method-param>int</method-param>
        </method-params>
      </method>
    </method-permission>

    <method-permission>
      <role-name>Manager</role-name>
      <method>
        <ejb-name>InventoryFacade</ejb-name>
        <method-intf>Local</method-intf>
        <method-name>deleteCars</method-name>
        <method-params>
            <method-param>java.lang.String[ ]</method-param>
        </method-params>
      </method>
    </method-permission>
    <method-permission>
      <role-name>Manager</role-name>
      <method>
        <ejb-name>InventoryFacade</ejb-name>
        <method-intf>Remote</method-intf>
        <method-name>deleteCars</method-name>
        <method-params>
            <method-param>java.lang.String[ ]</method-param>
        </method-params>
      </method>
    </method-permission>

    <method-permission>
      <role-name>Manager</role-name>
      <method>
        <ejb-name>InventoryFacade</ejb-name>
```

Example 9-15. ejb-jar.xml (continued)

```
          <method-intf>Local</method-intf>
          <method-name>saveCar</method-name>
          <method-params>
              <method-param> com.jbossatwork.dto.CarDTO</method-param>
          </method-params>
        </method>
    </method-permission>

    <method-permission>
      <role-name>Manager</role-name>
      <method>
        <ejb-name>InventoryFacade</ejb-name>
        <method-intf>Remote</method-intf>
        <method-name>saveCar</method-name>
        <method-params>
            <method-param>com.jbossatwork.dto.CarDTO</method-param>
        </method-params>
      </method>
    </method-permission>

    <method-permission>
      <role-name>guest</role-name>
      <role-name>Manager</role-name>
      <method>
        <ejb-name>InventoryFacade</ejb-name>
        <method-intf>Local</method-intf>
        <method-name>buyCar</method-name>
        <method-params>
            <method-param>int</method-param>
            <method-param>double</method-param>>
        </method-params>
      </method>
    </method-permission>

    <method-permission>
      <role-name>guest</role-name>
      <role-name>Manager</role-name>
      <method>
        <ejb-name>InventoryFacade</ejb-name>
        <method-intf>Remote</method-intf>
        <method-name>buyCar</method-name>
        <method-params>
            <method-param>int</method-param>
            <method-param>double</method-param>
        </method-params>
      </method>
    </method-permission>

    ...

</assembly-descriptor>
```

As we did in `web.xml`, we're creating `<security-role>` elements for the guest and Manager security roles in the JAW Motors application. The `<security-role-ref>` elements define the security roles (guest, Manager) for the `InventoryFacade` Bean. The `<method-permission>` elements specify that:

- Only users with the (unauthenticated) guest or (authenticated and authorized) Manager roles can invoke the non-secure `create()`, `listAvailableCars()`, `findCar()`, and `buyCar()` methods when using the Remote and Local Component Interface.

- Only users with the (authorized) Manager roles can invoke the administrative/ secure `deleteCars()` and `saveCar()` method when using the Remote and Local Component Interface.

These security settings in `ejb-jar.xml` ensure that someone with the Manager role has full access to both the secure and non-secure methods in `InventoryFacadeBean`, and that a guest user can only create the EJB and access its non-secure methods.

What About EJB-Based Programmatic Security?

The EJB API enables you to go farther with security and add more fine-grained control to resources that use the following methods on javax.ejb.EJBContext:

- `isCallerInRole()`
- `getCallerPrincipal()`

These methods determine the caller's identity or whether she plays a particular role in the system.

We don't want to use Programmatic Security in the EJB Tier for the same reasons why we didn't use it in the Web Tier. We'd rather let the container do the work so we can avoid writing our own infrastructure.

Automating EJB Security Settings with XDoclet

We already have an Ant-based build process that works with XDoclet, so we just have to add a couple of XDoclet tags to the `InventoryFacadeBean` in Example 9-16 so the Ant build process generates the new security settings in the `ejb-jar.xml` J2EE standard EJB deployment descriptor.

Example 9-16. InventoryFacadeBean.java

```
/**
 * …
 *
 * @ejb.security-role-ref
 *   role-name="Manager"
```

Example 9-16. InventoryFacadeBean.java (continued)

```
 *  role-link="Manager"
 *
 * @ejb.security-role-ref
 *  role-name="guest"
 *  role-link="guest"
 */
public class InventoryFacadeBean implements SessionBean {
    …

    /**
     * @ejb.create-method
     * @ejb.permission
     *  role-name="guest,Manager"
     *
     */
    public void ejbCreate( ) throws CreateException {}

    …

    /**
     * …
     * @ejb.permission
     *  role-name="guest,Manager"
     *
     */
    public List listAvailableCars( ) throws EJBException {
        …
    }
    …

    /**
     * …
     * @ejb.permission
     *  role-name="guest,Manager"
     *
     */
    public CarDTO findCar(int id) throws EJBException {
        …
    }

    /**
     * …
     * @ejb.permission
     *  role-name="Manager"
     *
     */
    public void deleteCars(String[ ] ids) throws EJBException {
        …
    }

    /**
     * …
```

Example 9-16. InventoryFacadeBean.java (continued)

```
 * @ejb.permission
 *  role-name="Manager"
 *
 */
public void saveCar(CarDTO car) throws EJBException {
    …
}

/**
 * …
 * @ejb.permission
 *  role-name="guest,Manager"
 *
 */
public void buyCar(int carId, double price) throws EJBException {
    …
}

}
```

The class-level @ejb.security-role-ref XDoclet tags associate the InventoryFacade
Bean with the Manager security role. The @ejb.permission tag on the ejbCreate( ),
listAvailableCars( ), findCar( ), and buyCar( ) methods makes them accessible only
to users in the guest and Manager roles. The @ejb.permission tag on the deleteCars( )
and saveCar( ) methods makes them accessible only to users in the Manager role.

Testing Secure EJB Methods

Now that we've propagated the correct user credentials and restricted access to the
InventoryFacadeBean's secure methods, let's test our application to ensure that everything still works properly. Here are the steps you should follow to build and deploy
the application:

- Type ant in the root directory of ch09-c to build the project.
- Shut down JBoss so the Ant script can clean up the JBoss deployment area.
- Type ant colddeploy to deploy the EAR file (jaw.ear) to the *$JBOSS_HOME/
  server/default/deploy* directory.
- Start JBoss back up.
- Visit *http://localhost:8080/jaw* in a web browser.

Click on the "Modify Inventory" link on the JAW Motors home page and everything
should work properly.

EJB Security Checklist

To secure the EJB tier, we did the following:

- Deployed the JAAS-based security realm with the JBoss container.
- Protected the EJB in `ejb-jar.xml`:
  - Added security roles.
  - Allowed callers with the unauthenticated guest or authorized `Manager` role to access non-secure methods.
  - Restricted access to administrative methods to users in the `Manager` role.
- Automated extra `ejb-jar.xml` settings with XDoclet.

Looking Ahead...

In this chapter, we secured the "Car Inventory" and "Add/Edit Car" pages so that only authorized users can modify cars in the inventory. We discussed J2EE web-based security, JAAS, and EJB security. Along the way, we showed how to deploy these security mechanisms on JBoss.

We've developed and secured the JAW Motors application. In the next and final chapter, we'll show how to expose a portion of the application as a Web service.

CHAPTER 10

Web Services

JAW Motors has a fully functional, secure J2EE-based web site and the business is doing well. Harry Schmidlap, the company President, now wants to expand JAW Motors' business beyond the web site and boost sales by displaying its inventory on other related web sites. Another company, Virtual Big Auto Dealership (VBAD), has a high-traffic web site that consolidates the inventory of many auto dealerships. Thousands of customers use VBAD's service to find and purchase cars. Mr. Schmidlap views VBAD as an ideal trading partner due to the sheer volume of potential new customers they could bring to JAW Motors.

One problem currently prevents JAW Motors from sharing its inventory—VBAD doesn't use J2EE. So none of the technologies we've shown so far will enable JAW Motors and VBAD to communicate. But VBAD has an experienced IS staff and knows how to use Web Services. Mr. Schmidlap has instructed Gunther Toady (with apologies to the restaurant chain and the cast of "Car 54, Where are You?"), the JAW Motors CTO, to look into Web Services and report back to the Board of Directors within two weeks with his results and findings.

This chapter shows how to deploy a portion of the JAW Motors application as a Web Service so it can work with non-Java clients. We'll show how to expose an EJB as a Web Service by using XDoclet and Java Web Services Developer Pack (JWSDP) to deploy it on JBoss. We'll finish by writing an Axis client that uses/consumes our Web Service.

Although we're going to show all deployment descriptors, including the WSDL, we're not covering them in any depth because our focus is on how to deploy a J2EE-based Web Service. We recommend J2EE Web Services by Richard Monson-Haefel, if you want to know the gory details of WSDL and you'd like a detailed description of all the elements in the Web Service deployment descriptors.

Web Services Architecture

Figure 10-1 shows how the VBAD client uses Web Services to access the JAW Motors inventory.

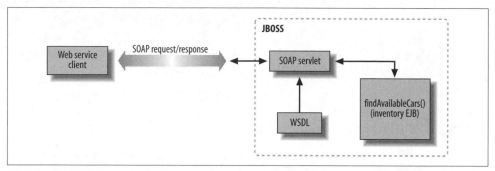

Figure 10-1. Web Service invocation

VBAD's web site acts as an external client that invokes the JAW Motors findAvailableCars( ) Web Service to get information about all JAW Motors cars. Underneath the covers, the client uses a Web Service proxy object to marshal the method findAvailableCars( ) call as a Simple Object Access Protocol (SOAP) Request and sends it to the JBoss application server. The SOAP Servlet picks up the SOAP Request, looks up the findAvailableCars service in the Web Services Definition Language (WSDL) file and invokes the findAvailableCars( ) method on behalf of the client. The findAvailableCars( ) method finds all unsold cars in the JAW Motors database, packages them into CarDTO objects, and returns control to the SOAP Servlet. The SOAP Servlet then marshals the CarDTO objects into a SOAP Response and returns it to the caller. On the client side, the Web Service proxy object unmarshals the SOAP Response into CarDTO objects to be displayed on the VBAD web site.

Web Services has its own terminology, so let's wade through the alphabet soup:

SOAP
> SOAP is an XML-based, platform-neutral, wire protocol that enables remote communication. Client and server communicate using SOAP Messages that contain a Header and a Body. The Header has routing information and the Body holds the request/response data.

WSDL
> WSDL is an XML-based interface descriptor that describes a web service interface along with its parameters. WSDL registers your Web Service with your server in the same way web.xml registers Servlets and ejb-jar.xml registers EJBs.

Web Service Proxy

A Web Service Proxy is a set of objects that work together to encapsulate low-level SOAP communication details and invokes a Web Service on behalf of a client. The client just uses the Web Service proxy and is oblivious to the low-level network API. SOAP toolkits are available for most programming languages that use the WSDL (for the Web Service) to generate Web Service proxy code for that language.

SOAP Servlet

As of J2EE 1.4, most application servers use a Servlet to listen for SOAP Requests, route them to a Web Service, and return the result(s) as a SOAP Response.

JBoss 4.x and Web Services

In previous versions of JBoss (pre 4.x), developers deployed Web Services by using a JBoss-specific tool called JBoss.NET (not to be confused with Microsoft .NET). Although JBoss.Net worked well and provided a highly automated way to create Web Services on JBoss, it was proprietary technology. In JBoss 4.x, JBoss.Net is deprecated in favor of JBossWS, JBoss's new J2EE 1.4-compliant Web Service implementation. JBossWS is based on Apache Axis (*http://ws.apache.org/axis*) and uses J2EE standard deployment descriptors and technologies.

JBoss and Web Services Issues

Bugs are a fact of life, and even though JBoss is an excellent product, JBoss 4.0.0 and 4.0.1 have problems deploying Web Services that use Custom Data types. Specifically, these versions of JBoss can't find serializers that convert custom data types between Java and WSDL. So you can't access Web Services that use Custom Data types with JBoss 4.0.0 and 4.0.1. This problem is fixed in JBoss 4.0.1sp1, so as long you use JBoss 4.0.1sp1 or later, everything will work properly.

J2EE 1.4 and Web Services

The main purpose of the J2EE 1.4 specification was to standardize Web Service deployment so Web Services would be portable and interoperable. With J2EE 1.4, you now use a set of standard deployment descriptors to deploy a Web Service so it can be deployed on any J2EE-compliant application server. The J2EE 1.4 specification mandates interoperability with other platforms, so a Web Service deployed on a J2EE application server will work and be compatible with non-Java clients written in: C#, Python, Perl, C++, and so on.

We'll introduce the new J2EE-Web Service deployment descriptors as we go through the process of deploying JAW Motors Inventory-related Web Services. On

---

the server-side, we have to create a Service Endpoint Interface and register it with the deployment descriptors. In J2EE 1.4, you can implement a Service Endpoint as a Servlet or POJO deployed in a WAR file, or as a Stateless Session Bean, but we'll limit our discussion to EJB Service Endpoints.

Let's start by working our way down through the architecture.

Implementing J2EE 1.4 Web Services

To expose the `InventoryFacadeBean`'s `findAvailableCars()` method as a J2EE 1.4-compliant Web Service, we need to do the following:

- Create a Service Endpoint Interface (SEI) to expose EJB methods as Web Service operations.
- Add a `<service-endpoint>` element to `ejb-jar.xml` to tell JBoss that the `InventoryFacadeBean` EJB implements the `InventoryEndpoint` Service Endpoint Interface.
- Generate the `webservices.xml` to register the Web Service and tie the `InventoryEndpoint` Service Endpoint Interface to an implementation—the `InventoryFacadeBean`.
- Create the JAX-RPC Mapping File to define JAX-RPC type mappings for the parameters and return values for the `InventoryEndpoint`'s methods.
- Generate the WSDL to define the Web Service and tie it to XML Schema data types.
- Set the Web Service URL by modifying `jboss.xml` with the Inventory Web Service URL.
- Modify the `InventoryFacadeBean`:
  - Add Web Services-related XDoclet tags.
  - Add the `findAvailableCars()` method and use an XML Schema-compatible data type.
- Upgrade Deployment by modifying the Ant build script:
  - Fix XDoclet-generated descriptors.
  - Modify the Web Service URL in `jboss.xml`.
  - Use JWSDP to generate the JAX-RPC and WSDL files.

As you'll see in the upcoming sections, the extra interface and descriptors required to deploy a Web Service are tedious and would be almost impossible to develop by hand. But don't lose heart—we can automate Web Service deployment with a combination of Ant, XDoclet, and JWSDP. However, before we show our new deployment process, it's important to know what we're automating—let's start with the Service Endpoint Interface.

Service Endpoint Interface (SEI)

A Service Endpoint Interface exposes business methods as Web Services that can be accessed by external clients. Example 10-1 shows the InventoryService interface.

Example 10-1. InventoryEndpoint.java

```
package com.jbossatwork.ws;

/**
 * Service endpoint interface for InventoryFacade.
 */
public interface InventoryEndpoint
   extends java.rmi.Remote
{

   public com.jbossatwork.ws.CarDTOArray findAvailableCars( )
      throws java.rmi.RemoteException;
}
```

A Service Endpoint Interface acts as a server-side stub that shows your business methods to clients and serves the same purpose for a Web Service that an EJB Remote Interface does for an EJB. The InventoryEndpoint interface is a Remote interface, and the findAvailableCars( ) method throws a RemoteException. The CarDTOArray (that holds an array of CarDTO objects) returned by the findAvailableCars( ) method may look odd to you—see the "Web Services and Collections" section for more information.

Modifying ejb-jar.xml

Although we're already generating the J2EE-standard ejb-jar.xml descriptor to deploy EJBs, we have to add a <service-endpoint> element to Example 10-2 to tell JBoss that the InventoryFacadeBean EJB implements the InventoryEndpoint interface.

Example 10-2. ejb-jar.xml

```
<enterprise-beans>
   …
   <session>
      …
      <display-name>InventoryFacadeSB</display-name>

      <ejb-name>InventoryFacade</ejb-name>
       …

         <service-endpoint>com.jbossatwork.ws.InventoryEndpoint</service-endpoint>

       …
   </session>
   …

</enterprise-beans>
```

Now that we've created a Web Service Endpoint, we have to register it with JBoss.

webservices.xml

The J2EE-standard `webservices.xml` file defines and registers the `InventoryService` Web Service, and ties the Service Endpoint Interface class (`com.jbossatwork.ws.InventoryEndpoint`) to the `InventoryFacadeBean` EJB. The `webservices.xml` file in Example 10-3 also tells JBoss where to find the WSDL and JAX-RPC Mapping files in the EJB JAR file.

Example 10-3. webservices.xml

```
<?xml version="1.0" encoding="UTF-8"?>

<webservices
 xmlns="http://java.sun.com/xml/ns/j2ee"
 xmlns:xsi="http://www.w3.org/2001/XMLSchema-instance"
 xsi:schemaLocation="http://java.sun.com/xml/ns/j2ee
http://www.ibm.com/webservices/xsd/j2ee_web_services_1_1.xsd"
 version="1.1">
    <webservice-description>
        <webservice-description-name>InventoryService</webservice-description-name>
        <wsdl-file>META-INF/wsdl/InventoryService.wsdl</wsdl-file>
        <jaxrpc-mapping-file>META-INF/inventory-mapping.xml</jaxrpc-mapping-file>
        <port-component>
            <port-component-name>Inventory</port-component-name>
            <wsdl-port>InventoryEndpointPort</wsdl-port>
            <service-endpoint-interface>
                com.jbossatwork.ws.InventoryEndpoint
            </service-endpoint-interface>
            <service-impl-bean>
                    <ejb-link>InventoryFacade</ejb-link>
            </service-impl-bean>
        </port-component>
    </webservice-description>
</webservices>
```

We've registered the Web Service endpoint and told the server about the JAX-RPC mapping and WSDL files, and now we need to create these extra descriptors.

JAX-RPC Mapping File

The J2EE-standard JAX-RPC mapping file helps the JAX-RPC compiler map Java objects to WSDL objects. If the Java objects are complex, the JAX-RPC and WSDL files also will be complex. Example 10-4 is the `inventory-mapping.xml` JAX-RPC mapping file that the JAW Motors application uses.

Example 10-4. inventory-mapping.xml

```xml
<?xml version="1.0" encoding="UTF-8"?>
<java-wsdl-mapping xmlns="http://java.sun.com/xml/ns/j2ee"
xmlns:xsi="http://www.w3.org/2001/XMLSchema-instance"
xsi:schemaLocation="http://java.sun.com/xml/ns/j2ee
 http://www.ibm.com/webservices/xsd/j2ee_jaxrpc_mapping_1_1.xsd" version="1.1">

  <package-mapping>
    <package-type>com.jbossatwork.ws</package-type>
    <namespaceURI>http://localhost:8080/jbossatwork-ws/types</namespaceURI>
  </package-mapping>
  <package-mapping>
    <package-type>com.jbossatwork.ws</package-type>
    <namespaceURI>http://localhost:8080/jbossatwork-ws</namespaceURI>
  </package-mapping>
  <java-xml-type-mapping>
    <java-type>com.jbossatwork.dto.CarDTOArray</java-type>
    <root-type-qname xmlns:typeNS="http://localhost:8080/jbossatwork-ws/types">
      typeNS:CarDTOArray
    </root-type-qname>
    <qname-scope>complexType</qname-scope>
    <variable-mapping>
      <java-variable-name>cars</java-variable-name>
      <xml-element-name>cars</xml-element-name>
    </variable-mapping>
  </java-xml-type-mapping>
  <java-xml-type-mapping>
    <java-type>com.jbossatwork.dto.CarDTO</java-type>
    <root-type-qname xmlns:typeNS="http://localhost:8080/jbossatwork-ws/types">
      typeNS:CarDTO
    </root-type-qname>
    <qname-scope>complexType</qname-scope>
    <variable-mapping>
      <java-variable-name>id</java-variable-name>
      <xml-element-name>id</xml-element-name>
    </variable-mapping>
    <variable-mapping>
      <java-variable-name>make</java-variable-name>
      <xml-element-name>make</xml-element-name>
    </variable-mapping>
    <variable-mapping>
      <java-variable-name>model</java-variable-name>
      <xml-element-name>model</xml-element-name>
    </variable-mapping>
    <variable-mapping>
      <java-variable-name>modelYear</java-variable-name>
      <xml-element-name>modelYear</xml-element-name>
    </variable-mapping>
    <variable-mapping>
      <java-variable-name>status</java-variable-name>
      <xml-element-name>status</xml-element-name>
    </variable-mapping>
  </java-xml-type-mapping>
```

Example 10-4. inventory-mapping.xml (continued)

```
    <service-interface-mapping>
      <service-interface>com.jbossatwork.ws.InventoryService</service-interface>
      <wsdl-service-name xmlns:serviceNS="http://localhost:8080/jbossatwork-ws">
        serviceNS:InventoryService
      </wsdl-service-name>
      <port-mapping>
        <port-name>InventoryEndpointPort</port-name>
        <java-port-name>InventoryEndpointPort</java-port-name>
      </port-mapping>
    </service-interface-mapping>
    <service-endpoint-interface-mapping>
      <service-endpoint-interface>
        com.jbossatwork.ws.InventoryEndpoint
      </service-endpoint-interface>
      <wsdl-port-type xmlns:portTypeNS="http://localhost:8080/jbossatwork-ws">
        portTypeNS:InventoryEndpoint
      </wsdl-port-type>
      <wsdl-binding xmlns:bindingNS="http://localhost:8080/jbossatwork-ws">
        bindingNS:InventoryEndpointBinding
      </wsdl-binding>
      <service-endpoint-method-mapping>
        <java-method-name>findAvailableCars</java-method-name>
        <wsdl-operation>findAvailableCars</wsdl-operation>
        <wsdl-return-value-mapping>
          <method-return-value>com.jbossatwork.dto.CarDTOArray</method-return-value>
          <wsdl-message xmlns:wsdlMsgNS="http://localhost:8080/jbossatwork-ws">
            wsdlMsgNS:InventoryEndpoint_findAvailableCarsResponse
          </wsdl-message>
          <wsdl-message-part-name>result</wsdl-message-part-name>
        </wsdl-return-value-mapping>
      </service-endpoint-method-mapping>
    </service-endpoint-interface-mapping>
</java-wsdl-mapping>
```

This JAX-RPC mapping file tells JBoss that the InventoryEndpoint Service Endpoint Interface has a findAvailableCars( ) method that takes no parameters and returns a CarDTOArray.

Mapping between WSDL data types and Java object types is tedious. Notice how one return type, CarDTOArray, explodes into two <java-xml-type-mapping> elements—one for the CarDTOArray itself and the other for the CarDTO. Besides mapping a Java object to a WSDL data type, each <java-xml-type-mapping> element lists each of the object's data members with a <variable-mapping> sub-element.

WSDL File

The WSDL file describes a Web Service interface along with its parameters and registers the web service with JBoss. If you thought the previous descriptors were tedious and painful to look at, then you're in for a treat—the WSDL file is much worse.

Example 10-5 is the InventoryService.wsdl WSDL file used to deploy the Inventory Web Services.

Example 10-5. InventoryService.wsdl

```
<?xml version="1.0" encoding="UTF-8"?>

<definitions name="InventoryService"
targetNamespace="http://localhost:8080/jbossatwork-ws"
xmlns:tns="http://localhost:8080/jbossatwork-ws"
xmlns="http://schemas.xmlsoap.org/wsdl/"
xmlns:xsd="http://www.w3.org/2001/XMLSchema"
xmlns:ns2="http://localhost:8080/jbossatwork-ws/types"
xmlns:soap="http://schemas.xmlsoap.org/wsdl/soap/">
  <types>
    <schema targetNamespace="http://localhost:8080/jbossatwork-ws/types"
            xmlns:tns=http://localhost:8080/jbossatwork-ws/types
            xmlns:soap11-enc="http://schemas.xmlsoap.org/soap/encoding/"
            xmlns:xsi="http://www.w3.org/2001/XMLSchema-instance"
            xmlns:wsdl="http://schemas.xmlsoap.org/wsdl/"
            xmlns="http://www.w3.org/2001/XMLSchema">
     <complexType name="CarDTOArray">
       <sequence>
         <element name="cars" type="tns:CarDTO" nillable="true" minOccurs="0"
                  maxOccurs="unbounded"/></sequence></complexType>
     <complexType name="CarDTO">
       <sequence>
         <element name="id" type="int"/>
         <element name="make" type="string" nillable="true"/>
         <element name="model" type="string" nillable="true"/>
         <element name="modelYear" type="string" nillable="true"/>
         <element name="status" type="string"
                  nillable="true"/>
       </sequence>
     </complexType>
   </schema>
 </types>
 <message name="InventoryEndpoint_findAvailableCars"/>
 <message name="InventoryEndpoint_findAvailableCarsResponse">
   <part name="result" type="ns2:CarDTOArray"/></message>
 <portType name="InventoryEndpoint">
   <operation name="findAvailableCars">
     <input message="tns:InventoryEndpoint_findAvailableCars"/>
     <output message="tns:InventoryEndpoint_findAvailableCarsResponse"/>
   </operation>
 </portType>
 <binding name="InventoryEndpointBinding" type="tns:InventoryEndpoint">
   <soap:binding transport="http://schemas.xmlsoap.org/soap/http" style="rpc"/>
   <operation name="findAvailableCars">
     <soap:operation soapAction=""/>
     <input>
       <soap:body use="literal" namespace="http://localhost:8080/jbossatwork-ws"/>
     </input>
```

Example 10-5. InventoryService.wsdl (continued)

```
      <output>
        <soap:body use="literal" namespace="http://localhost:8080/jbossatwork-ws"/>
      </output>
    </operation>
  </binding>
  <service name="InventoryService">
    <port name="InventoryEndpointPort" binding="tns:InventoryEndpointBinding">
      <soap:address location="REPLACE_WITH_ACTUAL_URL"/>
    </port>
  </service>
</definitions>
```

This WSDL file ties the InventoryService web service to the InventoryEndpoint interface and maps the CarDTO and CarDTOArray WSDL types to XSD data types. In the Client section, we'll use the WSDL file to generate proxy code that encapsulates the details of communicating with the Web Service.

The following line in the WSDL file tells JBoss that it can choose its own URL for the web service:

```
      <soap:address location="REPLACE_WITH_ACTUAL_URL"/>
```

By default, JBoss deploys our WSDL to the following URL:

http://localhost:8080/jaw/ejb/Inventory?wsdl

But we don't like the URL that JBoss uses, and we want to set the URL ourselves so it's meaningful to our clients.

Set the Web Service URL

We want to use a meaningful URL that matches our Web Services namespace—jbossatwork-ws. So we modify jboss.xml in Example 10-6 (the JBoss-specific EJB deployment descriptor) as follows.

Example 10-6. jboss.xml

```
<?xml version="1.0" encoding="UTF-8"?>
<!DOCTYPE jboss PUBLIC "-//JBoss//DTD JBOSS 4.0//EN"
                      "http://www.jboss.org/j2ee/dtd/jboss_4_0.dtd">

<jboss>

  <enterprise-beans>
    …

    <session>
      <ejb-name>InventoryFacade</ejb-name>

      <port-component>
        <port-component-name>Inventory</port-component-name>
```

Example 10-6. jboss.xml (continued)

```
        <port-component-uri>jbossatwork-ws/InventoryService</port-component-uri>
      </port-component>
      …
  </session>
  …
  </enterprise-beans>
  …
</jboss>
```

The `<port-component>` element and its sub-elements tell JBoss to deploy our WSDL to the jbossatwork-ws namespace at the following URL:

http://localhost:8080/jbossatwork-ws/InventoryService?wsdl

Although modifying the `jboss.xml` file to set the URL is helpful, it is purely optional. You could successfully deploy a Web Service without changing `jboss.xml`.

At this point we've shown all the Web Services-related deployment descriptors. We now have to upgrade `InventoryFacadeBean` to expose its `findAvailableCars()` method as a Web Service.

Modifying the InventoryFacadeBean EJB

Example 10-7 shows the new and upgraded XDoclet tags in the `InventoryFacadeBean` EJB that support Web Services deployment.

Example 10-7. InventoryFacadeBean.java

```
/**
 * @ejb.bean
 *   name="InventoryFacade"
 *   …
 *   view-type="all"
 *   …
 *
 * @wsee.port-component
 *   name="Inventory"
 *   wsdl-port="InventoryEndpointPort"
 *   service-endpoint-interface="com.jbossatwork.ws.InventoryEndpoint"
 *   service-endpoint-bean="com.jbossatwork.ejb.InventoryFacadeBean"
 *
 * @ejb.interface
 *   service-endpoint-class="com.jbossatwork.ws.InventoryEndpoint"
 *
 */
public class InventoryFacadeBean implements SessionBean {
    …

    /**
     * @ejb.interface-method
```

Example 10-7. InventoryFacadeBean.java (continued)

```
   * view-type="all"
   * …
   *
   */
  public CarDTOArray findAvailableCars( ) throws EJBException {
      CarDTOArray carDTOArray = new CarDTOArray( );
      CarDTO[ ] cars = (CarDTO[ ]) listAvailableCars( ).toArray(new CarDTO[0]);

      carDTOArray.setCars(cars);

      return carDTOArray;
  }

  /**
   * @ejb.interface-method
   * view-type="both"
   * …
   *
   */
  public List listAvailableCars( ) throws EJBException {
      …
  }

      …

}
```

We've added a new method called findAvailableCars( ) that we're exposing as a Web Service. This method doesn't do much—it wraps the call to the listAvailableCars( ) method (which won't be used as a Web Service) and converts its return value (a java.util.List) to a CarDTOArray. We added the findAvailableCars( ) method because Java 2 Collections are incompatible with J2EE 1.4 Web Services, and we didn't want to change the existing listAvailableCars( ) method. See the "Web Services Data Types" and "Web Services and Collections" sections for more details.

Setting the view-type to all in the class-level @ejb.bean tag tells XDoclet to generate the Service Endpoint Interface along with the EJB Remote and Local Component interfaces. The new class-level @ejb.interface tag specifies the Java file for the Service Endpoint Interface—com.jbossatwork.ws.InventoryEndpoint. In addition to generating the Service Endpoint Interface, we have to tell XDoclet which method to include and which methods to exclude. Thus we include the findAvailableCars( ) method in the Service Endpoint Interface along with the EJB Remote and Local Component interfaces by setting the view-type to all in their method-level @ejb. interface-method tags. We exclude all other business methods (such as listAvailableCars( )) from the Service Endpoint Interface by setting the view-type to both in their method-level @ejb.interface-method tags. That way, these business methods show up only in the EJB Remote and Local Component interface files.

The class-level `@wsee.port-component` tag provides data that XDoclet uses to generate the `webservices.xml` file so it can associate the `InventoryFacadeBean` EJB with the `InventoryEndpoint` Service Endpoint Interface.

Web Services Data Types

We've now shown all the steps needed to deploy a Web Service, and at this point we'd love to close our eyes and declare success, but that wouldn't be honest. We could have just shown a simplistic "Hello World" Web Service method like Example 10-8.

Example 10-8. HelloWorldEndpoint.java

```
...

public void hello() throws java.rmi.RemoteException {
}

...
```

The `hello()` method doesn't return anything, nor does it take any parameters. We could have also shown the same method using primitive Java data types (such as `int`, `float`, or `boolean`), Java wrappers (such as `Integer`, `Float`, or `Boolean`), or `java.lang.String`, but that's not realistic. In our everyday jobs, we develop Java objects for our application domain and use them as parameters and return values for our business methods. So rather than shying away from the hard issues of exchanging custom Java objects through a Web Service, we have a method like Example 10-9.

Example 10-9. InventoryEndpoint.java

```
...
  public com.jbossatwork.dto.CarDTOArray findAvailableCars()
    throws java.rmi.RemoteException;
...
```

The `findAvailableCars()` method returns a `CarDTOArray` object that encapsulates an array of `CarDTO` objects. We'll cover the `CarDTOArray` in greater detail in the "Web Services and Collections" section, but if you can exchange custom data types and arrays of custom data types, then you can do anything else. This is easy once you understand the rules for serializing and deserializing custom objects. Each application-specific class must follow the JavaBeans conventions:

- It must have a default constructor.
- Each private or protected data member must have a corresponding public getter and setter.

For example, the `CarDTO`'s make data member is a `String`, so the getter and setter must look like Example 10-10.

Example 10-10. CarDTO.java

```
    private String make;
    ...

    public String getMake( )
    {
        return make;
    }

    public void setMake(String make)
    {
        this.make = make;
    }
```

Web Services and Collections

J2EE Web Services can't exchange Java 2 Collections or arrays of custom data types due to portability concerns. WSDL uses XML Schema data types but it has no mappings for Collections or arrays of application-specific types. To get around these restrictions, we wrap an array of CarDTOs in a CarDTOArray object in Example 10-11 that follows the Java Bean conventions.

Example 10-11. CarDTOArray.java

```
package com.jbossatwork.dto;

import java.io.Serializable;

import com.jbossatwork.dto.CarDTO;

public class CarDTOArray implements Serializable {

    private CarDTO[ ] cars;

    public CarDTOArray( ) { }

    public CarDTO[ ] getCars( ) {
        return cars;
    }

    public void setCars(CarDTO[ ] cars) {
        this.cars = cars;
    }

}
```

Wrapping an array of DTOs in a JavaBean is inconvenient and tedious, but sometimes you have to sacrifice for the sake of interoperability. Remember that the main reason for Web Services is that it provides the ability for a service written in one programming language to be used by clients written in other languages.

We've shown all the components to deploy an EJB as a Web Service, but where do all the pieces belong?

Web Services Deployment

The new files go into the EJB JAR file as follows:

- In addition to the `ejb-jar.xml`, `jboss.xml`, and JAR Manifest files, the `META-INF` directory now contains `webservices.xml` and `inventory-mapping.xml` (the JAX-RPC mapping file). The WSDL file, `InventoryService.wsdl`, is in `META-INF/wsdl`.

- The `com/jbossatwork/ws` directory holds the `InventoryService` (Service Endpoint Interface) class file.

- Everything else remains unchanged.

The new `CarDTOArray` object class has been added to the `com.jbossatwork.dto` package, so its class file resides in the Common JAR's `com/jbossatwork/dto` directory.

At this point, we've shown all the Web Services-related deployment descriptors and upgraded `InventoryFacadeBean`. Let's show how to generate the descriptors and package the Web Service for deployment with Ant, XDoclet, and JWSDP.

Automating Web Services Deployment

As we've seen so far, deploying a Web Service requires writing very little code (just the Service Endpoint Interface), but it adds a complex set of deployment issues:

- Create three new descriptors (`webservices.xml`, the JAX-RPC Mapping file, and the WSDL file)

- Modify both EJB deployment descriptors (`ejb-jar.xml` and `jboss.xml`).

Although it's possible to develop everything by hand, it's not very practical because the new deployment descriptors are interrelated, and the XML elements are tedious and error-prone. In previous chapters, we've automated everything with Ant and XDoclet, but the current XDoclet version, XDoclet 1.2.3, falls short when it comes to Web Services. XDoclet has Ant tasks that are supposed to generate the JAX-RPC Mapping and WSDL files, but these XDoclet tasks don't work properly. Bug reports have been submitted to the XDoclet project, and we hope to see a resolution to these issues in the next production version of XDoclet. As you'll see in the "Web Services Ant Script" section, we'll add another technology to our toolkit—the Java Web Services Developer's Pack (JWSDP)—to complete our deployment by generating the JAX-RPC Mapping and WSDL files. Even though XDoclet doesn't do everything, we still use it to generate the Service Endpoint Interface, modify `ejb-jar.xml`, and generate `webservices.xml`.

Before you can use the JWSDP from our Ant build script, you need to download JWSDP 1.5 from *http://java.sun.com/webservices/downloads/webservicespack.html* and add the JAR files to your CLASSPATH by doing one of the following:

- In the Ant build script below, set the jwsdp.lib.dir property to your JWSDP 1.5 installation.

- Copy the lib sub-directory from your Axis 1.1 installation to /Library/jwsdp-1.5/ (the jwsdp.lib.dir property in the Ant build script currently points to /Library/ jwsdp-1.5).

Web Services Ant Script

We now modify the EJB deployment process to include Web Service deployment. Example 10-12 shows the upgraded build.xml script from the ejb sub-project.

Example 10-12. ejb/build.xml

```
...
<property name="jwsdp.lib.dir" value="/Library/jwsdp-1.5"/>
...
<target name="run-ejbdoclet" ...>
  <ejbdoclet ...>

    ...

    <service-endpoint/>

    ...

  </ejbdoclet>

  <!-- Fix problems with XDoclet-generated Service Endpoint Interface  -->

  <replace
        file="${gen.source.dir}/com/jbossatwork/ws/InventoryEndpoint.java">

    <replacetoken><![CDATA[throws javax.ejb.EJBException,
java.rmi.RemoteException]]></replacetoken>
        <replacevalue><![CDATA[throws java.rmi.RemoteException]]></replacevalue>
        </replace>

    <!-- Fix WS URL in jboss.xml -->

    <replace file="${gen.source.dir}/jboss.xml">
      <replacetoken><![CDATA[<ejb-name>InventoryFacade</ejb-name>]]>
</replacetoken>
        <replacevalue><![CDATA[
                    <ejb-name>InventoryFacade</ejb-name>
                    <port-component>
                      <port-component-name>Inventory</port-component-name>
                      <port-component-uri>jbossatwork-ws/InventoryService
```

Example 10-12. ejb/build.xml (continued)

```
</port-component-uri>
                        </port-component>
                    ]]></replacevalue>
        </replace>
    </target>

    <target name="run-wseedoclet" depends="run-ejbdoclet">
        <taskdef name="wseedoclet"
                classname="xdoclet.modules.wsee.WseeDocletTask"
                classpathref="xdoclet.lib.path"/>

        <wseedoclet wsdlFile="META-INF/wsdl/InventoryService.wsdl"
                    jaxrpcMappingFile="META-INF/inventory-mapping.xml"
                    wseeSpec="1.1"
                    destdir="${gen.source.dir}"
                    excludedtags="@version,@author"
                    addedtags="@xdoclet-generated at ${TODAY}"
                    verbose="true">

            <fileset dir="${source.dir}">
                <include name="**/*Bean.java"/>
            </fileset>

            <deploymentdescriptor name="InventoryService"/>
        </wseedoclet>

        <!-- Fix problems with XDoclet-generated webservices.xml -->

        <replace file="${gen.source.dir}/webservices.xml">
            <replacetoken><![CDATA[<wsdl-file>WEB-INF/]]></replacetoken>
            <replacevalue><![CDATA[<wsdl-file>]]></replacevalue>
        </replace>

        <replace file="${gen.source.dir}/webservices.xml">
            <replacetoken><![CDATA[<jaxrpc-mapping-file>WEB-INF/]]></replacetoken>
            <replacevalue><![CDATA[<jaxrpc-mapping-file>]]></replacevalue>
        </replace>

        <replace file="${gen.source.dir}/webservices.xml">
            <replacetoken><![CDATA[<icon>]]></replacetoken>
            <replacevalue><![CDATA[ ]]></replacevalue>
        </replace>

        <replace file="${gen.source.dir}/webservices.xml">
            <replacetoken><![CDATA[</icon>]]></replacetoken>
            <replacevalue><![CDATA[ ]]></replacevalue>
        </replace>

        <replace file="${gen.source.dir}/webservices.xml">
            <replacetoken><![CDATA[Port</wsdl-port>]]></replacetoken>
            <replacevalue><![CDATA[EndpointPort</wsdl-port>]]></replacevalue>
        </replace>
```

Example 10-12. ejb/build.xml (continued)

```
    </target>

    <target name="run-wscompile" depends="compile">
        <echo message="Generating JAX-RPC Mapping and WSDL files."/>

        <path id="wscompile.task.classpath">
            <fileset dir="${jwsdp.lib.dir}">
                <include name="**/*.jar"/>
            </fileset>
            <fileset dir="${java.home}/../lib" includes="tools.jar"/>
        </path>

        <taskdef name="wscompile"
                 classname="com.sun.xml.rpc.tools.ant.Wscompile"
                 classpathref="wscompile.task.classpath"/>

        <wscompile base="${build.dir}"
                   fork="true"
                   server="true"
                   features="rpcliteral"
                   mapping="${gen.source.dir}/inventory-mapping.xml"
                   config="wscompile-config.xml"
                   nonClassDir="${gen.source.dir}">

            <classpath>
                <path refid="wscompile.task.classpath"/>
                <path refid="compile.classpath"/>
                <pathelement location="${classes.dir}"/>
            </classpath>

        </wscompile>
    </target>
    ...

    <!-- Build EJB JAR. -->
    <target name="build-ejb-jar" depends="run-ejbdoclet, compile, run-wseedoclet,
run-wscompile"
            description="Packages the EJB files into a EJB JAR file">
        <mkdir dir="${distribution.dir}" />

        <jar destfile="${distribution.dir}/${ejb.jar.name}"
             basedir="${classes.dir}">
            <metainf dir="${gen.source.dir}" includes="*.xml"/>
            <zipfileset dir="${gen.source.dir}" includes="*.wsdl"
                        prefix="META-INF/wsdl"/>
        </jar>
    </target>
    ...
```

Even though we're adding Web Services to our EJB deployment, the overall process stays the same. We still execute run-ejbdoclet to generate all the EJB-based deployment descriptors and the EJB Remote and Local Component Interface files. The compile task compiles the EJBs, and the `run-wseedoclet` task generates the `webservices.xml` file. The `run-wscompile` target uses the `wscompile` task to create the JAX-RPC Mapping and WSDL files. Finally, `build-ejb-jar` takes all the descriptors and `.class` files, and creates an EJB JAR file.

In the `run-ejbdoclet` target, we've added a new `<ejbdoclet>` subtask called `<service-endpoint>` that generates the Service Endpoint Interface file and adds the `<service-endpoint>` element to `ejb-jar.xml` based on the XDoclet tags we added to our EJB. After executing `<ejbdoclet>`, the `run-ejbdoclet` target then uses the Ant `<replace>` task to set the Web Services URL in `jboss.xml`.

The `run-wseedoclet` target generates the `webservices.xml` file from the `@wsee.port-component` XDoclet tag we added to the EJB. But XDoclet doesn't generate the `webservices.xml` incorrectly (it doesn't conform to the W3C specification), so we used Ant's built-in `<replace>` task to fix each syntactical problem.

Since the XDoclet Ant tasks that generate the JAX-RPC Mapping and WSDL files don't work properly, the `run-wscompile` target uses the `wscompile` Ant task from JWSDP 1.5 to generate the JAX-RPC Mapping and WSDL files. Add the JWSDP JAR files to your `CLASSPATH` by doing one of the following:

- In the Ant build script above, set the `jwsdp.lib.dir` property to your JWSDP 1.5 installation.
- Copy the `jwsdp-shared`, `jaxrpc`, and `saaj` sub-directories from your JWSDP 1.5 installation to `/Library/jwsdp-1.5` (the `jwsdp.lib.dir` property in the Ant build script currently points to `/Library/jwsdp-1.5`).

The `wscompile` task takes the `wscompile-config.xml` file in Example 10-13 (which resides in the ejb sub-directory) as input.

Example 10-13. wscompile-config.xml

```
<?xml version="1.0" encoding="UTF-8"?>
<configuration xmlns="http://java.sun.com/xml/ns/jax-rpc/ri/config">
  <service name="InventoryService"
          targetNamespace="http://localhost:8080/jbossatwork-ws"
          typeNamespace="http://localhost:8080/jbossatwork-ws/types"
          packageName="com.jbossatwork.ws">
    <interface name="com.jbossatwork.ws.InventoryEndpoint"/>
  </service>
</configuration>
```

The `wscompile-config.xml` file provides the XML Schema namespace, Java package name, and the name of the Service Endpoint Interface Java file for each Web Service. The `wscompile` task uses the contents of the `wscompile-config.xml` file to generate the JAX-RPC Mapping and WSDL files.

J2EE Web Services Checklist

Before we move on to test the JAW Motors application's new Web Service functionality, let's recap what we've done to implement a J2EE 1.4 Web Service:

- Created the `InventoryEndpoint` Service Endpoint Interface (SEI) to expose EJB methods as Web Service operations
- Added a `<service-endpoint>` element to `ejb-jar.xml` to tell JBoss that the `InventoryFacadeBean` EJB implements the `InventoryEndpoint` Service Endpoint Interface
- Generated the `webservices.xml` to register the Web Service and tie the `InventoryEndpoint` Service Endpoint Interface to an implementation—the `InventoryFacadeBean`
- Created the JAX-RPC Mapping File to define JAX-RPC type mappings for the parameters and return values for the `InventoryEndpoint`'s method
- Generated the `inventory-mapping.xml` WSDL file to define the Web Service and tie it to XML Schema data types
- Set the Web Service URL by modifying `jboss.xml` with the Inventory Web Service URL
- Modified the `InventoryFacadeBean`:
  - Added Web Services-related XDoclet tags
  - Added the `findAvailableCars()` method and used an XML Schema-compatible data type
- Upgraded deployment by modifying the Ant build script:
  - Fixed XDoclet-generated descriptors
  - Modified the Web Service URL in `jboss.xml`
  - Used JWSDP to generate the JAX-RPC and WSDL files

Testing Web Services Deployment

It's taken us a while to get here, but now that we have the core infrastructure in place to deploy a Web Service, let's test our deployment. Here are the steps to build and deploy the application:

- Type ant in the root directory of ch10 to build the project.
- Shut down JBoss so the Ant script can clean up the JBoss deployment area.
- Type ant colddeploy to deploy the EAR file (jaw.ear) to the *$JBOSS_HOME/server/default/deploy* directory.
- Start JBoss back up.

You should see the following output in the JBoss console:

```
...
23:08:11,921 INFO  [WSDLFilePublisher] WSDL published to: file:/C:/jboss-
4.0.2/server/default/data/wsdl/jaw.ear/ejb.jar/InventoryService.wsdl

23:08:12,182 INFO  [AxisService] WSDD published to: C:\jboss-
4.0.2\server\default\data\wsdl\jaw.ear\ejb.jar\Inventory.wsdd

23:08:12,632 INFO  [AxisService] Web Service deployed:
http://localhost:8080/jbossatwork-ws/InventoryService
...
```

Now point your browser to *http://localhost:8080/ws4ee* to see the JBossWS page as shown in Figure 10-2.

Welcome to JBossWS

This is the JBoss J2EE-1.4 compatible webservice implementation based on Axis.

- Validate the local installation's configuration
- View the list of deployed Web services

Figure 10-2. JBossWS page

Clicking on the "View the list of deployed Web services" link takes you to the JBoss Deployed Web Services Page, as depicted in Figure 10-3.

And now... Some Services

- Version *(wsdl)*
  - getVersion
- ch10.ear/ejb.jar#Inventory *(wsdl)*
  - findAvailableCars

Figure 10-3. JBoss Deployed Web Services page

At this point, you'll see our Web Service (findAvailableCars) listed under jaw.ear/ejb.jar#Inventory. Click on the *wsdl* link, and you'll see the WSDL for our Web Service.

Now that we've successfully deployed our Web Service and viewed the WSDL, keep JBoss running. We now move on to develop an external client that calls the findAvailableCars Web Service.

Web Services Client

We viewed the Web Service's WSDL, so we know that it deployed properly. However, now we need to make sure that the Web Service really works. So, we're going to add an external client application that tests the Web Service. Running a client against our Web Service will flush out any Web Service-related issues like custom data type serialization/de-serialization errors (caused by using data types that aren't compatible with XML Schema data types).

For our client, we'll use a well-known API for invoking the Inventory Web Service methods. Here are some of our choices:

JNDI

We could add <service-ref> elements to our EJB and client deployment descriptors so an external client could use a JNDI name like java:comp/env/service/ Inventory to look up our service endpoint and invoke its methods.

JAX-RPC

We could use JAX-RPC calls that look up the service by using its port name from the WSDL, and then specify serializers/deserializers to handle the custom data types.

Apache Axis

We could download the WSDL from *http://localhost:8080/jbossatwork-ws/ InventoryService?wsdl* and use the Apache Axis toolkit to generate proxy and custom data type objects that communicate with the Web Service.

Perl, Python, C#

Clients could have been written in any language that supports Web Services, but since this is a Java book, we decided to stick with Java.

JNDI and JAX-RPC are too Java/J2EE-centric, so these approaches don't provide a good test for the interoperability of our Web Service. Besides, the main reason for using Web Services is to enable clients to seamlessly use a service, regardless of the programming language used on either side. We chose Axis because:

- Axis code generation is based on WSDL, making it platform-neutral.
- The generated proxy and custom data type objects make it much easier to write the client.

Our client is written in Java, but non-Java clients written in other languages like C# could also take our WSDL, generate a proxy using their own language-specific tools, and use our Web Service. WSDL completely decouples a Web Service from its clients because:

- Each client generates a proxy and any associated custom data types from the WSDL into its native language.
- There are no language- or platform-specific dependencies between a Web Service and its clients.

Before we develop a Web Service client, let's explore the new directory structure we'll use for our Web Service client development environment.

Exploring the New Directory Structure

In previous chapters, we had subdirectories for building the Common JAR (common), the database (sql), the web application (webapp), and EJBs (ejb).

If you change to the ch10 directory, you'll see that we've added a client sub-directory—this is our Web Service client development environment. The goal is to keep each portion of the application as autonomous as possible. By providing individual Ant scripts, we have the opportunity to build each portion of the project separately.

The client sub-project

Take a moment to explore the client sub-project. There is a single class in it— MyAxisClient. Notice that we've created a new package structure for our client code—com.jbossatwork.client.

The Ant build script in the client sub-directory generates Web Service proxy code, compiles the MyAxisClient class, and invokes the MyAxisClient's main( ) method to run the client. Don't run the Ant script just yet—we'll show how the Web Service client build works in the next section. The main build.xml script in the ch10 directory doesn't require any changes because the Web Service and the client are two separate builds.

Now that we've shown the Web Service client development environment, let's implement the client.

Implementing a Web Service Client

To implement a Web Service Client, we need to do the following:
- Download the WSDL from *http://localhost:8080/jbossatwork-ws/InventoryService?wsdl*.
- Generate Web Service proxy and custom data type objects by using the Axis WSDL2Java Ant task.
- Write a Web Service client that uses the Axis-generated proxy and custom data type objects to call the Web Service.

After downloading the WSDL and saving it to client/InventoryService.wsdl under the ch10 project root directory, we use the Axis 1.1 WSDL2Java Ant task in the client build.xml file to generate our Web Service proxy objects and custom data types (Example 10-14).

Example 10-14. client/build.xml

```
...
<property name="axis.lib.dir" value="/Library/axis-1_1/lib"/>
...

<path id="axis.classpath">
    <fileset dir="${axis.lib.dir}">
        <include name="**/*.jar"/>
    </fileset>
</path>
...

<target name="run-wsdl2java" description="Generates WS proxy code from WSDL">
    <path id="wsdl2java.task.classpath">
        <path refid="axis.classpath"/>
    </path>

    <taskdef name="wsdl2java"
             classname="org.apache.axis.tools.ant.wsdl.Wsdl2javaAntTask">
        <classpath refid="wsdl2java.task.classpath"/>
    </taskdef>

    <mkdir dir="${gen.source.dir}" />

    <wsdl2java output="${gen.source.dir}"
               url="InventoryService.wsdl"
               verbose="true">

        <mapping namespace="http://localhost:8080/jbossatwork-ws"
                 package="com.jbossatwork.client"/>

        <mapping namespace="http://localhost:8080/jbossatwork-ws/types"
                 package="com.jbossatwork.client"/>

    </wsdl2java>

</target>
```

The `<run-wsdl2java>` target uses the Axis `<wsdl2java>` task to generate the Web Service proxy objects (InventoryServiceLocator, InventoryService, and InventoryEndpoint) and custom data types (CarDTOArray and CarDTO) for the client. The `<mapping>` elements map the namespace from the WSDL to our Java package name—com.jbossatwork.client. The namespace for each `<mapping>` element comes from the WSDL:

- *http://localhost:8080/jbossatwork-ws* is the WSDL namespace for the proxy objects.
- *http://localhost:8080/jbossatwork-ws/types* is the WSDL namespace for the custom data type objects.

The <mapping> elements coerce <wsdl2java> to generate the proxy and custom data type objects with a reasonable Java package name.

Download Axis 1.1 from *http://ws.apache.org/mirrors.cgi*, and add the Axis JAR files to your CLASSPATH by doing one of the following:

- In the Ant build script above, set the axis.lib.dir property to your Axis 1.1 installation.
- Copy the lib sub-directory from your Axis 1.1 installation to /Library/axis-1_1/ (the axis.lib.dir property in the Ant build script currently points to /Library/axis-1_1/lib).

After generating the Web Service proxy and custom data type objects, we then compile and use them in our client, as Example 10-15 demonstrates.

Example 10-15. MyAxisClient.java

```
package com.jbossatwork.client;

public class MyAxisClient {
    public static void main(String [] args) {

        try {
            System.out.println("Finding InventoryService ...\n");
            InventoryService service = new InventoryServiceLocator();
            System.out.println("Getting InventoryEndpoint ...\n");
            InventoryEndpoint endpoint = service.getInventoryEndpointPort();

            System.out.println("Getting Cars ...");
            CarDTOArray carDTOArray = endpoint.findAvailableCars();
            CarDTO[] cars = carDTOArray.getCars();
            for (int i = 0; i < cars.length; ++i) {
                System.out.println("Year = [" + cars[i].getModelYear() +
                        "], Make = [" + cars[i].getMake() +
                    "], Model = [" + cars[i].getModel() + "], status = [" +
                        cars[i].getStatus() + "]");
            }
        } catch(Exception e) {
            e.printStackTrace();
        }
    }
}
```

Axis does all the heavy lifting for us by encapsulating the low-level Web Service calls and custom data type serialization/deserialization. The proxy and custom data type objects generated by Axis are easy to use, so Web Service invocation looks just like calling a POJO. The Axis-generated code is elegant and looks natural to anyone accustomed to OO programming languages. The InventoryServiceLocator() constructor returns an InventoryService object that enables us to obtain an InventoryEndpoint, a remote handle for accessing the service. We then use the

InventoryEndpoint object to access JAW Motors' car inventory by invoking our findAvailableCars() Web Service operation that returns a CarDTOArray. The CarDTOArray contains an array of CarDTO objects, so we call the CarDTOArray.getCars() method to extract the array of CarDTO objects. We finish by printing the contents of each CarDTO element in the array.

Hey! My Web Service Client Doesn't Work with Java 5!

Time and technology didn't stand still for us while we were writing this book. We tested our examples with J2SE 1.4, but some things have changed with Java 5 (also known as J2SE 5.0) and Axis. First, Java 5 is incompatible with Axis 1.1 (it doesn't understand enums), so you'll need to upgrade to Axis 1.2 or higher. Second, the <wsdl2java> task under Axis 1.2 works a bit differently—it now optimizes away the CarDTOArray. The generated InventoryEndpoint'sfindAvailableCars() method now returns an array of CarDTO objects—CarDTO[]. Here are the relevant changes to MyAxisClient:

```
public class MyAxisClient {
    public static void main(String [] args) {
        try {
            …
            CarDTO[] cars = endpoint.findAvailableCars();
            …
        } catch (…) {
        }
    }
}
```

We've left comments in the client/build.xml and MyAxisClient.java files to help you upgrade to Java 5. Please note that the server side remains the same—the InventoryFacadeBean's findAvailableCars() method still returns a CarDTOArray for serializing the CarDTO array.

We've tested these changes, and they work properly with Java 5 and Axis 1.2.1 (available at *http://www.apache.org/dyn/closer.cgi/ws/axis/1_2_1*).

Web Service Client Checklist

Before we move on to test the Web Service Client, let's recap what we've done:

- Downloaded the Web Service's WSDL from *http://localhost:8080/jbossatwork-ws/InventoryService?wsdl*
- Generated Web Service Web Service proxy and custom data type objects by using the Axis WSDL2Java Ant task
- Wrote a Web Service client that uses the Axis-generated proxy and custom data type objects to call the Web Service.

Testing the Web Service Client

We've generated Web Service proxy code and written a client to call the findAvailableCars Web Service. Go to the ch10/client sub-directory, and compile and run the client by typing: ant run-client.

Ant runs the client (by MyAxisClient's main( ) method) after generating and compiling the client code. You should see the following output in the client console:

```
...
[java] Finding InventoryService ...

[java] Getting InventoryEndpoint ...

[java] Getting Cars ...
[java] Year = [2005], Make = [Toyota], Model = [Camry], status = [Available]
[java] Year = [1999], Make = [Toyota], Model = [Corolla], status = [Available]
[java] Year = [2005], Make = [Ford], Model = [Explorer], status = [Available]
```

Final Thoughts on J2EE 1.4 Web Services

Here are the lessons we learned from deploying a J2EE 1.4 Web Service:

- Adding Web Services to your application doesn't have a huge impact on your server-side code, but it increases the complexity of your deployment.
- If you already have a Stateless Session Bean, you only have to modify and add some XDoclet tags to expose its methods as Web Services.
- Make sure that the Java classes you're using as parameters and return values follow the Java Beans conventions.
- Java 2 Collections and arrays of custom data types are incompatible with Web Services, so wrap an array of custom data types in a Java Bean.
- If your Web Service uses custom data types as parameters or return values, make sure you use JBoss 4.0.1sp1 or higher.
- Set your Web Service URL to something meaningful in jboss.xml.
- The tools that generate Web Services server-side deployment artifacts are still maturing.
- XDoclet 1.2.3 has limited support for Web Services. Use XDoclet to:
    - Generate the <service-endpoint> element in ejb-jar.xml.
    - Create webservice.xml.
    - Generate the Service Endpoint Interface.
- Due to XDoclet's limitations, use JWSDP's wscompile tool to generate the JAX-RPC Mapping and WSDL files.

- Check your Web Service deployment by viewing the JBossWS Page (*http://localhost:8080/ws4ee*) on your JBoss instance.
- On the client side, use the WSDL to generate proxy and custom data type objects in your native programming language to communicate with a Web Service. Using WSDL-based client code tests the interoperability of your Web Service.
- Even if you're using Java, using the Axis toolkit to invoke a Web Service gives you a simple, elegant Object Oriented interface that hides the low-level API calls.
- If you're using Java 5, make sure you use Axis 1.2 or higher.
- If you're using J2SE 1.4, use Axis 1.1.

Conclusion

In this chapter we showed how to expose a portion of the JAW Motors application as a Web Service so JAW Motors can share its inventory with its online trading partners and work with non-Java clients. We exposed an EJB as a Web Service by using Ant, XDoclet, and JWSDP to deploy it on JBoss. We finished by writing an Axis client that invoked our Web Service.

Congratulations!

Congratulations—you did it! You started off this book by deploying an EAR and serving up simple content with hardcoded data for demonstration purposes. Then you progressed to using a JDBC connection to get data from JBoss' built-in HyperSonic database. You wired up the database using Hibernate to make the database access easier, more platform-independent, and to more easily automate the application. You added Session Beans to the application to manage transactions. Then you used JMS to send a message to a Credit Card approval system and sent an email with JavaMail to indicate the success or failure of the credit check. You then added security to the application to prevent unauthorized access to certain portions of the application. You finished by exposing a portion of the application as a Web Service so JAW Motors could share its inventory with its online trading partners. We hope that you can take what you've learned in this book and apply it to your real-world JBoss projects.

ClassLoaders and JBoss

When a Java application references Java classes, the Java Virtual Machine (JVM) uses a ClassLoader to load them into memory. The Delegation Model was introduced in Java 2 and organizes ClassLoaders into the following tree/hierarchy by using parent/child relationships, as shown in Figure A-1.

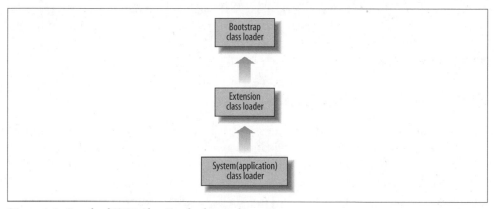

Figure A-1. Standard J2SE ClassLoader hierarchy

The J2SE ClassLoaders do the following:

- The Bootstrap (also called the *primordial*) ClassLoader has no parent, is the root of the ClassLoader tree, and loads core Java classes (java.*) into the JVM.

- The Extension ClassLoader loads extension classes:

  - Classes that extend core Java classes—*javax.**.

  - Classes from the Java Runtime Environment (JRE) *lib/ext* directory in the standard J2SE installation.

- The System (also called the Application) ClassLoader loads classes and JARs from the system CLASSPATH—the CLASSPATH environment variable and the classpath argument on the java command line.

If the current ClassLoader previously loaded a class, then the ClassLoader returns the class to the client. If a class has not been previously loaded, then according to the Java specification, a ClassLoader must defer (or delegate) to its parent before trying to load the class itself. For example, if an application references `java.lang.String`, the System ClassLoader delegates to the Extension ClassLoader, which in turn defers to the Bootstrap ClassLoader to load the String class. The child ClassLoader gets a chance to load a class only if the parent hasn't already loaded the class or couldn't load the class. A class is loaded only once per ClassLoader.

Namespaces

The JVM recognizes a class by its runtime identity—the class' full name (the package plus class name), along with the instance of the ClassLoader that instantiated the class. Each ClassLoader has its own namespace consisting of the classes it loads, and each fully qualified class name MUST be unique within that namespace. This naming convention is required by the J2EE specification. Two ClassLoaders could each load the same class, and the JVM would treat each class as a distinct type. Thus the JVM considers class `com.jbossatwork.util.TextEmail` in ClassLoader 1 different from the `com.jbossatwork.util.TextEmail` in ClassLoader 2 because they have different runtime identities based on the ClassLoader name. We'll see why this distinction is important when we get to the section on the JBoss ClassLoaders.

Class Loading in the J2EE

Class Loading is one of the least understood aspects of J2EE deployment. Although not officially part of the J2EE specification, *most* application servers use a strategy similar to the ClassLoader hierarchy in Figure A-2 to support J2EE component deployment.

The J2EE-based ClassLoaders work as follows:

- The EAR ClassLoader loads the classes from JARs contained in the EAR file.
- The EJB ClassLoader loads EJBs and related classes that reside in the EJB JAR file.
- The WAR ClassLoader loads the web-specific classes and JARs in the WAR file's `WEB-INF/{class,lib}` directories.

Because each ClassLoader has no access to the classes loaded by its children or siblings, the classes in the WAR file are not visible to EJBs. Of course EJBs shouldn't try to reference things in the WAR in the first place because it is poor architecture. Each layer should not know about the invoking layer, and you can't assume that a web-based presentation layer will always be in your application.

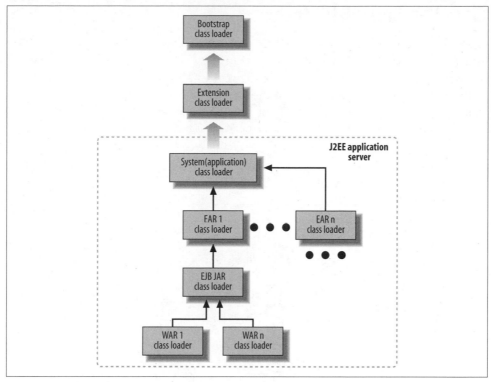

Figure A-2. Generic J2EE Application Server Class Loader Hierarchy

The J2EE specification is vague concerning the deployment order of the J2EE modules. Many application servers deploy the JARs and classes in the EAR, and then the classes in the EJB JAR, and finally, the classes and JARs in the WAR. In the JAW Motors application, the Common JAR strategy works because the EAR contains the Common JAR, so the application-specific dependency classes and the third party utility JARs get deployed first, then the EJBs in the EJB JAR are loaded, and the web components from the WAR—which depend on the EJBs and common classes and JARs—deploy last.

Here is a practical example that uses the class-loading scenario from Figure A-2. In the JAW Motors application, a JSP invokes a Servlet, which in turn uses an EJB; both the Servlet and the EJB use Log4J. Since the JSP and Servlet are packaged in the WAR, the WAR ClassLoader finds and loads the JSP and Servlet. When the Servlet instantiates the EJB, the WAR ClassLoader cannot find the EJB, so WAR ClassLoader defers to its parent—the EJB ClassLoader. The EJB JAR contains the EJB, so the EJB ClassLoader finds and loads the EJB on behalf of the WAR ClassLoader. When the Servlet instantiates the Log4J Logger to log messages, neither the WAR ClassLoader nor the EJB ClassLoader can find the Log4J JAR, so they delegate to their parent, the EAR ClassLoader. Since The Common JAR contains the Log4J JAR, the EAR ClassLoader finds and loads the Log4J Logger on behalf of the child ClassLoaders.

Class Loading with JBoss

JBoss' class loading scheme is similar to the strategy used by other J2EE application servers, as shown in Figure A-3.

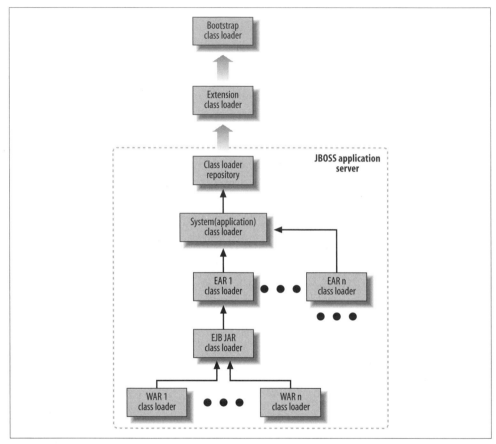

Figure A-3. JBoss ClassLoader Hierarchy

JBoss' ClassLoader hierarchy differs from the strategy used by other J2EE application servers in the following ways:

The ClassLoader Repository

The ClassLoader Repository contains all classes loaded by a JBoss instance, including:

- JBoss' internal boot classes, including its J2EE component implementations
- Any classes or JARs specified on the command line when starting JBoss
- All classes or JARs from each deployed application

By default, only one ClassLoader Repository covers the entire server. But you are free to declare any number of repositories and associate any deployed applications with a repository. To keep deployment simple, the JAW Motors application uses the default ClassLoader Repository.

Cross-referencing between EJB JAR and WAR files

Within an EAR, an EJB could access classes and/or properties packaged in a WAR file (Log4J for example). The converse is true as well—web components could access resources bundled in an EJB JAR. However, we do not recommend this practice because it ties you to JBoss—your application will not deploy on other application servers.

Loading classes

The WAR, EJB JAR, and EAR ClassLoaders do NOT load any classes. When an application loads its classes, each ClassLoader adds its contextual information (classes, property files, and JARs) to the ClassLoader context and defers to its parent. Finally, control passes to the JBoss Application ClassLoader, which loads the class from the ClassLoader Repository.

We still recommend using a Common JAR (that resides in the EAR), which contains all JARs and classes common to both an application's EJB JAR and WAR, because:

- Some form of packaging JARs in an EAR file works with most J2EE application servers.

- It enables you to share classes between applications. For example, if EAR 1 and EAR 2 both use `com.jbossatwork.util.TextEmail.class`, you could factor it out of both applications into a separate deployment. Then you would be free to cycle the EAR files independently and never have to worry about `ClassCastExceptions` when you hot deploy one of the applications.

Common ClassLoader Issues

ClassLoader issues are difficult to find and take a long time to debug. They fall into one of two categories:

Not enough visibility

You'll see one of the following exceptions:

    ClassNotFoundException

Java API methods such as `Class.forName()` or `ClassLoader.loadClass()` throw a `ClassNotFoundException`. This exception happens when a class loader tries to load a class and can't find the class. Here are some possible causes:

- A JAR or directory for the class is not available, so the ClassLoader asked to load the class, or to its parent(s).

- The wrong ClassLoader is used to load the class.

NoClassDefFoundError

A `NoClassDefFoundError` has the same causes as the `ClassNotFoundException`, but there is an additional reason—a class depends on other classes that are inaccessible from the current ClassLoader. The other classes may reside only in a child or sibling ClassLoader, neither of which is available to the current ClassLoader.

Too much visibility

This happens when you have a duplicate class and the problem manifests as a ClassCastException. For example, you could include the same JAR file (bundled with several libraries) more than once in your deployment.

ClassLoader Options

In the Java API, you can explicitly use either the System (or Application), Current, or the Thread Context ClassLoader.

You can access the System ClassLoader by calling ClassLoader.getSystemClassLoader( ). In most J2EE application servers, the System ClassLoader is too high in the hierarchy and will not find the resources packaged in your application's EJB JAR or WAR. In JBoss, using the System ClassLoader is still a problem because the ClassLoader Repository holds references to all deployed applications, so you could easily have a naming conflict if more than one application uses the same class.

The Current ClassLoader is the ClassLoader that loaded the class that contains the method that's currently executing. Class.getResource( ) and the one-parameter version of Class.forName( ) use the Current ClassLoader by default. The Current Class-Loader is a better choice than the System ClassLoader, but there are still problems with using the Current ClassLoader:

- You may not know who calls your class, and the current ClassLoader could be up too high in the ClassLoader to find the resources that your class needs.

- In JBoss, you could have the same naming conflict with Class Loader Repository that you had with the System ClassLoader.

You gain access to the current Thread Context ClassLoader by calling Thread.currentThread( ).getContextClassLoader( ). The Thread Context ClassLoader is the ClassLoader used by the creator of the Thread that runs your code. The Thread Context ClassLoader works in a way that's contrary to the Delegation Model by enabling a parent ClassLoader to access classes from any of its child ClassLoaders. Sometimes a parent ClassLoader needs to see classes that one of its child ClassLoaders instantiates at runtime. Use the Thread Context Class Loader for the following reasons:

- In JBoss, you're guaranteed to load the class or property file from your application by using the Thread Context ClassLoader. Even though the JBoss Class-Loader Repository may have the same class or property from several applications, the Thread Context ClassLoader picks the class or property that belongs to your application.

- The EJB specification forbids EJBs to use the Current Class Loader, and since the System Class Loader isn't a workable option, you're left with the Thread Context ClassLoader. See the Programming Restrictions section in the EJB specification for further details.

Here are a couple of practical uses of the Thread Context ClassLoader:

- If you have a factory method that uses `Class.forName( )` to instantiate classes dynamically, pass the Thread Context ClassLoader as a parameter to `Class.forName( )`.

- To load a Properties file in your application's CLASSPATH, call `Thread.currentThread( ).getContextClassLoader( ).getResourceAsStream( )` to find the Properties file, and use the resulting `InputStream` when calling `Properties.load( )`.

Solving ClassLoader Issues

The best way to solve ClassLoader issues is to reduce their likelihood by following good deployment practices:

- Know the basics of ClassLoaders and how your particular deployment environment uses them. Even though it sounds boring, make a deployment plan and stick with it. Know the dependencies for each J2EE module. Then factor out the common classes and utility JARs into a Common JAR that resides in the EAR. When you add new dependency classes or third party utility JARs, update the plan and refactor. Planning where your classes and utilities reside reduces the chance that you'll have `ClassNotFoundException` and `NoClassDefFoundError` issues.

- Make sure that there are no duplicate classes or JAR files. Third party libraries typically cause this problem because they each may have their own copy of a particular JAR file. For example, many Apache libraries have their own copy of files such as Log4J and Commons Lang. Make sure there is only one copy of these classes or JAR files across the entire EAR deployment. This process is tedious and requires upgrading Ant build scripts, but it saves serious headaches later on. Without duplicate classes or JARs, you're less likely to see problems like the `ClassCastException`.

- Encapsulate/Minimize Visibility to avoid `ClassCastExceptions`.
  - Put web-specific classes in the WAR file's *WEB-INF/classes* directory and web-specific third party JARs (like Struts, for example) in the WAR file's *WEB-INF/lib* directory. There's no need to put web-specific classes and JARs in the Common JAR because other J2EE modules don't depend on them.
  - Put extra EJB-specific utility classes and dependent JAR files in EJB JAR's root directory because the web components don't need to access them.

- Use a Common JAR that contains all utility classes and JARs used in both the EJB JAR and the WAR.

- Use the correct ClassLoader to avoid the `ClassNotFoundException` and `NoClassDefFoundError`. Use the Thread Context ClassLoader (`Thread.currentThread( ).getContextClassLoader( )`). If you use `Class.forName( )`, pass in the Thread Context ClassLoader as a parameter. To load a Properties file in your application's `CLASSPATH`, use the `Thread Context ClassLoader` to get an `InputStream` for loading the Properties file.

Conclusion

In this Appendix, we covered J2SE and J2EE ClassLoaders. We then showed how Class Loading works in JBoss, and finished by discussing how to reduce the probability of ClassLoader problems in your applications.

Logging and JBoss

Most J2EE applications use some form of logging or tracing API that stores messages to a persistent medium (such as DBMS or file). Logging provides the following benefits:

Debugging
Developers generate log messages to debug their programs.

Reviewing
System personnel examine log messages to check for problems.

Auditing
Security personnel can review log messages to see what actions a user performed in the system.

This chapter covers two of the most common logging APIs and how to use them with JBoss:

- Jakarta Commons Logging (JCL) API
- Apache Log4J

Jakarta Commons Logging (JCL) API

The Jakarta Commons Logging (JCL) package from the Apache Jakarta project provides a standard interface to the various logging libraries, hiding the details of the logging implementation from an application. Many logging APIs are available, and at some point an application may need to change to another logging technology. The main benefit of the JCL is that it enables developers to switch between logging implementations without impacting their code.

Using the Apache JCL

Example B-1 is an example from the JAW Motors InitServlet that uses the JCL to print out a log message.

Example B-1. InitServlet.java

...

```
import org.apache.commons.logging.*;

...

public class InitServlet extends GenericServlet {
    private Log log = LogFactory.getLog(InitServlet.class);

    private ServletContext servletContext;

    public void init( ) {
        ...
        log.info("Testing Logging Setup ...");
    }
}
```

The call to `LogFactory.getLog( )` creates a concrete implementation of the `org.apache.commons.logging.Log` interface so we can log messages. The `init( )` method then uses the `Log` instance to log an informational message by calling `log.info( )`—this method then does the real work of logging the message to its destination. See the next section for more information about `org.apache.commons.logging.Log` interface. See the Initialization Servlet section for more information on the `InitServlet`.

Using a Logging Implementation

A logging package must implement the `Log` interface to work with the JCL, which comes bundled with four usable concrete logger instances that encapsulate the underlying logging package:

`Log4JLogger`
>   Delegates to a Log4J Logger

`Jdk14Logger`
>   Wraps the standard logger that comes with the J2SE

`LogKitLogger`
>   Encapsulates the Avalon logkit logger

`SimpleLogger`
>   The default logger that dumps all messages to `System.err`

Several options logging implementations are available, but we chose Log4J for the JAW Motors application because of Log4J's widespread use and robust features. Each logger implements the JCL's `Log` interface so the caller doesn't know about the logger that JCL uses. The JCL uses the following algorithm to determine which logger to use:

```
If the org.apache.commons.logging.Log property was set, THEN
    Instantiate the logger defined by the org.apache.commons.logging.Log property.
```

```
ELSE IF Log4J is available (on the CLASSPATH) THEN
    Use Log4JLogger.
ELSE IF JDK 1.4 or later is available THEN
    Use Jdk14Logger.
ELSE
    Use SimpleLogger.
```

Property File

The Commons Logging package uses a property file, commons-logging.properties (which resides in the appb project's common/conf sub-directory), to configure and instantiate the underlying logging mechanism to use. The JAW Motors application places this properties file in the base directory of its Common JAR file so that Apache Commons Logging can find the file on the CLASSPATH and configure itself properly (for more details see the "Logging Deployment" section). In Example B-2, Log4J is the logging implementation.

Example B-2. commons-logging.properties

```
org.apache.commons.logging.Log=org.apache.commons.logging.impl.Log4JLogger
```

Logging Levels

Logging levels have no intrinsic universally accepted meaning. On each project, system personnel and developers need to determine what logging levels are meaningful and how to use to them. JCL's Log interface has six logging levels (in ascending order). Here's how we use them in the JAW Motors application:

trace
> This is the least serious/lowest level, and we don't see a need for trace because we use debug instead.

debug
> We use debug when we're debugging an application or to leave some bread crumbs when running an application. These messages are typically sent to a log file.

info
> The JCL development group recommends using info messages to log events that occur at system startup or shutdown.

warn
> This level represents minor errors. We feel that it is a bit too fine-grained, so we use the error logging level instead.

error
> This represents runtime failures in the application due to system failures or programming errors. The most common problems we've seen include: JNDI lookup failure, database is inaccessible, and NullPointerException. You usually want to log the error and notify system personnel with an email or pager message.

fatal

> This is the most serious/highest level, and it represents errors that cause an application to terminate abnormally. On our projects, we haven't seen any of these kinds of problems in the code. We've seen exceptions that terminate the deployment process show up in the JBoss console. So, we don't use fatal messages in the JAW Motors application.

Of course, if you want to apply different meanings and actions to these logging levels, do what works for your application. Although each logging API manages its logging levels in an implementation-specific manner, each logging system must work in an expected way. For example. if the debug level logging is enabled, the logging package logs debug and higher level messages, and ignores trace level messages.

Apache Log4J

Apache Log4J, a powerful logging framework, is the de-facto standard in the Java Open Source community. Recently promoted from the Jakarta project, Log4J has done so well that it has been ported to C, C++, Perl, PHP, Python, .NET, and Ruby. Log4J provides the following features:

Configurable Destinations
> Log4J logs messages to different output destinations, including files, JMS, and a DBMS.

Log Levels
> Log4J has logging levels that enable you to configure which messages are logged to the output destination. For example, if debug-level logging is enabled, Log4J logs debug and higher level messages, and ignores trace-level messages.

Powerful Formatting
> The formatting classes enable developers to specify the look and feel of logging messages.

Because a thorough discussion of Log4J is outside the scope of this book, please see the References section for complete documentation.

Log4J Core Concepts

Log4J's key classes and interfaces include:

Logger
> Log4J's main class. Logger logs messages to an Appender based on the message's logging level.

Appender
> An Appender sends logging messages to a particular destination. Here are some of the Appender interface's concrete implementations:

JDBCAppender

> Stores logging messages in a database table.

FileAppender

> Writes logging messages to a file.

DailyRollingFileAppender

> Writes logging messages to a file that is rolled over at a user-defined interval. Most people let the log file roll over every 24 hours so you have a separate log file for each day.

JMSAppender

> Publishes logging messages to a JMS Topic.

SMTPAppender

> Sends an email message that contains a logging message.

Layout

> An Appender uses a Layout to format a logging message. Here are some of the Layout interface's concrete implementations:

SimpleLayout

> Creates log messages that consist of the log level followed by a dash, and then the message itself. For example:
>
> ```
> FATAL—Something went terribly wrong.
> ```

HTMLLayout

> Outputs log messages into an HTML table.

PatternLayout

> Formats log messages based on a conversion pattern.

PatternLayout

PatternLayout is the most common way to format messages, so that's what we use for the JAW Motors application. Table B-1 shows some of the most common conversion patterns.

Table B-1. Log4J PatternLayout

Pattern	Meaning
%c	Category of the log message.
%C	Fully qualified class name of the caller (caution: extremely slow).
%d	Date of the log message. This uses the default ISO 8601 format (YYYY-mm-dd HH:mm:ss,SSS) if none is specified.
%F	File name from where the logging request was issued (caution: extremely slow).
%L	Line number from where the logging request was issued (caution: extremely slow).
%m	The message text.
%M	Method name from where the logging request was issued (caution: extremely slow).

Pattern	Meaning
%n	Line separator—this is Operating System neutral.
%p	Log level (priority) of the log message.
%%	A single percent sign.

The JAW Motors application uses the following conversion pattern to output messages to a log file:

```
%d %-5p [%c] - %m%n
```

Here is a sample message from the log file:

```
2005-06-06 17:24:02,923 INFO  [com.jbossatwork.InitServlet] - Testing Logging Setup
...
```

This message consists of: the date/time (%d), the logging level (%-5p), the category ([%c]) of the message (this is configured as the class name), a dash, the message text (%m), and the line separator (%n). Example B-3 shows the call from the InitServlet (see the Initialization Servlet section) that generated the message.

Example B-3. InitServlet.java

```
log.info("Testing Logging Setup ...");
```

Log4J Configuration File

Log4J configures the Appender (destination) and Layout (format) for Log4J messages in an external file. Originally, Log4J used a Java properties file (log4j.properties), but now the preferred way is to use an XML configuration file, log4j.xml. The JAW Motors application uses log4j.xml file because:

- Non-Java applications can work with XML files.
- Most people prefer the XML configuration file rather than the properties file.

There are two options for configuring Log4J with JBoss:

- Modify JBoss' log4j.xml file (located in the conf directory within the JBoss server configuration—for the JAW Motors application, this is in $JBOSS_HOME/server/default/conf).
- Create an application-specific log4j.xml.

Modifying JBoss' log4j.xml file is undesirable for the following reasons:

- You don't want to co-mingle your application-specific log messages with JBoss' log messages because your messages will be harder to find.
- The JBoss log4j.xml file contains JBoss-specific Log4J setup details that you don't care about.

- You have to make the same changes for your application to the JBoss `log4j.xml` file every time you upgrade JBoss.

- You could copy the JBoss `log4j.xml` to your project directories, modify it with your application setup, and then include this file as part of application deployment. However, you still need to change your local version of `log4j.xml` whenever you upgrade JBoss.

- Using the JBoss `log4j.xml` file ties an application to JBoss.

The JAW Motors application uses its own Log4J XML configuration file, `jbossatwork-log4j.xml`, to keep its configuration and log messages separate from JBoss. We named our file `jbossatwork-log4j.xml` rather than `log4j.xml` because:

- We use a ClassLoader to locate the file.

- We don't know if the configuration file comes before or after JBoss' `log4j.xml` file on the CLASSPATH, so we don't know which file (ours or JBoss') the Class-Loader will use.

- Using a different file name guarantees that the ClassLoader loads our Log4J XML configuration file.

Example B-4 shows the Log4J XML configuration file for the JAW Motors application.

Example B-4. jbossatwork-log4j.xml

```xml
<?xml version="1.0" encoding="UTF-8"?>
<!DOCTYPE log4j:configuration SYSTEM "log4j.dtd">
<log4j:configuration xmlns:log4j="http://jakarta.apache.org/log4j/" debug="true" >

    <appender name="STDOUT" class="org.apache.log4j.ConsoleAppender">
        <param name="Target" value="System.out"/>
        <param name="Threshold" value="INFO"/>
        <layout class="org.apache.log4j.PatternLayout">
            <param name="ConversionPattern" value="%d %-5p [%c] - %m%n"/>
        </layout>
    </appender>

    <appender name="ROLLING" class="org.apache.log4j.DailyRollingFileAppender">
        <param name="File" value="${log4j.log.dir}/jbossatwork.log"/>
        <layout class="org.apache.log4j.PatternLayout">
            <param name="ConversionPattern" value="%d %-5p [%c] - %m%n"/>
        </layout>
    </appender>

    <category name="com.jbossatwork">
        <priority value="DEBUG"/>
        <appender-ref ref="ROLLING"/>
    </category>

    <category name="org.apache">
        <priority value="WARN"/>
```

```
    </category>

    <root>
        <priority value="WARN"/>
        <appender-ref ref="STDOUT"/>
    </root>

</log4j:configuration>
```

The above `jbossatwork-log4j.xml` file defines two Appenders:

- The `DailyRollingFileAppender` logs messages using the specified format to a file defined as `${log4j.log.dir}/jbossatwork.log`. We use a property because we don't want to hardcode the log file's directory path. At midnight, Log4J closes the previous day's log file (tagging it with the date) and creates a new one for the next day. The property `log4j.log.dir` is a System property that specifies the directory where the log file resides. Log4J looks in System Properties to find the value for any properties mentioned in a Log4J XML configuration file. The `log4j.log.dir` property can be set in one of two ways:

    - By passing in the value of the `log4j.log.dir` property as a `-D` option on the Java command line in the JBoss startup script (`run.bat` or `run.sh`). You can pass in the value by adding the following code to the `JAVA_OPTS` environment variable (the script uses `JAVA_OPTS` to build the Java command line):

        ```
        Dlog4j.log.dir=C:\rev2\logs
        ```

    - But this has the same drawbacks (see above) as the JBoss `log4j.xml`.

    - By putting the `log4j.log.dir` property in a property file and including it in the application's `CLASSPATH`. The JAW Motors application specifies `log4j.log.dir` in a property file, `log4j.extra.properties` (which resides in `common/conf`). This properties file is deployed in a Common JAR that resides in an EAR file. The Initialization Servlet (see the Initialization Servlet section) then adds the `log4j.log.dir` property to System Properties at runtime before initializing Log4J. This type of deployment removes the tight coupling between the application and JBoss.

- `ConsoleAppender` logs messages by using the specified format to `System.out` (the default setting).

The `log4j.extra.properties` file is an application-specific properties file that holds extra properties to configure Log4J. The `log4j.extra.properties` file resides in the appb project's `common/conf` subdirectory and looks like Example B-5.

Example B-5. log4j.extra.properties

```
log4j.log.dir=C:/rev2/logs
```

The log4j.log.dir property represents the directory where the JAW Motors application's log file resides. You'll want to set the log4j.log.dir property to a valid path on your filesystem—if you don't do this, Log4J will not log your messages. This log directory MUST exist before starting JBoss or Log4J can not create the logfile. However, you don't have to create the directory because appb Ant build script does it for you. The log4j.log.dir property's key and value must be added to System Properties so Log4J can configure itself properly by using jbossatwork-log4j.xml (which uses log4j.log.dir as a System Property to configure its File Appender).

A Category logs messages to one or more Appenders. The JAW Motors application's jbossatwork-log4j.xml file (which resides in the appb project's common/conf subdirectory) defines three Categories:

com.jbossatwork
> By using com.jbossatwork (the JAW Motors application's root package name) as the category name, Log4J sends all messages from the JAW Motors application's classes to the "ROLLING" appender—a DailyRollingAppender that uses the jbossatwork.log file (in the directory specified by log4j.log.dir) as its output destination. For the com.jbossatwork category, Log4J logs only messages with a logging level of INFO or higher.

org.apache
> By using org.apache (the Apache Project's root package name) as the category name, Log4J sends all messages from the Apache Project's classes to the Root Category. In this case, Log4J logs only messages with a logging level of WARN or higher.

root
> The Root Category has no name and is the default for messages that don't match any other Category. For the Root Category, Log4J logs only messages with a logging level of WARN or higher to the "STDOUT" appender—this is a ConsoleAppender that uses Standard Output (the terminal) as its output destination.

Log4J Initialization

You can initialize Log4J with JBoss in several ways:

- Several options include setting the log4j.configuration system property with the -D option on the Java command line in the JBoss startup script (run.bat or run.sh) by adding the following to the JAVA_OPTS environment variable (the script uses JAVA_OPTS to build the Java command line):

      -Dlog4j.configuration=jbossatwork-log4j.xml

- Use the CLASSPATH. In this case, you put the Log4J configuration file on the application CLASSPATH and access the file with a ClassLoader at application startup.

Using the -D mechanism is unacceptable because it forces you to modify the JBoss startup script (JBOSS_HOME/bin/run.bat or run.sh)—see the Log4J Configuration File section for a full discussion on the problems with modifying JBoss files. Getting a resource on the CLASSPATH with a ClassLoader is a better option because it separates an application's deployment (EAR/WAR/EJB JAR) from the application server.

Initialization Servlet

JBoss loads—instantiates the Servlet and invokes init( )—the InitServlet at startup before invoking any other Servlet or other J2EE component. The InitServlet extends javax.servlet.GenericServlet because it doesn't respond to HTTP requests—its only purpose is to set up the JAW Motors application. Initializing Log4J with a Servlet that executes at startup time sets up Log4J for all J2EE components in the application. The following extra settings in web.xml (Example B-6) ensure that InitServlet runs at startup time.

Example B-6. web.xml

```
...
<servlet>
    <servlet-name>InitServlet</servlet-name>
    <servlet-class>com.jbossatwork.InitServlet</servlet-class>
    <load-on-startup>1</load-on-startup>
</servlet>
...
```

We've already seen the basic <servlet> tags in the Web Application Chapter. Any positive integer value (0 or greater) for the <load-on-startup> tag causes JBoss to instantiate InitServlet and invoke its init( ) method when JBoss starts the web application. For further information on loading Servlets on startup, see one of the Servlet books in the References section.

The Web Application Chapter showed how to use XDoclet tags for core Servlet deployment. In keeping with XDoclet-based development, the InitServlet now uses an additional attribute—load-on-startup="1"—on the @web.servlet XDoclet tag to generate the <load-on-startup> element in web.xml (Example B-7).

Example B-7. InitServlet.java

```
package com.jbossatwork;

import javax.servlet.*;

import java.io.*;

import org.apache.commons.logging.*;

import com.jbossatwork.util.*;

/**
 * InitServlet sets up Log4J for the application.
```

```
 *
 * @web.servlet
 *   name="InitServlet"
 *   load-on-startup="1"
 *
 */
public class InitServlet extends GenericServlet {
    private Log log = LogFactory.getLog(InitServlet.class);

    private ServletContext servletContext;

    public void init() {
        servletContext = getServletContext();
        SystemPropertiesUtil.addToSystemPropertiesFromPropsFile(
                                    "log4j.extra.properties");

        Log4jConfigurator.setup("jbossatwork-log4j.xml");
        log.info("Testing Logging Setup ...");
    }

    public void service(ServletRequest request, ServletResponse response)
    throws ServletException, IOException {
    }
}
```

Rather than putting all the low-level setup code in the InitServlet, the init( ) method defers to utility objects:

- Calls SystemPropertiesUtil.addToSystemPropertiesFromPropsFile( ) to add the properties from the log4j.extra.properties file to the System Properties.
- Calls Log4jConfigurator.setup( ) to configure Log4J with our Log4J configuration file, jbossatwork-log4j.xml.

J2EE Design Notes

We could have used a JMX MBean (Managed Bean) to initialize the JAW Motors application instead of using a Servlet. An MBean is similar to an initialization Servlet because both run when JBoss starts up. An MBean differs from an initialization Servlet because an MBean enables you to use the JMX Console to change settings such as Log4J Levels while the application is still running. We chose an initialization Servlet because we didn't need to dynamically change application properties and settings at runtime. If you need this level of flexibility, though, an MBean would be the best technology for the job.

We've shown the Log4J Configuration file, the Initialization Servlet, and application-specific properties for setting up Log4J. Now let's look closely at the SystemPropertiesUtil utility class.

Adding Application-Specific Properties to System Properties

The InitServlet uses SystemPropertiesUtil to add the log4j.log.dir property (that represents the directory that holds the log file) from the log4j.extra.properties to the System Properties. The SystemPropertiesUtil utility looks like Example B-8.

Example B-8. SystemPropertiesUtil.java

```
package com.jbossatwork.util;

import java.util.*;

public class SystemPropertiesUtil {

    /**
     * Making the default (no arg) constructor private
     * ensures that this class cannnot be instantiated.
     */
    private SystemPropertiesUtil( ) {}

    public static void addToSystemPropertiesFromPropsFile(String propsFileName) {
        Properties props = ResourceLoader.getAsProperties(propsFileName),
                sysProps = System.getProperties( );

        // Add the keys/properties from the application-specific properties  to
        // the System Properties.

        sysProps.putAll(props);
    }
}
```

The SystemPropertiesUtil's addToSystemPropertiesFromPropsFile( ) method adds the keys/properties from an application-specific properties file to the System Properties. The application-specific properties file MUST reside in a directory listed on the CLASSPATH. The SystemPropertiesUtil uses the ResourceLoader.getAsProperties( ) method to retrieve application-specific properties file from the CLASSPATH. We'll cover the ResourceLoader utility after we show the Log4jConfigurator.

Now that we have the logging infrastructure in place, let's look more closely at the Log4jConfigurator.

Configuring Log4J with a Configuration File

The InitServlet uses the Log4jConfigurator to set up Log4J with our Log4J Configuration file, jbossatwork-log4j.xml. Example B-9 shows the Log4jConfigurator class.

Example B-9. Log4jConfigurator.java

```java
package com.jbossatwork.util;

import java.net.*;

import org.apache.log4j.BasicConfigurator;
import org.apache.log4j.xml.DOMConfigurator;

public class Log4jConfigurator {

    /**
     * Making the default (no arg) constructor private
     * ensures that this class cannnot be instantiated.
     */
    private Log4jConfigurator() { }

    /**
     * Configures Log4J for an application using the specified Log4J XML
     * configuration file.
     *
     * @param log4jXmlFileName The specified Log4J XML configuration file.
     */
    public static void setup(String log4jXmlFileName) {
        URL url = ResourceLoader.getAsUrl(log4jXmlFileName);

        if (url != null) {

            // An URL (from the CLASSPATH) that points to the Log4J XML
            // configuration file that was provided, so use Log4J's
            // DOMConfigurator with the URL to initialize Log4J with the
            // contents of the Log4J XML configuration file.

            DOMConfigurator.configure(url);
        } else {

            // An URL that points to the Log4J XML configuration file wasn't
            // provided, so use Log4J's BasicConfigurator to initialize Log4J.

            BasicConfigurator.configure();
        }
    }
}
```

The Log4jConfigurator.setup( ) method configures Log4J for the JAW Motors application. The ResourceLoader.getAsUrl( ) method retrieves the Log4J configuration file from the CLASSPATH. If the configuration file is found, the Log4jConfigurator.setup( )

method uses the Log4J `DOMConfigurator.setup( )` method to configure Log4J with our Log4J configuration file. Otherwise, the `Log4jConfigurator.setup( )` method uses Log4J's `BasicConfigurator.configure( )` method to configure Log4J with default settings.

Loading Resources from the CLASSPATH

Both the `SystemPropertiesUtil` and `Log4jConfigurator` utilities use `ResourceLoader` to find resources (a property file and the Log4J configuration file) on the application CLASSPATH. The `ResourceLoader` utility looks like Example B-10.

Example B-10. ResourceLoader.java

```
package com.jbossatwork.util;

import java.io.*;
import java.net.*;
import java.util.*;

public class ResourceLoader {

    /**
     * Making the default (no arg) constructor private
     * ensures that this class cannnot be instantiated.
     */
    private ResourceLoader( ) { }

    public static Properties getAsProperties(String name) {
        Properties props = new Properties( );
        URL url = ResourceLoader.getAsUrl(name);

        if (url != null) {
            try {
                // Load the properties using the URL (from the CLASSPATH).

                props.load(url.openStream( ));
            } catch (IOException e) {
            }
        }

        return props;
    }

    public static URL getAsUrl(String name) {
        ClassLoader classLoader = Thread.currentThread( ).getContextClassLoader( );

        return classLoader.getResource(name);
    }
}
```

The `ResourceUtil.getAsProperties()` method calls `ResourceUtil.getAsUrl()` to find a properties file as an URL on the application `CLASSPATH`. The `props.load(url.openStream())` call first opens the `URL` as an `InputStream` and then loads the properties file.

The `ResourceUtil.getAsUrl()` method uses the Thread Context ClassLoader to find a properties file as an URL on the `CLASSPATH` application. The call to `Thread.currentThread().getContextClassLoader()` gets the current Thread's ClassLoader, and the `classLoader.getResource(propsFileName)` call searches for a properties filename on the application `CLASSPATH` and returns a `java.net.URL` that points to a resource (a properties file, data file, .class file, and so on). The Thread Context ClassLoader is the ClassLoader used by the creator of the Thread that runs your code. By using the Thread Context ClassLoader, we're guaranteed to load the resource as long as it's on the application's `CLASSPATH`. For more information on deployment, please see Chapter 3. See Appendix A for more information on ClassLoaders.

Packaging properties files in a JAR is cleaner than using external property files that reside on a disk directory because the directory structure for your deployment environment could differ on each machine where you deploy your application. Using JAR files for packaging is a standard technique for both J2SE and J2EE applications.

We've shown all the components to use Apache Commons Logging and Log4J, but where do all the pieces belong?

Logging Deployment

The new files go into the Common JAR file, as follows:

- The root directory holds the following:
  - The Apache Jakarta Commons Logging JAR files
  - The Log4J JAR file
  - The `log4j.extra.properties` file that defines the property where the log file resides
  - The `commons-logging.properties` file that tells Jakarta Apache Commons Logging to use Log4J
  - The Log4J Configuration file, `jbossatwork-log4j.xml`
- Everything else remains unchanged.

The new `SystemPropertiesUtil`, `Log4jConfigurator`, and `ResourceLoader` objects are part of the `com.jbossatwork.util` package, so their class files reside in the Common JAR's `com/jbossatwork/util` directory. See Chapter 3 for more information on the Common JAR file.

Logging Checklist

Before moving on to test the JAW Motors application's new logging functionality, let's recap what we've done to add logging to the application:

- Created the `commons-logging.properties` file that tells Apache Jakarta Commons Logging (JCL)) to use Log4J as its implementation.
- Used Apache JCL calls in the JAW Motors application code.
- Added a Log4J Configuration file, `jbossatwork-log4j.xml`, to tell Log4J to format messages and where to log them.
- Developed a `log4j.extra.properties` file that defines where the log file resides.
- Wrote an Initialization Servlet to configure Log4J at JBoss startup, deferring the low-level setup details to utility classes.
- Deployed the logging implementation in the Common JAR:
  - The Apache JCL and Log4J JARs, properties files, and new utility classes go in the root directory.

Testing Logging

Now that we've developed all the logging code and infrastructure, let's test the application to ensure that everything still works properly. Here are the steps to build and deploy the application:

- Type ant in the root directory of `appb` to build the project.
- Shut down JBoss so the Ant script can clean up the JBoss deployment area.
- Type ant `colddeploy` to deploy the EAR file (jaw.ear) to the *$JBOSS_HOME/server/default/deploy* directory. Notice that the Ant build script also creates the logfile directory (specified by `log4j.log.dir` in the `log4j.extra.properties` file).
- Start JBoss back up.

The Initialization Servlet runs at startup time, and you should see this message in the JAW Motors logfile, `${log4j.log.dir}/jbossatwork.log`:

```
2005-06-06 17:24:02,923 INFO  [com.jbossatwork.InitServlet] - Testing Logging Setup
...
```

Now point your browser to *http://localhost:8080/jaw*—this takes you to the JAW Motors home page. After running a credit check and buying a car, the log messages in the `${log4j.log.dir}/jbossatwork.log` file should now look like this:

```
2005-06-06 17:24:02,923 INFO  [com.jbossatwork.InitServlet] - Testing Logging Setup
...
2005-06-06 17:25:19,163 INFO  [com.jbossatwork.ControllerServlet] - Credit Check:
2005-06-06 17:25:19,163 INFO  [com.jbossatwork.ControllerServlet] - Name = [Tom]
2005-06-06 17:25:19,163 INFO  [com.jbossatwork.ControllerServlet] - SSN =
[[345834[958[34]]
```

```
2005-06-06 17:25:19,163 INFO  [com.jbossatwork.ControllerServlet] - Email =
[fred@acme.org]
2005-06-06 17:25:19,293 INFO  [com.jbossatwork.ejb.CreditCheckProcessorBean] -
CreditCheckProcessorBean.onMessage( ): Received message.
2005-06-06 17:25:19,293 INFO  [com.jbossatwork.ejb.CreditCheckProcessorBean]—
Credit Check:
2005-06-06 17:25:19,293 INFO  [com.jbossatwork.ejb.CreditCheckProcessorBean]—Name
= [Tom]
2005-06-06 17:25:19,293 INFO  [com.jbossatwork.ejb.CreditCheckProcessorBean] - SSN
= [[345834[958[34]]
2005-06-06 17:25:19,293 INFO  [com.jbossatwork.ejb.CreditCheckProcessorBean]—
Email = [fred@acme.org]
2005-06-06 17:25:19,303 INFO  [com.jbossatwork.ejb.CreditCheckProcessorBean]—
Verifying Credit ...
2005-06-06 17:25:26,804 INFO  [com.jbossatwork.ejb.CreditCheckProcessorBean]—
Credit Check Result = [Pass Credit Check]
2005-06-06 17:25:26,844 INFO  [com.jbossatwork.ejb.CreditCheckProcessorBean]—
Sending Email to [fred@acme.org] ...
2005-06-06 17:25:48,465 INFO  [com.jbossatwork.ControllerServlet] - carId = [99],
price = [13500.0]
```

Conclusion

In this appendix, we showed how to use Apache JCL as the high-level logging API
used by an application. We hid the Log4J logging implementation to enable migra-
tion to another technology without changing the code. We then showed how to configure Apache JCL and Log4J in a J2EE/JBoss environment, and how to instrument
your code with logging.

APPENDIX C

JAAS Tutorial

The Java Authentication & Authorization Service (JAAS) enables an application to protect its resources by restricting access to only users with proper credentials and permissions. JAAS provides a layer of abstraction between an application and its underlying security mechanisms, making it easier to change security technologies and realms without impacting the rest of the system.

JAAS

JAAS is a standard Java extension in J2SE 1.4, and it provides pluggable authentication that gives application designers a wide choice of security realms:

- DBMS
- Application Server
- LDAP
- Operating System (UNIX or Windows NT/2000)
- File System
- JNDI
- Biometrics

JAAS supports single sign-on for an application. Rather than forcing the user to log in to a web site, and then log in again to a forum or a backend legacy system used by the application, JAAS coordinates all these steps into one central login event to help coordinate access to all systems that the user needs.

We chose JAAS as the basis for our authentication strategy because:

- It provides a security context that covers the entire J2EE architecture from the web tier to the EJB tier.
- It is application-server neutral.

- It integrates with the Java 2 security model.

- It is part of the J2SE 1.4 extension API.

- It is more sophisticated than the other authentication mechanisms and provides more functionality.

- It supports single sign-on by coordinating multiple security realms.

- It addresses authorization in addition to authentication.

- It provides good encapsulation for authentication and authorization, enabling an application to be independent of the underlying security mechanisms it uses.

JAAS Core Concepts, Classes, and Interfaces

Here are the key pieces of the JAAS framework and the roles that they play:

javax.security.auth.Subject
> A Subject is a user ("John Smith") or outside entity ("Acme") that accesses the system. The Subject groups one or more Principals together and holds the user's credentials.

java.security.Principal
> Although not officially part of the JAAS packages (javax.security.*), the Principal acts as a role for a Subject (user).

Credentials
> A credential can be a password, certificate, or key that identifies the user to the system. The JAW Motors application uses passwords.

javax.security.auth.spi.LoginModule
> A LoginModule wraps an underlying security realm and authenticates a user.

javax.security.auth.callback.Callback
> A Callback holds user authentication credentials for the LoginContext.

javax.security.auth.callback.CallbackHandler
> A CallbackHandler manages the Callbacks associated with the LoginContext. LoginModules interact with the CallbackHandler to get Callback objects.

javax.security.auth.login.LoginContext
> A LoginContext coordinates the LoginModules and CallbackHandlers. An application uses the LoginContext to authenticate a user.

java.security.PrivilegedAction, java.security.PrivilegedExceptionAction
> These actions run code that's protected by a login. It is an implementation of the GoF Command pattern. The difference between these two interfaces is that PrivilegedExceptionAction runs code that can throw checked Exceptions, and PrivilegedAction does not run code that can throw checked Exceptions.

LoginContext

The JAAS `LoginContext` authenticates a user. The `LoginContext` instantiates the `LoginModule`(s) (that log the user into the security realm) based on the contents of the `LoginModule` Configuration file. By storing the `LoginModule` setup information in a configuration file, you can change the `LoginModule`(s) without modifying the application. The `LoginContext` invokes the `LoginModule`(s) for an application, and acts as the controller for the logon process. If the application accesses multiple security realms, the `LoginContext` coordinates the logon process across multiple `LoginModule`(s) (one per security realm).

LoginModule

The `LoginModule` logs a user/Subject into a security realm based on their username and password. A `LoginModule` could interact with an operating system, a database, JNDI, LDAP, or a biometric device like a retinal scanner or touch pad. Application developers normally don't need to know very much about `LoginModules` because the `LoginContext` invokes them on behalf of an application. Thus your code never interacts with `LoginModules`. To add or remove a LoginModule used by your application, you only need to modify the LoginModule Configuration file—your code remains unchanged. This indirection enables an application to be independent of the underlying security mechanisms used

Although you could write your own `LoginModule`, doing so is usually unnecessary because of the abundance of quality third-party Open Source implementations available. You only need to know how to configure (in the `LoginModule` Configuration file) and deploy them for your particular runtime environment. If the Open Source `LoginModule` implementations don't provide all the functionality you need, you can either modify the code from that library or write your own `LoginModule`. Since this topic is outside the scope of this book, please see the JAAS `LoginModule` Developers' Guide (*http://java.sun.com/j2se/1.4.2/docs/guide/security/jaas/JAASLMDevGuide. html*) for further details.

Tagish

> Tagish has a set of Open Source JAAS `LoginModules` released under the GNU (Lesser GNU Public License (LGPL) found at: *http://free.tagish.net/jaas*. The Tagish collection has the following `LoginModules`:
>
> - DBMS
> - File System
> - Windows NT/2000 domain

Sun Microsystems

> Sun bundles several `LoginModules` with J2SE 1.4. However, they are in the `com.sun.security.auth.module` package and not officially part of J2SE 1.4 because

they're Sun's implementation of the JAAS interfaces. Sun provides the following `LoginModules`:

- Kerberos
- Key Store
- JNDI
- Windows NT
- UNIX

JBoss

JBoss provides several `LoginModules` with its distribution, including:

- DBMS
- File-based
- Key Store
- LDAP
- External Client

We could easily configure the Tagish, Sun, or JBoss `LoginModules` and use them with the JAW Motors application. We chose the JBoss `LoginModules` because they're already bundled with JBoss and we don't need to configure any third party JARs. Even though we use `LoginModules` provided by JBoss, the application code remains vendor-neutral because:

- The `LoginModules` are configured in an external configuration file.
- The application code doesn't change if you use different `LoginModules`.

Callback

The `Callback` interface enables other JAAS components to retrieve user authentication information, such as usernames and passwords. The `Callback` implementations include:

`ChoiceCallback`
Enables `LoginModules` to display a list of choices and receive a response.

`ConfirmationCallback`
Allows `LoginModules` to ask for a confirmation like YES/NO or OK/CANCEL.

`NameCallback`
Enables `LoginModules` to ask for a username and receive a response.

`PasswordCallback`
Allows `LoginModules` to ask for a password and receive a response.

The external application uses the `NameCallback` to hold the username and the `PasswordCallback` to hold the password. As you'll see in the next section, we use these `Callbacks` a bit differently than the standard JAAS documentation, so it works in a command-line application.

CallbackHandler

The `CallbackHandler` is an interface that enables `LoginModules` to retrieve authentication information such as a username and password entered by the user. The `CallbackHandler` is the most confusing part of the JAAS API because its whole design premise is that you don't have user authentication data yet, and that the application needs to query the user for this information.

However, this type of user interaction flies in the face of the client application's design because the user already entered her username and password on the command line. The external client just needs to pass the user's data to the `LoginContext`. To make JAAS compatible with our application, we strip out the functionality that queries for a user name and password that you would see in a typical JAAS API tutorial. We'll implement a passive `CallbackHandler` that acts as a simple pass-through that holds only the username and password without querying the user for further information. The `LoginModule`(s) simply call the `CallbackHandler`'s handle( ) method to retrieve the username and password that the user previously entered on the command line, as in Example C-1.

Example C-1. MyPassiveCallbackHandler.java

```
import javax.security.auth.*;
import javax.security.auth.callback.*;

// Simple placeholder that stores userName and password.
public class MyPassiveCallbackHandler implements CallbackHandler {
    private String userName;
    private String password;

    public MyPassiveCallbackHandler(String userName,
                                    String password) {
        this.userName = userName;
        this.password = password;
    }

    public void handle (Callback[ ] callbacks)
        throws UnsupportedCallbackException {

        for (int i = 0; i < callbacks.length; ++i) {
            if (callbacks[i] instanceof NameCallback) {
                NameCallback nc = (NameCallback) callbacks[i];

                nc.setName(userName);
            } else if (callbacks[i] instanceof
                       PasswordCallback) {
```

Example C-1. MyPassiveCallbackHandler.java (continued)

```
                PasswordCallback pc =
                        (PasswordCallback) callbacks[i];

                pc.setPassword(password.toCharArray( ));
        } else {
            throw new UnsupportedCallbackException(callbacks[i],
                            "Unrecognized Callback");

        }
      }
    }
}
```

Once you get past this indirection, the rest of the JAAS API is straightforward. Figure C-1 shows the interactions in the API.

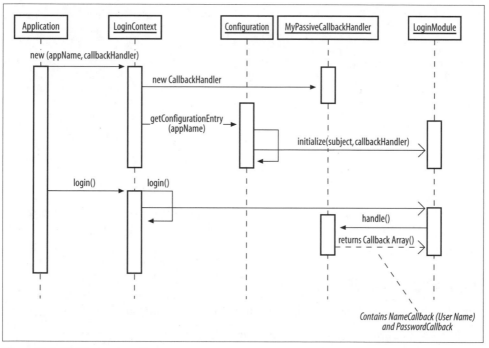

Figure C-1. JAAS sequence diagram

The application instantiates a LoginContext with the application name and an application-specific CallbackHandler (in our case, we instantiate MyPassive-CallbackHandler with a username and password entered from the login form). The LoginContext reads the LoginModule Configuration file and instantiates the LoginModule(s). The application then calls LoginContext's login( ) method, which in turn calls the login( ) method of each LoginModule. MyPassiveCallbackHandler returns the NameCallback (with the username) and PasswordCallback to each LoginModule when it calls MyPassiveCallbackHandler's handle( ) method.

JAAS LoginModule Configuration and Deployment

The JAAS LoginModule Configuration file configures the LoginModule(s) used by a J2SE application, specifies their runtime behavior, and optionally provides them with initialization parameters. The template in Example C-2 shows the format of a LoginModule Configuration file.

Example C-2. LoginModule Configuration file

```
Application1 {
    ModuleClassInvokedFirst Flag
        ModuleOption1=value1
        …
        ModuleOptionN=valueN
    ;

    ModuleClassInvokedLast Flag
        ModuleOption1=value1
        …
        ModuleOptionN=valueN
    ;
};
…

ApplicationN {
    …
};
```

The LoginContext invokes the LoginModules in the order declared in the Configuration file. The Module Options are initialization parameters (with values) for each LoginModule.

LoginModule Configuration Flags

The Flag in the LoginModule Configuration file serves two purposes:

- It gives the runtime behavior of each LoginModule.
- It tells the LoginContext how to coordinate the LoginModule stack.

Here are the options available for LoginModule Configuration Flags:

Required
> The LoginModule has to succeed. The LoginContext executes other LoginModules in the stack, regardless of the success or failure of a Required LoginModule. The overall authentication process fails if a Required LoginModule fails.

Requisite

> The LoginModule must succeed. If it succeeds, the LoginContext continues executing other LoginModules. If it fails, the LoginContext immediately returns control to the caller without invoking any other LoginModules.

Sufficient

> The LoginModule is not required to succeed. If it succeeds, the LoginContext immediately returns control to the application, and does not invoke the rest of the LoginModules in the stack. If it fails, the LoginContext continues executing other LoginModules.

Optional

> The LoginModule does not have to succeed. The LoginContext executes other LoginModules in the stack, regardless of the success or failure of an Optional LoginModule.

Although JAAS provides a sophisticated set of options, we're going to be conservative and set our LoginModule(s) to Required because we don't want to allow the user to access sensitive portions of an application unless they successfully log on to all the security realms.

When filled in with real LoginModules and settings, the above LoginModule Configuration file template works in a J2SE environment when you add it your application's CLASSPATH. We use a J2SE-style LoginModule Configuration file when we create an external application client, but this won't work with most J2EE application servers. Refer to the Security chapter to see how to configure a server-side LoginModule on JBoss.

Client-Side JAAS

To use JAAS from an external client, we need to take the following steps:

- Write the client code, using the MyPassiveCallbackHandler from the CallbackHandler section.
- Configure a client-side LoginModule.
- Set up a J2SE Security Policy file.

External Client Application that Uses JAAS

The following code snippet shows how an external application would use JAAS authentication, assuming that the user already entered his username and password. We first instantiate an application-specific CallbackHandler implementation, MyPassiveCallbackHandler, with the userName and password. We then create the JAAS LoginContext by using the application name along with our CallbackHandler. The "Client-JBossAtWorkAuth" application name comes from the LoginModule Configuration file—see the "Client-Side LoginModule Configuration" section for details.

The LoginContext's login( ) method then authenticates the user. If login( ) throws a LoginException, then the logon process failed. If the logon succeeds, the application calls the code the user is allowed to access, as in Example C-3.

Example C-3. Sample external client

```
import javax.security.auth.login.*;
import javax.security.auth.*;
import java.security.*;

...

try {
    MyPassiveCallbackHandler myCallbackHandler = null;

    // Set Security Association CallbackHandler-specific settings
    myCallbackHandler = new MyPassiveCallbackHandler(userName, password);

    // Get Login Context (NOTE: Client-JBossAtWorkAuth is the application
    // name in the client-auth.conf LoginModule Configuration file)
    System.out.println("Creating the JAAS Login Context");
    LoginContext loginContext = new LoginContext("Client-JBossAtWorkAuth",
                                                 myCallbackHandler );

    // Login
    System.out.println("Logging in as user [" + userName + "]");
    lc.login( );

    // Protected code goes here.

} catch (LoginException le) {
    System.out.println(le.getMessage( ));
}
```

We've now written the core client code and the CallbackHandler, but there's still a little more work to do before we can run the client. We need to take the following steps:

- Configure a client-side LoginModule.
- Create a J2SE Security file.
- Set up the Client's CLASSPATH.

Client-Side LoginModule Configuration

We have to configure a client-side LoginModule in Example C-4 so the client application can instantiate a LoginContext.

Example C-4. client-auth.conf

```
Client-JBossAtWorkAuth {
    org.jboss.security.ClientLoginModule required;
};
```

When called by the client application, the LoginContext's constructor reads this LoginModule Configuration file to set up a JBoss-specific JAAS LoginModule that communicates with the JBoss server. The application then uses the LoginContext to log on to the JBoss server using JAAS.

J2SE Security Policy File

The Security Policy File in Example C-5 gives the client the privileges it needs to use the JAAS API.

Example C-5. security.policy

```
grant codeBase "file:.${/}-" {
  permission javax.security.auth.AuthPermission "createLoginContext";
  permission javax.security.auth.AuthPermission "doAs";
  permission javax.security.auth.AuthPermission "doAsPrivileged";
  permission javax.security.auth.AuthPermission "modifyPrincipals";
  permission javax.security.auth.AuthPermission "getSubject";
  java.util.PropertyPermission "read";
  java.security.auth.debug "read";
};
```

The javax.security.auth.AuthPermission settings in this file grant permissions to:

- Create a LoginContext.
- Call Subject.doAs() and doAsPrivileged() so the client can access protected code.
- Allow a CallbackHandler to modify Principals.
- Enable the client to get the Subject from the LoginContext.

The java.util.PropertyPermission setting enables the client to read Properties files, and the java.security.auth.debug setting enables the client to read the java.security.auth.debug System property—see the next section for details.

Setting the Client CLASSPATH

The client requires the following CLASSPATH settings to run properly:

```
java -classpath.;$JBOSS_HOME/client/jbosssx-client.jar \
-Djava.security.manager \
-Djava.security.policy="security.policy" \
-Djava.security.auth.policy="security.policy" \
-Djava.security.auth.login.config="client-auth.conf" \
-Djava.security.auth.debug="all" com.jbossatwork.client.JaasClient
```

The jbosssx-client.jar contains the JBoss JAAS client-side classes, and the java.security.manager System property tells the JVM to use a security policy file. The java.security.policy and java.security.auth.policy System properties tell the Java Security Manager to use our security policy file, security.policy. The `java.security.auth.login.config` System property tells the Java Security Manager to use our client-side LoginModule Configuration file, `client-auth.conf`.

To check for any client-side configuration problems, we turn on JAAS debug options by specifying the `java.security.auth.debug` System Property. Here are some of the valid values for `java.security.auth.debug`:

all
> Turn on all JAAS debugging.

logincontext
> Enable `LoginContext` debugging.

policy
> Configure access control policy debugging.

We're setting `java.security.auth.debug` to `all` so we can see everything. You can turn this setting off later on if you'd like.

Conclusion

In this appendix, we reviewed portions of the Security chapter and added detailed coverage of other aspects of the JAAS API, including client-side `LoginModule` configuration and classes such as the `Callback`, `CallbackHandler`, and `LoginContext`.

Index

A

ACCOUNTING table, 141
AccountingDAO,
        HibernateAccountingDAO, 142
AccountingDTO object, 141
Ant
    automated deployment and, 38
    build script, XDoclet and, 122–123
    databases and, 60
    EAR task, 36
    EJB JAR file creation, 125
    HBM file, 70
    installation, 5
    WAR and, 23
Apache
    Axis, Web Services client and, 235
    Commons Logging, 253
    JCL API, 251
    Log4J, 254–262
        Appender interface, 254
        Common Jar file, 265
        configuration, 263–264
        configuration file, 256–259
        initialization, 259
        Layout interface, 255
        Logger class, 254
        PatternLayout, 255–256
        resource loading, 264–265
Appender interface (Log4J), 254
application.xml file, 33
applications
    presentation tier, 15
    three-tier, 14

application-specific properties, System
        properties and, 262
architecture, JMS, 150
archives, HARs (Hibernate Archives), 71
asynchronous processing, EJBs and, 98
<attribute name> element,
        hibernate-service.xml file, 71
authentication
    declarative, web.xml and, 191
    form-based, 190
        login form, 191
    J2EE security, 185
    web-based, 190
authorization
    declarative, web.xml and, 191
    J2EE security, 185

B

Bean Class, 114
bin/ directory, 7
BMPs (Bean-Managed Persistence), 46
BMTs (Bean-Managed Transactions), 119
    MDBs and, 167
Bootstrap ClassLoader, 243
build.xml files, 34
    common.jar and, 35
business logic, removing from Controller
        Servlet, 128–138
Business tier, 99–100
Buy Car page, JAW Motors
        example, 139–144

We'd like to hear your suggestions for improving our indexes. Send email to *index@oreilly.com*.

X

XDoclet, 40–44
Ant build script, 122–123
EJB security automation, 210
installation, 5
JavaMail-based JNDI references, 181
MDB deployment, 170
Servlet deployment, 260
Stateless Session Beans, deployment automation, 120–122
Web Services deployment and, 228
XML, application.xml file, 33

Y

YAGNI (You Ain't Gonna Need It), 98

About the Authors

Tom Marrs, a 20-year veteran in the software industry, is the Principal and Senior Software Architect at Vertical Slice, a consulting firm that designs and implements mission-critical business applications using the latest J2EE and open source technologies, along with providing architecture evaluation and developer training and mentoring services. Tom teaches Java/J2EE/JBoss training classes, speaks regularly at software conferences such as No Fluff Just Stuff (*http://www.nofluffjuststuff.com*), and is a blogger on java.net and ONJava. An active participant in the local technical community, Tom is the President of the Denver JBoss User Group and has served as President of the Denver Java Users Group (*http://www.denverjug.org*).

Scott Davis is a senior software engineer in the Colorado front range. He is passionate about open source solutions and agile development. He has worked on a variety of Java platforms, from J2EE to J2SE to J2ME (sometimes all on the same project).

Scott is a frequent presenter at national conferences and local user groups. He was the president of the Denver Java Users Group in 2003 when it was voted one of the Top 10 JUGs in North America. After a quick move north, he is currently active in the leadership of the Boulder Java Users Group. Keep up with him at *http://www.davisworld.org*.

Colophon

Our look is the result of reader comments, our own experimentation, and feedback from distribution channels. Distinctive covers complement our distinctive approach to technical topics, breathing personality and life into potentially dry subjects.

The animal on the cover of *JBoss at Work: A Practical Guide* is a golden eagle (*Aquila chrysaetos*), named for the golden feathers on the back of its neck. This large bird of prey is one of the two eagle breeds found in the United States, inhabiting parts of the West as well as Canada, Alaska, Eurasia, and northern Africa. The golden eagle makes its home in desert grasslands and above the timberline. There it can stretch its wings (7 feet across) and go for a nice swoop at 200 mph, or catch a rising mass of warm air called a thermal and spiral upward into the sky.

Golden eagles build large stick nests in trees or cliff walls. They may build multiple nests within a nesting range and alternate among them, depending on the year. Since golden eagles continually elaborate on their nests, the nests can grow quite large, reaching 8 to 10 feet across and 3 to 4 feet in depth. Both the male and female participate in the rearing of the eaglets, with the male doing most of the hunting and the female doing most of the incubating. If food is scarce, the larger of the eaglets may commit siblicide.

The young fledge when 72 to 84 days old and depend upon their parents for another 3 months. After this period they either migrate or move out of their parents' territory, but they generally winter in their natal area. At four years of age, golden eagles mate. They often stay paired with the same mate for life—about 30 years. Golden eagles are excellent hunters and for this reason are rarely forced to migrate far from their nesting territory. They feast on over 50 species of mammals, 48 birds, 5 reptiles, and 2 fish. Among these are included prairie dogs, rabbits, ground squirrels, grouse, ducks, chukars, marmots, foxes, skunks, cats, meadowlarks, and snakes. Golden eagles are protected in the U.S. through the U.S. Fish and Wildlife Service. Possessing a feather or any other body part belonging to this bird will incur a $10,000 fine or a jail term of up to 10 years. (There are some exceptions for Native American traditions.)

Colleen Gorman was the production editor and proofreader, and Ann Schirmer was the copyeditor for *JBoss at Work: A Practical Guide*. Jamie Peppard and Genevieve d'Entremont provided quality control. Loranah Dimant provided production assistance. Johnna VanHoose Dinse wrote the index.

Karen Montgomery designed the cover of this book, based on a series design by Edie Freedman. The cover image is a 19th-century engraving from Johnson's Natural History. Karen Montgomery produced the cover layout with Adobe InDesign CS using Adobe's ITC Garamond font.

David Futato designed the interior layout. This book was converted by Joe Wizda to FrameMaker 5.5.6 with a format conversion tool created by Erik Ray, Jason McIntosh, Neil Walls, and Mike Sierra that uses Perl and XML technologies. The text font is Linotype Birka; the heading font is Adobe Myriad Condensed; and the code font is LucasFont's TheSans Mono Condensed. The illustrations that appear in the book were produced by Robert Romano, Jessamyn Read, and Lesley Borash using Macromedia FreeHand MX and Adobe Photoshop CS. The tip and warning icons were drawn by Christopher Bing. This colophon was written by Lydia Onofrei.

Better than e-books

Buy *JBoss at Work: A Practical Guide* and access
the digital edition FREE on Safari for 45 days.

Go to www.oreilly.com/go/safarienabled
and type in coupon code DACG-BCXD-NFAX-DWDY-SBMN

Search
thousands of
top tech books

Download
whole chapters

Cut and Paste
code examples

Find
answers fast

Search Safari! The premier electronic reference
library for programmers and IT professionals.

Related Titles from O'Reilly

Java

Ant: The Definitive Guide,
2nd Edition

Better, Faster, Lighter Java

Beyond Java

Eclipse

Eclipse Cookbook

Eclipse IDE Pocket Guide

Enterprise JavaBeans,
4th Edition

Hardcore Java

Head First Design Patterns

Head First Design Patterns Poster

Head First Java

Head First Servlets & JSP

Head First EJB

Hibernate: A Developer's
Notebook

J2EE Design Patterns

Java 1.5 Tiger: A Developer's
Notebook

Java & XML Data Binding

Java & XML

Java Cookbook, *2nd Edition*

Java Data Objects

Java Database Best Practices

Java Enterprise Best Practices

Java Enterprise in a Nutshell,
3nd Edition

Java Examples in a Nutshell,
3rd Edition

Java Extreme Programming
Cookbook

Java in a Nutshell, *5th Edition*

Java Management Extensions

Java Message Service

Java Network Programming,
2nd Edition

Java NIO

Java Performance Tuning,
2nd Edition

Java RMI

Java Security, *2nd Edition*

JavaServer Faces

Java ServerPages, *2nd Edition*

Java Servlet & JSP Cookbook

Java Servlet Programming,
2nd Edition

Java Swing, *2nd Edition*

Java Web Services in a Nutshell

JBoss: A Developer's Notebook

Learning Java, *2nd Edition*

Mac OS X for Java Geeks

Maven: A Developer's
Notebook

Programming Jakarta Struts,
2nd Edition

QuickTime for Java: A
Developer's Notebook

Spring: A Developer's
Notebook

Swing Hacks

Tomcat: The Definitive Guide

WebLogic: The Definitive Guide

Keep in touch with O'Reilly

Download examples from our books

To find example files from a book, go to: *www.oreilly.com/catalog* select the book, and follow the "Examples" link.

Register your O'Reilly books

Register your book at *register.oreilly.com* Why register your books? Once you've registered your O'Reilly books you can:

- Win O'Reilly books, T-shirts or discount coupons in our monthly drawing.
- Get special offers available only to registered O'Reilly customers.
- Get catalogs announcing new books (US and UK only).
- Get email notification of new editions of the O'Reilly books you own.

Join our email lists

Sign up to get topic-specific email announcements of new books and conferences, special offers, and O'Reilly Network technology newsletters at:

elists.oreilly.com

It's easy to customize your free elists subscription so you'll get exactly the O'Reilly news you want.

Get the latest news, tips, and tools

www.oreilly.com

- "Top 100 Sites on the Web"—PC Magazine
- CIO Magazine's Web Business 50 Awards

Our web site contains a library of comprehensive product information (including book excerpts and tables of contents), downloadable software, background articles, interviews with technology leaders, links to relevant sites, book cover art, and more.

Work for O'Reilly

Check out our web site for current employment opportunities:

jobs.oreilly.com

Contact us

O'Reilly Media, Inc.
1005 Gravenstein Hwy North
Sebastopol, CA 95472 USA
Tel: 707-827-7000 or 800-998-9938
   (6am to 5pm PST)
Fax: 707-829-0104

Contact us by email

For answers to problems regarding your order or our products:
order@oreilly.com

To request a copy of our latest catalog:
catalog@oreilly.com

For book content technical questions or corrections: **booktech@oreilly.com**

For educational, library, government, and corporate sales: **corporate@oreilly.com**

To submit new book proposals to our editors and product managers:
proposals@oreilly.com

For information about our international distributors or translation queries:
international@oreilly.com

For information about academic use of O'Reilly books:
adoption@oreilly.com
or visit:
academic.oreilly.com

For a list of our distributors outside of North America check out:
international.oreilly.com/distributors.html

Order a book online

www.oreilly.com/order_new